THE ILL-FRAMED KNIGHT

THE ILL-FRAMED KNIGHT

A skeptical inquiry into
the identity of Sir Thomas Malory

by

WILLIAM MATTHEWS

It is not unlikely that the name has its origin in the Old French verb *orer* (= to frame, to surround) and that *Maloret* was a nickname meaning "ill-framed" or "ill-set."

Eugène Vinaver, *Malory* (1929)

UNIVERSITY OF CALIFORNIA PRESS
Berkeley and Los Angeles

1966

University of California Press
Berkeley and Los Angeles, California
Cambridge University Press
London, England

© 1966 by The Regents of the University of California
Library of Congress Catalog Card Number: 66-23179

Designed by Pamela F. Johnson

*To my admired adversaries,
the established wits—
coupled with the unassaulted name
of a good and generous friend,
Majl Ewing*

PREFACE

Informed that Mrs Montagu, Queen of the Blues, First of Literary Women, was coming to dine at the Thrales', Dr Johnson, then approaching seventy, began to seesaw with suppressed mirth. Finally he turned to his new favorite, the 26-year-old authoress of a recent bestseller called *Evelina*, and burst out with animation:

"Down with her, Burney!—down with her!—spare her not!—attack her, fight her, and down with her at once! You are a rising wit, and she is at the top; and when I was beginning the world, and was nothing and nobody, the joy of my life was to fire at all the established wits . . . to vanquish the great ones was all the delight of my poor little dear soul! So at her, Burney,—at her, and down with her!". . .

"Miss Burney," cried Mr Thrale, "you must get up your courage for this encounter! I think you should begin with Miss Gregory; and down with her first."

Dr Johnson: "No, no, always fly at the eagle!"
Bertrand Bronson, Johnson Agonistes, 1946.

The simple-seeming question that led to this book popped up while I was assembling a chapter in *The Tragedy of Arthur*. That was in 1957, and since then it has drawn me from library to library, country to country, one fewmet to another, a Pellinore hunt that still goes on. The book raises more problems than it settles, and that it is put out now is mainly because vanishing years and thinning resources cry halt for the nonce.

Simple questions come in with so lamblike an air, that one really ought to be wary of them: all too often they lead to quite dragonish answers. This simple question certainly has done so. The pleasures I have been graced with as I assembled this book have been varied and rich; and if the reader should come to suspect that one of them has been the gamin's delight in spotting a mote in an eminent eye, I trust he will forgive me.

Preface

Where motes dance, beams may surely dazzle. I therefore owe more than I can easily acknowledge to outspoken friends who have borne with my talk about this book or read it in its rougher forms. Among these, I would single out for particular thanks these my companions in scholarly piety: Ralph Rader, Helaine Newstead, Florence Ridley, Majl Ewing, Hugh Trevor-Roper, Albert Friedman, Francis Utley, Harold Hungerford, my colleagues in a linguistic group and two literary societies at University of California, Los Angeles, and Lois, poor wretch, the readiest victim of all my lamblike questions.

Many scholars have helped me with information. Sir Anthony Wagner, Garter-Principal King-of-Arms, has supported my amateur probings into genealogy with his own splendid professionalism. The following, professors and friends, have cleared up for me many small matters in topography, documents, linguistics, and history: John Butt, C. H. Gillies, Angus McIntosh, Norman Davis, K. B. Macfarlane, A. G. Dickens, R. S. Loomis, John Crow, C. D. Ross, Helen Heath, Elizabeth Brunskill, Canon Bartlett and Canon Wilkinson of Ripon, Canon Bailey of Wells. For all these, I take pleasure in refreshing my posy of forget-me-nots, and do the like for numerous archivists and librarians, particularly those at York Minster, the Borthwick Institute, Leeds Public Library, the Yorkshire Historical Society, Lincoln Cathedral, Delapré Abbey, Warwick County Archives, the Bodleian, the British Museum, Cambridge University, Lambeth Palace, the Public Record Office, the Institute for Historical Research, Winchester College, Mercers' Hall, the College of Arms, the Huntington Library, and UCLA. To the Honorable Henry Vyner, and Mr. Browne his agent at Studley Royal, I am deeply obliged for their warm hospitality in a famously cold winter: I trust they will regard this book as a suitable thanks-offering. I am also indebted to Ruth Pryor for her care and skill in rechecking the endless details in the appendixes. So I am to the Research Committee at UCLA for financial support.

I trust the book will give readers some of the pleasure and excitement it has given me in assembling it. It is not a last word, for sure, and the final pleasure I would hope to have from it is to hear scholarly voices, some as yet unbroken, give tongue: "Gone away! The Hunt is Up!"

William Matthews

Department of English
University of California, Los Angeles
April 1, 1965

CONTENTS

I. THE ILL-FRAMED KNIGHT 3

II. PROS AND CONS 35

III. THE LOCALE OF LE MORTE DARTHUR 75

IV. ANOTHER MAN OF THE SAME NAME 115

Appendixes 155

Bibliographical Notes 239

Index 253

THE ILL-FRAMED KNIGHT

A Malory Map of England

I

THE ILL-FRAMED KNIGHT

The question with which this book deals, "Who was the Sir Thomas Malory who wrote *Le Morte Darthur?*" is one that has teased the curiosity of scholars for four centuries at least. As the question is answered in this book, it will involve the reader in a double whodunit.

The book itself and its first editor do little to answer the question, overtly at least. Malory himself gives almost the sum total of his information in his last words:

> I praye you all jentylmen and jentylwymmen that redeth this book of Arthur and his knyghtes from the begynnyng to the endynge, praye for me whyle I am on lyve that God send me good delyveraunce. And whan I am deed, I praye you all praye for my soule. For this book was ended the ninth yere of the reygne of King Edward the Fourth, by Syr Thomas Maleore, knyght, as Jesu helpe hym for His grete myght, as he is the servaunt of Jesu bothe day and nyght.

And Caxton's preface has but little to add. It tells us merely that the book was printed according to a copy delivered to Caxton, "whyche copye syr Thomas Malorye dyd take oute of certeyn bookes of Frensshe and reduced it into Englysshe."

This is all the direct information that appears in any edition of *Le Morte Darthur* based upon Caxton's first edition of 1485. From a late fifteenth-century manuscript that was discovered at Winchester College in 1934, however, a little more can be gleaned. First, two further variations in the spelling of the author's surname, *Maleorre* and *Malleorre*. Second, a variation in the name of his social rank, *shyvalere*. Third, and most important, a series of prayers which confirm the prayer for good deliverance which has been quoted from the Caxton print. One—"And I praye you all that redyth this tale to pray for hym that this wrote, that God sende hym good delyveraunce sone and hastely"—occurs at the end of the tale of Sir Gareth. A second—"Here endyth the secunde boke off syr Trystram de Lyones whyche was drawyn oute of Freynshe by sir Thomas Malleorre, knyght, as Jesu be hys helpe"—comes at the end of the *Tristram*. A third concludes the Quest of the Holy Grail: "by sir Thomas Maleorre, knight: O Blessed Jesu helpe hym thorow hys myght." A fourth refers to "the moste pyteous tale of the Morte Arthure Saunz Gwerdon par le shyvalere sir Thomas Malleorre, knyght" and goes on, "Jesu ayede ly pur voutre bone mercy." Although there is significance in the fact that these four additional prayers are spread throughout Malory's book, none is any more specific than the prayer that appears solely at the end of the Caxton text. Their obscurity concerning the circumstance that induced Malory to call for pity and help seems to be clarified, however, by a further prayer, which occurs fairly early in the Winchester manuscript, at the end of the section which in Vinaver's edition is entitled *The Tale of King Arthur*. This runs:

> And this booke endyth whereas sir Launcelot and sir Trystrams com to courte. Who that woll make ony more lette hym seke other bookis of kynge Arthure or of sir Launcelot or sir Trystrams; for this was drawyn by a knyght presoner sir Thomas Malleorre, that God sende hym good recover.

The effect of this passage is to make almost certain what a generation of scholars had guessed even from the final words in the Caxton print: that *Le Morte Darthur*, or at least a great deal of it, was written while the author was a prisoner.

This thimbleful of details is merely tantalizing. It does little but whet the thirst of our first question. Granted that the author was a knight, that he translated his book while he was a prisoner, and that he completed it between March 4, 1469, and March 3, 1470, the question still remains: Who was he, and what kind of life did he lead? The question has produced several answers, and recently it has evoked several brilliant essays in literary detection and a covey of ingenious arguments, all of which will be discussed in the course of this book.

So far, three answers have been proposed: that Sir Thomas was a Welshman; that he came from Huntingdonshire; that he was Sir Thomas Malory of Newbold Revel in Warwickshire. The simple objective of this our first chapter is to report what has been discovered about these three candidates. Discussion of their claims is left to the second chapter.

That Malory was Welsh was first proposed in 1548, in a Latin *Catalogus* of the illustrious writers of Great Britain.* The cataloguer, John Bale—antiquary, playwright, and bishop—declared that Malory was *Britannus, i.e.* Welsh, by race, and that he was born near the River Dee, at Maloria in Wales. Bale apparently had no further biographical details to offer, and none has been discovered during the four centuries that have elapsed. Nor did the old antiquary pinpoint the position of Maloria-on-Dee, an omission that is not a little frustrating since it cannot now be located. However, when Professor John Rhys edited Malory's work in 1893, he both revived Bale's proposal, stating that he had himself long thought that Malory might be Welsh, and did something to give Maloria a local habitation and new name. Rhys, distinguished both as an Arthurian scholar and a Welshman, proposed that *Maleore*, Caxton's second spelling (and to this we might now add the two new Winchester spellings, *Maleorre* and *Malleorre*), may be referred to two districts that straddle the border of England and North Wales, Maleor in Flintshire and Maleor in Denbigh. A place-name can easily become a surname, he points out. As for Caxton's trisyllabic spelling, *Malorye*, that can be explained as derived from a Latinized adjective, *Mailorius*. For Professor Rhys, therefore, the author of *Le Morte Darthur* was a compatriot and namesake of Edward ab Rhys Maelor, Edward Price of Maelor, the fifteenth-century Welsh poet.[1]

The claim on behalf of the second candidate, Thomas Malory of Papworth St. Agnes in Huntingdonshire, was first put forth by A. T. Martin, an English antiquary, in two articles. The first, a communication to the *Athenaeum* for September 11, 1897, reported the discovery of the Papworth man's will and argued from its contents that this might be the author. The second article, published a year later in *Archaeologia*, reaffirmed the proposal, added a good deal of biographical information about this candidate and also about Sir Thomas Malory of Newbold Revel, and came

---

* Oskar Sommer, in his 1890 edition of Malory, was the first modern scholar to draw attention to the Welsh proposal made by Bale.

to the opinion that the Papworth Malory was a more likely candidate than the Newbold Revel knight. Martin's contribution, based upon most extensive investigation of many Malory families of the Midland counties and drawing upon manuscripts in the Public Records and Somerset House, is a sterling job of research. Had it not been that his choice between the two Malorys was to be rejected almost immediately by the scholarly world, his work might have better enjoyed the acclaim it so richly deserves.

Martin's searches produced this brief biography of the Papworth Thomas Malory. He was born on December 6, 1425, at Morton Corbet, a small place in Shropshire where his family owned property, some few miles north of Shrewsbury and not far from the borders of Wales. He was baptized at Morton Corbet church and apparently spent a good deal of his boyhood in the vicinity, probably in the home of his sister Margaret, who was married to John Corbet of Morton Corbet. Despite this association with the West Country, however, his main tie was with the East Midlands. His father was Sir William Malory (1386-1445), who held lands at Shawbury and Upton Waters, near Morton Corbet, and also owned manorhouses at Sudburgh in Northamptonshire and Shelton in Bedfordshire. Sir William's principal estate and home, however, was at Papworth St. Agnes, in the fen-and-farm country on the flat borderlands of Cambridge and Huntingdon. These he held by knight service of the King. Sir William, very clearly, was a knight of some substance, and the fact is reflected in his being returned to Parliament in 1433 as one of the gentry of Cambridgeshire.

Thomas the son succeeded to the family estates in 1445. Then only twenty, he was therefore put first into the custody and wardship of Leo Louthe, acting on behalf of the King. For reasons unknown, he continued under this wardship for most of his life, for although he went to Shrewsbury on May 17, 1451, and there proved his age, he did not obtain full release of his lands at Papworth until May 31, 1469, four months before he died. In his will, dated September 16, 1469, and probated the next month, he describes himself as of Pappesworth in the county of Huntingdon, asks to be buried in the church of St. Mary's at Huntingdon, appoints two London drapers as his trustees, and makes provision for his wife Margaret, his son Anthony, and eight other children, one still at nurse and all under age.

During his restudy of every candidate's life and claims, the present writer came across a few more details about the Papworth claimant. From the character of his trustees and the career of his son Anthony, it may be judged that he was somehow concerned in the mercer's trade. He held a few minor offices in the counties of Cambridge, Huntingdon, and Bedford: escheator, member of a commission *de kidellis* (fishtraps), and so on. In one legal document he is described as *armiger*, or esquire, despite his holding his lands by knight service from the King. None of these details changes the impression, given by Martin's evidence and the succession of children, that this Thomas Malory was an average county gentleman of bourgeois inclinations.

This impression of placidity may not be the true picture, however, for in a bundle of *Early Chancery Proceedings* the present writer discovered a document that seems to indicate that Thomas Malory of Papworth was in no wise immune from that overbearing violence which was so common in his time. One November (the document does not record the year) he lay in wait, "as hit had been in londe of werre," and accosted Richard Kyd, the parson of Papworth. Malory was armed with *launsettys* and an armory of other formidable weapons. The terrified Kyd thought that he was being led to the slaughter immediately. Changing his mind, however, Malory carried him first to Papworth, thence to Huntingdon, Bedford, and Northampton, and so on and on, all the way to Leicester. Throughout the whole scarifying tour, he continued to threaten death to the terrified cleric. Simply to save his life, Parson Kyd, who relates all this in a petition, agreed to resign his parish church to Malory or else to forfeit a hundred pounds. The petition pleads that Kyd might be released from the enforced commitment.[2]

The third candidate, Sir Thomas Malory of Newbold Revel, is the one of whom we know most. The reasons are simple: In the 1890's, when the cases for all these candidates were stated or restated in their various strengths, his was the one that seemed distinctly the strongest. Moreover, he was lucky enough to have a most skillful advocate. The result has been that research into the biography of the author of *Le Morte Darthur* has been concentrated exclusively upon him. Whatever the correctness of the identification, whatever the merit of preferring him above the others, the outcome has been extraordinary. We now know more about Sir Thomas Malory of Newbold Revel than about any other Warwickshireman of his time. The only possible competitor is Richard Neville, Warwick the Kingmaker; but he, so far as he belonged to any county, was really a Yorkshireman.

Although scholars had known of the Warwickshire knight for some time (Sommer, for instance, mentions him in his standard 1890 edition of Malory's work), the credit for proposing and supporting the case for his being thought the author of the great romance belongs to the eminent Harvard scholar George Lyman Kittredge. He first broached the thesis in a thumbnail biography in Johnson's *Universal Cyclopoedia*, 1894. A little later, he presented a fuller report in a lecture at Columbia College. His full statement appeared in 1897 as a lengthy essay in the testimonial volume presented to Francis James Child, the famous ballad scholar. This distinguished essay, which set Kittredge on his highroad of scholarly fame, came first only by a handspan; for at the time it was published, A. T. Martin was making his investigations into this Thomas Malory as well as his own, quite unaware of what Kittredge had done.

Biographically Kittredge's essay is not particularly rich except that it reports those details which make the Newbold Revel candidate seem the likeliest among the three that have so far been proposed. These details derive from the biographical sketch of Sir Thomas Malory that appears in Sir William Dugdale's old book on the antiquities of Warwickshire, and their essence is that in his youth Sir Thomas soldiered at Calais with a great chivalric figure, Richard Beauchamp, earl of Warwick, that he later served as Member of Parliament for his county, and that he died in 1471 and was buried at the Greyfriars in London.

There the biography rested for nearly a quarter of a century. But during the 1920's—partly under the stimulus of those exciting revelations about Christopher Marlowe that Leslie Hotson unearthed from the Public Records Office—a number of startling new discoveries were made which seemed to bespatter most sadly the chivalric picture that Dugdale and Kittredge had painted.

In 1920, Edward Cobb, one of Kittredge's students at Harvard, came upon a Northamptonshire *De Banco* roll for 1443 which recorded that Sir Thomas Malory, together with Eustace Burnaby, was charged with having by force and arms insulted, wounded, and imprisoned Thomas Smythe and made off with goods and chattels to the value of forty pounds. Independently, and only two years later, E. K. Chambers reported two documents which indicate that during the years 1451 and 1452 Sir Thomas had had further brushes with the law: a warrant was issued for his arrest, and he was ordered to provide guarantors that no hurt should be done to the prior and convent of the Carthusian house at Axholme in Lincolnshire.

So startling a lead, especially when it was matched by Hotson's Marlowe revelations from the Public Record Office, was not to be denied. In 1928, Edward Hicks, another of Kittredge's students, was able to bring in his harvest from the documentary haystacks in Chancery Lane. His lively biography, *Sir Thomas Malory, His Turbulent Career*, gave proof —documentary proof—that Malory had been charged with many more crimes than those that Cobb and Chambers had reported, and that as a result he had spent time in several jails. Even this was not the whole story. Two years later, the distinguished medievalist Albert C. Baugh, while he was looking for other things in the Public Record Office, came across a series of mislabelled documents relating to Warwickshire which both substantiated Hicks's discoveries and added further details of comparable kind. These new Malory gleanings, together with some information about the persons who were alleged to have collaborated with Sir Thomas in these criminal activities, were reported in an article published in 1932.

Although the total biography revealed by this sequence of studies is somewhat legal and specialized—few men would relish the prospect that their lives should be reported simply from legal records—it is detailed and remarkably lively. Here it is re-presented in a fuller form than before; with the addition of a few new details about Malory's parents and birth, some new facts about several persons with whom he was associated, some novel suggestions about his political connections and their relation to his own behavior, a few new details concerning his last years, and a series of social and topographical settings—this will, it is hoped, serve to root Sir Thomas in his time and place.

The Malorys had come to Warwickshire in the fourteenth century when Sir Stephen Malory of Winwick, whose family had been settled in Northamptonshire for going on two centuries, married Margaret Revell, heiress to an estate at Fenny Newbold that had been in Revel possession since 1299. Other Malorys, branches of the same family it seems, were settled throughout the Central Midlands, most of them in the counties of Northampton, Bedford, Huntingdon, Leicester, and elsewhere in Warwickshire. Several of their offspring had moved to London, largely to keep shop and trade. But in the 1460's, one Edward Malory was a member of the King's household and one Robert Malory was the Earl of Worcester's lieutenant at the Tower. With a few of these, the Leicestershire relatives mostly, the Malorys of Newbold maintained some family social connection.

After Sir Stephen's arrival, the Malorys gradually extended their holdings. Their estates never became large, although by the time of Sir

John, grandson to Sir Stephen, they owned a few small manors in addition to Newbold Revel: Swinford, Winwick, Cleahull, Stretton, Palyngton, Hardburgh. During the life of his son Thomas, some of these may have been sold, for the inventories of the 1470's list only the small family manor at Newbold and two slightly larger ones not far off: Winwick in Northamptonshire and Swinford in Leicestershire. The total value of all three was put at less than twenty pounds per annum, perhaps a thousand in our inflated money.

Their social and political standing was much the same; they had become a family of modest consequence in Warwickshire. Sir Stephen's grandson Sir John was in 1391 appointed a commissioner for conservation of the peace in the county, and next year he became sheriff. Twenty years later, when he was in his forties probably, he was chosen to represent Warwickshire in Parliament, and in 1417 he became sheriff once more. In 1420 he was entrusted with a corner in the county's financial welfare when he was appointed to a commission set up to treat with the people about a loan to Henry V. Thereafter he held a variety of unstartling local offices: escheator, sheriff again, commissioner of the peace. The last year that his name appears in the records is 1434; and, since his first recorded appearance was in 1383, it is likely that he died in 1434, upwards of seventy and a very ancient man as the Middle Ages reckoned such matters. His record is one of unspectacular economic advancement, of tenure of those respectable public offices that commonly went to solid citizens. In a window at Grendon church his wife was depicted as a heavy-set, blunt-featured woman, and he as an old man of rustic cast, with short beard, hair draped over the forehead, and deep-set eyes. The depictions may be conventional, but they do not conflict with the little that we know of their lives. Whether under this appearance of solidity there lay any excitement we shall probably never know. The only intimate details that the records vouchsafe about them are that the wife was Philippa (whose family name is not reported), and that they had two children. One was named Helen, and she married Robert Vincent of Barnack and later lived in Swinford. The other was named Thomas, and he is the man in whom we are chiefly interested.

The Warwickshire into which this Thomas was born was the same gently rolling county that it is now, watered by the Avon and other detergent streams, green with pastures and copses, humanized mainly by nibbling sheep and by the cows, horses, countrymen, and clergy that strolled slowly through its fields and winding lanes. In many ways it was different, however, especially in its northern stretches. Birmingham, Bromwich, Wolverhampton and Nuneaton were still ungrimed villages. The only substantial town was Coventry, one of the four great towns of England, although tiny by today's measurements. It was a town within walls, crowded with friaries, tall-steepled churches, halls, and high narrow houses; normally busy with markets and the manufacture of a famous cloth known as Coventry Blue, it was periodically excited by preparations for the Corpus Christi plays that were put on by its numerous guilds. The county was occupied mainly with farming and grazing. To its inhabitants it had two contrasting divisions: the feldon, a southern region which had long been settled and farmed; and the weldon in the north, much of which was still ancient woodland in spite of frontier penetration, which began in the twelfth century and had given rise to a pattern of scattered small hamlets and endless enclosures of ten acres or so. Coventry was a town easily accessible, for it was the hub of the nation's ancient road system, the place where the old Roman roads converged. Elsewhere ways were primitive, and for any but an untramelled traveler, journeys within and without the county were wearisome and long.

The population was much sparser than it is now even in the farmlands, and because the frontier was recent, the percentage of yeomen and franklins was high, almost a third. Nevertheless, the county was dominated by its magnates. In earlier days, abbeys and monasteries had embraced poverty in its remoteness; but, since the only tribute that the world can pay to voluntary poverty is to corrupt it, by Malory's time many of these retreats into poverty had become rich indeed. Among these, the Benedictine house at Coventry and the Cistercian abbeys at Combe and Stoneleigh were wealthier than most, commanding economic power beyond that of many princes. Castles and fortified manors outnumbered even the abbeys and friaries: Astley, Bagington, Brinklow, Caludon, Bromwich, Coleshill, Fillongley, Fulbrook, Hartshill, Henley, Kenilworth, Maxstoke, Rugby, Warwick, these are but some. Many of their owners were knights of small substance—men like the Peytos of Chesterton and their relatives, the Greswolds of Solihull, or indeed the Malorys of Newbold. Among the rest were some of the richest and most influential men in England.

The Mountfords of Henley were descendants of the great Simon de Montfort. The Mowbrays, although their seat as Earls of Norfolk was at Framlingham in Suffolk, were the owners of Brinklow. Maxstoke, still one of the most impressive of castles, was the home of the Staffords. In the 1450's it was occupied by Humphrey Stafford, Duke of Buckingham, who owned estates in twenty-seven counties, was the second richest man in England, and as a soldier and politician of Lancastrian bias was one of the most powerful men in the realm. Warwick was a royal borough, but the vast castle that had been built up over several centuries was the seat of the Earls of Warwick. During the fifteenth century, its owners included the two greatest men who have ever borne that title. The earlier was Richard Beauchamp, companion and comrade of Henry V, Captain of Calais and Rouen, guardian and tutor of Henry VI, statesman, patron of religion, commerce and the arts. A fifteenth-century genealogy claims that he was descended from Gothgallus, a Knight of the Round Table, and that the Warwick badge, the bear and ragged staff, was derived from Arthur himself—the King's name in Welsh means "bear." Whatever the truth of this, Beauchamp's fifteenth-century biographer stresses the qualities that made the Earl fit for so exalted an origin—his friendships with the princes of both Christendom and Islam, his love of ancient story, his pride in his ancestor Guy of Warwick, his predilection for tournaments and adventures of Arthurian kind, his *courtoisie*. The Emperor Sigismund, the biographer reports, told Henry V that "no prince christian, for wisdom, nurture, and manhood, had such another knight as he had of the Earl of Warwick," adding thereto that, "if all courtesy were lost, yet it might be found again in him." The second Earl, having married Richard Beauchamp's daughter and succeeding to the title upon the death of Beauchamp's son, was a man of different family. He was a man of different character too: Richard Neville, Yorkshireman, soldier, politician, the breaker and maker of kings, the Yorkist contriver who forced Henry VI off the throne, put Edward IV on it, and then put Henry back again.

For all its beauty, piety, wealth and power, Warwickshire was no quieter than some other counties. Strategically situated, it witnessed many great battles near its border: Evesham, Edgecot, Bosworth among others. Coventry, "flourishing with fanes and proud pyramids," was often disturbed by political, religious, and civilian conflicts. The two greatest magnates, Buckingham and Warwick, took opposite sides in the Wars of the Roses, and before then they were at serious odds in other matters too. The *fauxbourdon* of trouble however were the activities of lesser men. Fifteenth-century England has an ill reputation for misrule, and to this reputation Warwickshire made at least average contribution. The following instances typify a single decade. John Shaw of Coventry charged Richard the abbot of Combe with unlawfully seizing his goods. Margery Mariot accused Sir William Mountfort of falsely imprisoning her husband. Richard Clapham complained that Sir Simon Mountford and Richard Verney conspired to have men lie in wait to murder him on the road between Kenilworth and Barkswell. Sir John Gresley's tenants at Chesterton went to court about the riot that had been raised by Robert Danton, John Rounton, and William Rose. John Wykes petitioned for justice against Sir Robert Harecourt, a Warwickshire knight, who with a mob of sixty men had beaten and wounded Wykes's tenants at Carswell, carried off their two hundred sheep, and left them entirely destitute. Richard Dalby charged Sir Richard Verney with assault and seizure of sheep and cattle at Brockhampton. John Whalley accused the abbot and monks of Combe with seizing his cattle. And the great Forest of Arden was the refuge of many a man who came, not to tune any merry note, but simply to slip the knots of the law.[3]

The Warwickshire Malorys were modest members of this society: moderately prosperous landholders, respected, but not eminent for either wealth or family connections. Their parish, a very large one, was called Monks Kirby. It took its name from its priory, an alien foundation that adhered to the Carthusian abbey of Angers in France and was joined with the priory at Axholme in Lincolnshire. Thomas Cowper was the prior of both places in the mid-fifteenth century, and Thomas Mowbray was their patron. Ten small hamlets were scattered through the parish, and in one of these, Fenny Newbold, otherwise Newbold Revel, was the Malorys' manor house—three miles west of the Leicester border, eight east of Coventry, three northeast of Combe Abbey, eighteen northeast of Warwick. It is gone now, the area is all parkland. But in the fifteenth century it was probably a small manor house surrounded by rolling pastures, with farm buildings, a mill, and the priory and the square-towered church of St. Edith close by. Here and in the other hamlets of Monks Kirby lived most of the Malorys' friends and acquaintances: yeomen like the Sherds and Podmores and Warwicks and Leightons, and persons of such miscellaneous occupations as Hugh Smith, maybe a merchant, Maryot the bowmaker, John the cook, John the harper, Masshot the groom, and Richard, whose likeliest trait was that he was Irish.

As with many another famous man, we cannot be exact about when Thomas Malory was born, but the likeliest dates are 1393 or 1394. His boyhood companions were probably the children of the servants and laborers who looked after the manor house and tended its fields. With these and the children of yeomen he must, judging from his later career, have been a young man of mettle, sworn brother to a leash of drawers and footrakers. When his father died, apparently in 1434, Thomas succeeded to the estates and may also have succeeded to a title of knighthood —ever since Sir Stephen's day the head of the Warwickshire Malorys had been usually addressed as "Sir."[4]

Sometime in his youth he must have served as a soldier, one of the professional kind new to Henry V's time—a soldier who, for a salary and provisions, indentured himself to the King for a stated period: a month, a year, two years, sometimes longer. In this capacity he was at Calais under the command of Richard Beauchamp, Earl of Warwick and Captain of Calais. Dugdale gives the details. Thomas Malory was in the retinue of Richard Beauchamp at the siege of Calais, serving there with one lance and two archers, and receiving for his lance and one archer 20 pounds per annum and their diet, and for the other archer 10 marks and no diet. What exactly he did at Calais and how long he soldiered there and elsewhere we are not told. His military life must have begun before 1439, however, for in that year Richard Beauchamp died.

In 1442 he acted as elector in Northamptonshire, but the next thing we hear of him is less to his credit. It is the sordid detail, unearthed in 1920 by Edward Cobb, which set off a train of scholarly enquiry that was to lead to a portrait far different from the one that Dugdale gave or Kittredge knew. In 1443, according to a legal document from Northampton, Sir Thomas Malory of Monks Kirby, *miles*, and Eustace Burnaby of Watford, Northants, *esquire*, were charged by one Thomas Smythe with having by force and arms insulted, wounded, and imprisoned the plaintiff at Sprotton in Northants, and made off with goods and chattels to the value of £40. The charge was not proved, for Malory and Burnaby did not appear to answer it. The Sheriff of Northamptonshire ordered them to be attached, but nothing seems to have resulted—at least the records are silent.

To a modern social conscience, such a charge against a knight and a member of a county family seems particularly shocking. No doubt, to many fifteenth-century consciences it was as distressing as it is to us, even though, as we have seen, Warwickshire men who might have been expected to be particularly law-abiding—an abbot, a Verney, a Harecourt, a Mountford—were charged with offenses of much the same kind.

Around this time, or so it might seem by the paces of generation,

Thomas Malory married a lady named Elizabeth; her family name is unrecorded. They had a son Robert, who died during his father's lifetime, leaving a son named Nicholas. Elizabeth Malory survived her husband, and it is the documents relating to her death in 1479 that record the value of the properties she had inherited: the manor of Newbold Revel, worth a meager 6 pounds 13 shillings and 8 pence a year; the manor of Winwick, valued at 10 pounds per annum; the manor of Swinford, worth 4 marks a year—probably including the lands there which had been mortgaged to them in 1441 and conveyed outright in 1449 by their relations Helen and Robert Vincent; a messuage and two virgates of land at Stormfield in Leicestershire, worth 26 shillings and 8 pence a year. Lady Elizabeth had apparently died intestate: the property went to her thirteen-year-old grandson Nicholas. The values are interesting, and to realize what they might now mean it would be reasonable to multiply them by about fifty for pounds and about 140 for dollars. But what is even more interesting in the 1479 documents is the statement that the Malorys held the manor of Newbold Revel as lieges of John Mowbray, Duke of Norfolk and patron of the priory that adjoined Newbold Revel. This fact, as we shall see, may have been closely related to some things that Sir Thomas is said to have done and to some things that were done to him.

Despite any harms he may have done Thomas Smythe in 1443, Malory was in good repute with the men who ran Warwickshire. Two years later, in 1445, he was elected one of the two knights of the shire—the other was Sir William Mountford of Coleshill—and served in the parliament at Westminster for much of that year.

The rolls that record the proceedings of medieval parliaments are not like *Hansard* or the *Congressional Record*: They are restricted to brief notes on business and action, and do not mention any gestures or speeches that individual members may have made. So we must be content to know merely the business that Malory may have heard and participated in. Like most parliaments of the time, the session dealt with few of the really important national issues. Worsted, wine, sewers, and safe-conduct were the staple of its business, varied by discussion and confirmation of the marriage-treaty between Henry VI and Margaret of Anjou. Except for the splendor of Margaret's arrival and the three-day tournament that followed the coronation, the proceedings at Westminster seem rather dull now. From our own point of view the most interesting decision is that parliament confirmed the extensive endowments that Henry VI had bestowed on his two new colleges, The King's College of Our Lady at

Eton-beside-Windsor and The College Royal of Our Lady and St. Nicholas of Cambridge. Whether Eton and King's owe any debt of gratitude to Sir Thomas may be doubted. Judging by the record of his later life, he may have been rather more interested in the protest that came before the parliament about John Bolton, who had first been thrown into the Marshalsea for robbing a Peckham woman and attempting to rape her, and then had got a King's pardon by informing on his fellows in jail. However that may be, in the same year Sir Thomas was appointed (with Sir William Mountford and the Duke of Buckingham) to a royal commission charged with distributing money to the impoverished towns of Warwickshire, and the next year received a similar appointment.

Four years later, it is reported, Malory welcomed in the second half-century in a most rousing style. A King's Bench document for January 4, 1450 declares that Thomas Malory, knight, together with twenty-six other persons, had lain in ambush in the woods of Combe Abbey, armed with staves, bows and arrows, glaives, jacks, sallets, and crossbows, intending to murder Humphrey Stafford, Duke of Buckingham. The twenty-six are unnamed, so it is clear the complaint was directed against Malory as leader of the band. Buckingham was not only one of the richest and most powerful men in the realm, he also had been Sir Thomas' former colleague in charity. Who or what had provoked Malory into attempting to murder the great Duke is a question we cannot now answer. Some students suspect Richard Neville; some seem to believe that Buckingham imagined the assault. But these are airy guesses. All we know for sure is that during the next twenty months Malory was not brought to justice. Again we do not know why. Perhaps it was because he was too fast on his feet and the Forest of Arden was too near at hand; perhaps someone was protecting him.*

What seems as likely as anything else is that the attempted assassination was an item in the violence that broke out in many parts of England in the fall of 1449. England was doing very badly in France, and the Yorkists laid the blame on Lancastrian advisors. Young Richard Neville, who had just become Earl of Warwick, was active with the Yorkists; Humphrey, Duke of Buckingham, was in close correspondence with the

---

* So as not to plague the reader with a plethora of qualifying phrases, I have sometimes omitted to record the fact that the documents that report Malory's alleged crimes are charges, not judgments. It is hoped that this stylistic procedure will not prejudice the cause of those who believe that Sir Thomas was innocent.

Lancastrian lords. If Malory really did make this attempt on Buckingham's life, the Duke was luckier than some, for about the date of the charge against Malory, Bishop Moleyns was murdered.

Hardly five months had passed when Malory turned to a new color on the criminal spectrum: in company with William Weston of Newbold Revel, gentleman, Thomas Potter of Bernangle in Warwickshire, husbandman, and Adam Broun of Coventry, weaver, the records charge that he, Thomas Malory of Newbold Revel, knight, feloniously had broken into the house of Hugh Smyth at Monks Kirby and there raped Mistress Joan Smyth. This alleged offense, as some have supposed, may have been less offensive than it now seems. It may mean merely that the four men carried her off, with some violence perhaps. Then again, it probably means just what it seems to us to mean, for eight weeks later Malory was charged with doing the same thing to the same woman, alone and at Coventry, and again very clearly—*cum ea carnaliter concubuit*. Moreover, in for a penny, in for several pounds, he also seized the Smyths' goods and chattels to the value of 40 pounds, and carried them off to Barwell in Leicestershire. A woman's virtue, says the Bard, is a thing of naught; but 40 pounds was twice the annual value of Malory's three estates.

A little before this—and a little after, so the charges declare—Sir Thomas again varied the pattern of his activities with offenses against neighbors in Monks Kirby. On May 31, with the support of John Appleby, gentleman, he extorted by threats 100 shillings from Margaret Kyng and William Hales. On August 31, he used the same procedure with John Mylner, the take being this time a modest 20 shillings.

Six months gone, the law began to close in. On March 15, 1451, Thomas Malory of Newbold Revel, knight, and nineteen other persons, all listed by name, were ordered to be arrested for the divers felonies, transgressions, insurrections, extortions, and oppressions for which they had been previously indicted. No action seems to have resulted however, and the further writs that were issued later in the year had no better result.

At this point it may be instructive to scan the roster of Malory and his band. As the accusations show it, it was a loose confederation of about thirty men, with Malory the leader. Sometimes, though very rarely, he is reported to have operated alone; sometimes he worked with a single colleague, sometimes with three or four. For great and important activities, such as the attempt on the life of the Duke of Buckingham, almost the whole company went into action. And when the target itself was large, a mob drawn from the local population was ready to lend its fervor and mass to the core of stalwarts. Then the operations took on the character of a riot. Such an organization and such a methodology may have been approved patterns among professors of misrule in the fifteenth century, for in the parliamentary rolls and the Paston letters the same procedures are reported for other areas.[5]

Most of the company came from Monks Kirby. And, lest it be deduced from this that the district was inordinately given to crime, one needs to remember that it was a particularly large parish, some ten thousand acres. Malory's lieutenant, Poins to his Falstaff, was a fellow in the early twenties: John Appleby, gentleman, who came from Stoneleigh, half way to Warwick. His aide on occasion may have been William Weston of Newbold, also described as gentleman. Most of the supporters were from Newbold Revel, and they are likely to have been tenants or employees of Sir Thomas: Philip Burman, John Masshot, Thomas Leghton, William Podmore, John Sherd, Roger Sherd, Thomas Sherd, John Warwick, all of whom were yeomen; Geoffrey Griffin the Welshman, Richard the Irishman, and William Smith were all laborers; John Masshot, a groom; John, a harper; Robert, a smith; John, a cook. All these were Newbold men, and they must have formed the majority of that hamlet's male adults. Others lived in nearby villages: John Furneys the tailor was from Brinklow, as also were Gregory Walshale a yeoman and Thomas Partrych a husbandman; William Halle, a yeoman, came from Stoneleigh, the same village as John Appleby; John Tyncock and Thomas Potter, both husbandmen, lived at Wolvey and Bernangle respectively; Adam Broun, a weaver, hailed from Coventry; and Thomas Maryot, the necessary bowmaker, lived somewhere in the parish of Monks Kirby. The company was therefore essentially local; but it was reinforced at times by a few hands from over the border. Richard Malory esquire was one; he came from Radclyff in Leicester and was probably Sir Thomas' relative. Eustace Burnaby of Watford in Northampton was another esquire; he had apparently been sheriff of his county not long before, and there is reason to think that he too was a relative. John Arnesby and John Frysseby were yeomen of Leicestershire, one from Tyrlynton, the other from Carleton; they may have strung along with Richard Malory.

The company was thoroughly representative of country life at the time: lord of the manor, his gentleman friends, and his tenants, laborers and craftsmen. Their ordinary lives one must suppose were humdrum; had it not been for interest in their leader, their chronicle would be one of those panoramas of rural piety that nobody describes.

Before they fade from our view, it is simple decency to record the little more we can learn of them: about their leader we shall have much more to say. John Appleby, obviously an agile young man, slipped through the huge-holed legal net and in 1453 he was outlawed. He seems to have made his way to Carlisle and northern respectability, for in 1468 he was granted a royal pardon, ten years later he was elected member of parliament for Carlisle, and in 1500 or so he died. Eustace Burnaby, who had been sheriff of Northamptonshire three years before he went on jaunt with Sir Thomas, had a similar career. Never brought to trial or outlawed, he is said to have bought lands in Leicestershire, married a Malory, and again established respectability as sheriff in his own county of Northamptonshire. Richard Malory, Sir Thomas' Leicestershire cousin, was given a royal pardon in 1452, his guarantors being several of the Warwickshire gentry.

Thomas Maryot and Thomas Leghton gave themselves up and were sent to the Marshalsea. But within a year, in October 1452, they were pardoned by the King when a group of London swordmakers gave guarantees for their future good behavior. Earlier in the year Thomas Partrych had also been pardoned, and it is an interesting commentary on contemporary legal procedures that one of his guarantors was Thomas Leghton, who was still in prison on the same charge. Before the King's Bench in London, Gregory Walshale pleaded not guilty and demanded trial before a jury from his own county. He was temporarily released on the assurances of two London gentlemen, one of them a relative, and on the day appointed for trial he appeared with a royal pardon and so was released *sine die*. John Tyncok failed to answer an indictment and was outlawed. In 1454 he stated that he had been in prison at Bedford—possibly he was there on some other charge—and he was ordered to remain in the Marshalsea. In Easter term, 1458, he was brought to the bar by the Marshal and asked why he should not be outlawed. He replied that he had a pardon for all offenses he may have committed before February, and so he too was set free.

Many of the rest simply avoided the law's feeble clutches, and all we hear of them is that after the necessary succession of five writs, which may never have been served—the subjects may have been in the Forest of Arden—they were declared outlaws. The sheriff reported that on September 17, 1453, after two years of frustration in attempting to serve writs, he had outlawed John Appleby, John Frysseby, Goeffrey Gryffyn, John Masshot, and William Smith. Some of the others may have been outlawed a month or so earlier, for these names appear in the outlawry roll for Michaelmas term, 1453: John Cook, William Hall, John Harper, Richard Irishman, John Masshot, John Tyncock, and all the Sherd boys. Very surprisingly, all but eight of Malory's merry band enjoy a continuance in the roll of fame, something that people of their sort rarely achieve except by reports of unsanctioned variations from a respectable round.

The writ of March 15, 1451, did not impress Sir Thomas apparently, for in August, William Rowe and William Dowde of Shawell in Leicestershire came to court and made a grave charge against him. With the support of ten eyewitnesses they declared that Malory and four other men—John Masshot, William Smyth, Geoffrey Gryffyn, John Arnesley—had broken into the plaintiffs' property at Cosford and stolen seven cows, two calves, 335 sheep, and a cart worth 4 pounds. Cosford is near to the Leicester border, only five miles from Newbold, but it gives almost a "western" pleasure to imagine the dust, the curses, the sweat, and the bellows of that alleged cattle-rustling of a June 4 five centuries ago.

About the same time probably, though the date is uncertain, a larger echelon of the company, possibly emboldened by the success at Cosford, turned its attention to a more distant prospect, the property of the Peytos of Chesterton. Lady Katherine Peyto makes the complaint, and it is this fact that makes it likely that the actions complained of relate to 1451, for at that time her husband was away, a prisoner in France. Lady Katherine —she was Sir John Gresley's daughter—addresses herself to the Archbishop of Canterbury, declaring that, the Earl of Warwick being out of the country, she knows not where else to seek remedy. Her complaint, still raw with her distress, is that Sir Thomas Malory, "wyth force and armes and grate pepel arraied en fere of werre," had burst into her estate at Syburtoft in Northamptonshire—the hamlet is half way between the Malory manors at Swinford and Winwick—assaulted her bailiff, a farmer named John Dercet, and driven away into Warwickshire four rotherbestes—oxen, that is. All this was without cause and against law, and now Malory ". . . menaceth the said John Dercet: that if he come home, he will either maim him or slay him." And so she implores the archbishop "for the love of Almighty God and in the way of Saint Charity" to summon Malory to appear before him to give sureties of peace.

After his alleged attempt on Buckingham's life, Sir Thomas seems to have lowered his sights for a time. Now they were up again, and the next charge that is made against him is made by an important monastery. On July 13 of the same year a royal commission directed the Earl of Warwick and the Duke of Buckingham to arrest Sir Thomas and his servant John Appleby and to cause them to find guarantors that they would do no hurt to the prior and convent of the monastery of Axholme. There is something perplexing in this. Axholme, a Carthusian monastery in Lincolnshire, was considerably off Sir Thomas' usual beat. The explanation may lie in the fact that Thomas Cowper its prior also had under his jurisdiction the priory of Monks Kirby. It is a fair guess that whatever Malory may have done or threatened to do, he did it against the priory next door to his own house. However this may be, it is probably this writ that led to his arrest a few days later. Sir Thomas had done well so far with seculars, but he was to find the religious considerably more persistent in exacting revenge.

If Malory knew of this writ, his next reputed operation must have been prompted by insolence. For on July 20, according to a later charge, he broke into the park at Caludon* three miles east of Coventry, which Buckingham owned jointly with the Duke of Norfolk and the Archbishop of Canterbury. There he is said to have done damage extraordinary, with swords and sticks—the amount of it was estimated at the outrageous sum of £500—and carried off six does that had graced their lordships' plesance. This reported activity, which bears all the marks of malice, was too fresh even to appear in the list of charges that were presented when Malory was at length brought to book.

The record declares that the Caludon mayhem took place on a Tuesday. On the following Sunday, Warwick and Buckingham took action. Sir Thomas was arrested with John Appleby at Newbold Revel, taken to Coventry, and there put into the custody of the sheriff of Warwickshire, his old parliamentary colleague, Sir William Mountford. Mountford was ordered to keep the prisoner safe and to bring him before the King and his Council. Sir William transported Sir Thomas to Coleshill and shut him up for safekeeping in the great manor house there with its strong walls and moat: nearby Maxstoke Castle, it is interesting to note, was owned by Sir Thomas' intended victim, Humphrey Stafford, Duke of

---

* Represented as *Calendon* on Saxton's map.

Buckingham. Two nights later, on Tuesday, Malory broke out, swam the moat, and rejoined his band at Newbold.

Their parley must have been desperate and vengeful. According to the records, their sally the next day (Wednesday, July 28) was the most violent and comprehensive of all their ventures to date. Malory and ten of the band—Appleby, the three Sherds, Hall, Masshot, Tyncok, Walshale, Maryot, and Richard the Irishman—together with many other malefactors and breakers of the King's peace unnamed, rose in the manner of an insurrection and forced their way into the monastery and abbey of the Blessed Mary at Combe. With great wooden balks they burst in at night, entered divers gates and doors, and there and then broke into two chests and two bags which contained £46 in gold and silver coins and many other ornaments and jewels belonging to Abbot Richard. The loot, to the value of £40, they then carried away "in great destruction and spoliation of the monastery and abbey aforesaid."

Next day they repeated the maneuver. Some scholars, unmindful of Malory's seeming penchant for duplicating a satisfying achievement, have thought that a scribe may absent-mindedly have restated things. However that may be, the scribe's declaration is that on Thursday, Malory and a mob of about a hundred—the eighteen who are named are all old comrades—entered into the close of the abbey, armed with swords, lances, ropes, bows and arrows. They broke down eighteen doors; and, when Abbot Richard and his few monks and servants expostulated, they first insulted them and then proceeded violently to force open and rifle three iron chests. The plunder reads like a pawn ticket: forty-odd pounds in coin, three gold rings, two silver signets, two silver zones (belts presumably), three rosaries (one of them coral, one amber, the third jet), two bows and three sheaves of arrows. The product of the two sallies was, therefore, chattels and bullion to the value of £134, about £6,700 in present-day terms.

This was simply too much. Malory had now, or so the charges indicate, offended God and abbots as well as men, all of them substantially. Very soon after this his adventurous career narrowed from the expanses of Warwickshire to the confines of London jails.

On Monday, August 23, the charges against Sir Thomas Malory were brought before a court at Nuneaton. The bill included all but three of the offenses that we have so far described: the eight-year-old assault on Thomas Smythe and the more recent raids on Syburton and Caludon Park. The jury consisted of fifteen persons from Birmingham, Solihull, and other villages in northern Warwickshire. The four middle-aged men on the bench were Humphrey, duke of Buckingham; Sir William Birmingham, the sheriff-designate; Thomas Greswold, the coroner for Warwickshire; and Thomas Bate, a commissioner of the peace. In point of fact, Malory's offenses came before two juries on the same day and occasion. After the first jury had considered the bulk of the charges, an additional charge was brought before a smaller jury of nine persons.

The documents record no discussion or any decision taken by this court. It has often been assumed that Malory was present at the inquests, facing his accusers, one of whom was also an alleged victim. But the documents do not say who appeared as accusers or witnesses, nor that Sir Thomas was there in person. It is not impossible that he and the rest of his company, so far from standing in a Nuneaton dock, were in fact walking the Arden woods.

Much has been written of the iniquity of an accuser sitting in judgment on a man he accused. But it may not have been quite so unjust as it now seems. Buckingham and Richard Neville, the new and youthful earl of Warwick, had royal instructions to put Malory in custody. The most recent of Malory's offenses against the Duke does not appear in the Nuneaton bill. And although the allegation of attempted assassination is there, it is only one of nine charges, the rest being offenses that he is said to have committed against Combe Abbey and ordinary people of the county. The function of such inquests moreover was not to pass sentence. As with a modern grand jury, the job of an inquest was to decide whether there were grounds for committing the accused person to custody and later to trial.

Presumably the Nuneaton court found a true bill. Some recent scholars, rallying to Malory's defense, have urged that the inquest, like the charges, was rigged. That is as it may be: there is no evidence one way or the other. But there is a matter for reflection in the fact that three of the four men on the bench seem to have been Lancastrians. Bate was a lawyer and had held public offices for many a year—as prison commissioner, justice of the peace, recorder of Coventry, and member of parliament in 1442 and 1449. In politics he seems to have been Lancastrian. Greswold of Solihull and Tamworth was a lawyer, a King's Serjeant, coroner for Warwick, commissioner of the peace, and a man who later lent money to Malory and then had to sue for it. He was Yorkist in politics, the only one of that persuasion on the bench. Birmingham had been sheriff of Warwickshire and Leicester nine years before, and the abundance of his offices before 1460 and their total absence after Edward IV came to the throne hints strongly at his being Lancastrian. Buckingham, a colleague and a relative of Richard Beauchamp, had served with the great earl at Rouen, been captain of Calais, warden of the Cinque Ports, member of the Council. As a soldier he had suppressed several rebellions —without necessarily being wicked for so doing. In the conflict of Lancaster and York he first tried to patch up the differences between the rival political factions. When this proved useless, he took the opposite side from Richard Neville, the new earl of Warwick, and cast his lot with Henry VI and his queen, dying in their cause at St. Albans less than four years after the inquest at Nuneaton. That young allegiance may possibly have been the reason for any attempt on his life in Combe Abbey woods.

How and when Malory was seized is uncertain, but seized he must have been; for, by the end of the following January (1452), he was in the Marshalsea. The Marshalsea prison, which housed offenders of every kind from debtors to murderers, was in Southwark a little way beyond the Bridge out of London—a short walk southeast from the inn where Chaucer and his pilgrims are said to have met some sixty years earlier. Malory's whereabouts are stated in a document which reports that the Duke of Buckingham, the Archbishop of Canterbury, and the Duke and Duchess of Norfolk had laid complaint before the King's Bench at Westminster about the raid on Caludon Park in the preceding July. Sir Thomas appeared in person at the King's Bench, pleaded not guilty, and put himself upon the country. That is, he demanded that he should be tried before a jury made up from men who lived in Warwickshire. The court so ordered, and it appointed April 28 as the day when the jury should be ready at Westminster.

About the same time, another document records Malory's appearance on several other charges. The procedure ran the same course. Sir Thomas pleaded not guilty and demanded a trial before his countrymen; the court ordered such a jury to be summoned. But the court, and Sir Thomas too, must have known full well what would happen. Nothing was more difficult in those days than to persuade even a few men to drop their businesses, make the long journey to London (it took three full days from Warwick), and spend time and money there simply to uphold the principle of trial before local peers. What happened in this case was what had happened in hundreds of others: the twenty-four persons nominated as jurors failed to show up. The court ordered their goods to be distrained; and while it was in a punitive mood, it also ordered that all Sir Thomas' own goods should be distrained. That the orders were evaded or not implemented seems pretty sure; his widow continued to own his three manors right to her dying day.

Nothing happened at all, except that Malory rested in the Marshalsea. How long is uncertain, however: he was certainly at large a year later. On March 26, 1453, the Duke of Buckingham, Sir Edward Grey of Groby, and the sheriffs of Warwickshire and Leicestershire were ordered to arrest him and to bring him before the King and Council at Westminster. From the officers named we may conjecture that Sir Thomas had returned to his *patria*. How he got out can only be guessed. In May, 1452, he had borrowed sixty shillings from Robert Overton, undertaking to repay it in September. Overton, as the legal records show, was a London citizen and mercer who was notably busy in the London jails, lending smallish sums of money to prisoners and sometimes failing to get them back: his benefactions were something short of charity, it seems. Anyone who is acquainted with the tried and proven ways of securing release from medieval prisons may therefore venture a cautious conjecture. My own is that Malory bribed a jailer or two, possibly using Overton's loan, and just walked out.

Before the fall he must have been arrested again, for a document of the 1453 Michaelmas term reports that a jury was to be assembled to judge whether Sir Thomas Malory was guilty of the various felonies, insurrections, extortions, and oppressions with which he had been charged. Again no jury could be assembled; so the case was respited to the following January, and the Sheriff of London was ordered in the meantime to keep the prisoner in the Marshalsea. January came and then February, and, the jury being still not assembled, an order was again issued that Sir Thomas should be kept secure by the Marshal. The document denies bail and it also imposes a penalty on the Marshal if Malory should escape—a penalty that seems intentionally stiff: 1,000 medieval pounds. Some interested party was clearly being obdurate. Who it was may be guessed from the fact that in enumerating Sir Thomas' offenses strong stress is put upon his activities against the Abbot of Combe.

Within three months, on May 5 or 24, 1454, he contrived his liberty by a second well-tried means. He was released on bail of a kind. He swore to the court that he would maintain good behavior and that on October 29 he would come back for recommittal to the Marshalsea. The procedure presumably was prompted by a hope that a jury might be got together by then. As guarantee, Sir Thomas put himself under penalty of £200, and ten other persons were put under penalty of £20 each. The guarantors were men of some standing: one knight, three gentlemen, and six esquires. What is most interesting however is that while four of the guarantors were from Warwickshire and one lived in Essex, the five others all came from Framlingham in Suffolk: Edmund Fitzwilliam, Ralph Worthington, John Valens, William Worsop, and Sir Roger Chamberlain. Such an assembly could scarcely have been a gathering of Malory's own friends, nor does it seem likely that Sir Thomas could secure £200 without help. Behind the maneuver there must have been some man of substance, and who it was is not hard to guess: John Mowbray, earl of Norfolk. Mowbray's seat was at Framlingham, some of these guarantors are known to have been major officers of his, and Malory himself held his manor of Newbold Revel from the Duke. It is hardly stretching probability to suspect that Mowbray had decided to overlook Malory's offenses at Caludon and to effect his release. Even the reason seems plain. On January 19, 1454, a letter written from London to the Pastons in Norfolk reported the gathering of Lancastrian forces in London and warned that ". . . it is necessarie that my Lord loke wele to hym self and kepe hym amonge his meyné, and departe nat from theym, for it is to drede lest busshementes shulde be leide for hym." The writer was John Stodeley, and among his informants he lists John Leventhorpe, one of the men who went bail for Malory. Mowbray, very clearly, was counting on Sir Thomas' strong arm for his safety.

The appointed day came, October 29. No Malory appeared in court. Thomas Greswold demanded execution of the penalties to which Sir Thomas and his guarantors were liable. (Greswold, the reader will remember, had been on the bench at Nuneaton, but on this occasion he was the King's Serjeant, spokesman for the law.) Two guarantors however had come to explain why Malory was unable to meet the court that day: John Hampton would not let him. Hampton was governor of Colchester Jail, and Malory was in his charge on suspicion of felony. When the truth of this statement was confirmed, the court issued a writ of *habeas corpus* two days later, directing Hampton to produce his prisoner in three weeks time. The judge who issued the writ was Sir John Fortescue, best known to us as the author of an admirable treatise on absolute and limited monarchy, best known to his contemporaries as a forceful and independent chief justice and a politician who was fervently devoted to the cause of Henry VI and Queen Margaret.

How Malory came to be in Colchester Jail is an interesting tale and

The Ill-Framed Knight

seemingly typical of the man. It is recounted in a series of documents relating to three inquests that were held at Braintree and Chelmsford in the county of Essex. Twenty-nine witnesses combined to narrate the following saga, a sequel to Malory's release from the Marshalsea upon the assurances of Mowbray's officers at nearby Framlingham.

It begins with John Aleyn, recently of London, a yeoman—he may also be the John Aleyn, formerly of London, mercer and outlaw, whose name appears in Edward IV's general pardon of October 24, 1461. In May, 1454, so the justices were told, Aleyn broke into the close at Great Easton, which belonged to John the abbot of Tilty, and thence feloniously stole two horses—one a bay worth 40 shillings, the other a grey worth 100 shillings. Just over a month later he broke into the close of Richard Skott, the vicar of Gosfield, and thence stole a white horse worth 5 marks. On July 2, with swords and daggers, he stole a sorrel and a bay belonging to Thomas Bykenen and Thomas Strete at Gosfield. What Aleyn had in mind to do with this stable of horses is not stated; perhaps it was to spread his conquests further.

Sir Thomas Malory enters the story on July 9. He is described, delicately and perhaps obliviously, as "nuper de London." The record goes on to state, quite in saga style, that he was first seen riding with John Aleyn from Waltham Cross to Thaxted and thence to Braintree. That night Malory lodged with Aleyn, comforting him it is asserted and conspiring against William Grene, William Algore, and several other Essex worthies. Next Sunday, while all the Christians of Gosfield were in church partaking of the mass, Aleyn, Malory, and several associates armed with swords and daggers, broke into the close of John Grene, got into his house by means of various wire instruments, made their way to Grene's bedroom, and—had they not been interrupted—would have feloniously carried away the several coffers and chests in which Grene and his wife kept their goods and chattels. Only a week late John Addelsey, described as Malory's servant, broke into John Grene's close a second time.

Malory avoided retribution, possibly at Framlingham, for nearly three months. At long last the law caught up with him on October 16, when he was arrested and committed to the royal jail at Colchester by Sir Thomas Cobham, sheriff of Essex.

He remained there only a short time. Three years before it had taken him merely two days to break out of Coleshill Manor. Colchester was a grim and strong fortress, and it is said to have taken Sir Thomas a fortnight before he could remove himself from John Hampton's custody. In fact, the separation had to be effected with some violence, by force and arms, viz., with swords, longbills, and daggers. It is an interesting consideration whether this substantial armory was wrested, Lancelot-wise, from the enemy or sneaked in by confederates on the outside. Certainly the break must have involved more men than Malory, but it is satisfactory that it occurred on October 30, the very day that Sir John Fortescue issued the writ commanding John Hampton to bring Malory to court.

That Sir Thomas' impatient departure from Colchester was prompted by fear of missing an appointment at Westminster is not likely. He remained on French leave until November 18, when he was apprehended and entrusted to the care of the governor of the Marshalsea. As if in tribute to Malory's reputation for resolution and resource but in disapprobation of the ways that he used them, the court put the severe penalty of 1,000 medieval pounds on the Marshal should he let him escape.

For the next two years, the records suggest that Sir Thomas remained in close custody. In May, 1455, he was removed into the Tower, and the Constable was instructed to hold him secure. No reason is given, but it is not impossible that the shift to a prison that specialized in taking care of political prisoners may have had some connection with the activities of Malory's noble associates, the Duke of Norfolk and the Earl of Warwick. Three days after that removal, the battle of St. Albans was fought. That battle, though it was hardly more than a skirmish, was almost the official declaration of the Wars of the Roses. Henry VI, sick and crazy, was on one side and Warwick was on the other; supporting Warwick in his less martial way was Malory's patron, the duke of Norfolk.

On June 15, twenty-three days after the battle, Malory was again before the King's Bench at Westminster. A day was then appointed, October 13, when he should be tried before a jury drawn from his own countymen, and thereupon he was recommitted to the care of the Constable of the Tower. Such was the concern of the presiding judge—probably Sir John Fortescue, the sturdy Lancastrian—that the penalty on the Constable was increased to £2,000.

Efforts to recruit a Warwickshire jury must have failed once more, for a later document states that jurors were to be distrained again for January 27, 1456. On February 8 Malory must have been still in the custody of the Constable: on that date Thomas Gower brought him to the King's Bench to present a petition. Malory brought with him letters patent from the King dated November 24 of the previous year, instructing that "Thomas Malory nuper de Fenny Newbold in com. Warwick, miles alias

Thomas Malory nuper de London, miles" should be pardoned for transgressions, insurrections, and any other misdemeanors committed before July 9, 1455. He also presented, either by writing or in person, six men who were willing to act as his guarantors: Roger Malory of Ryton, gentleman; John Benford of London, gentleman; William Clyff of London, gentleman; Walter Boys of London, sadler; Thomas Pulton of London, tailor; and David John of London, tailor.

The court dismissed both the pardon and the offer of guarantees. If this seems surprising at first glance, it may seem less surprising at second. The pardon that Malory brought was a particular application of a document that the King had issued to the bailiffs of England, pardoning offenses committed before July 9, 1455. This general pardon was related to the battle of St. Albans, in which Warwick and the Yorkists had defeated Henry VI; and it was probably issued by the Duke of York who was then serving as Protector for the poor mad king. That the court rejected the pardon may relate to the politics of Sir John Fortescue, its presiding officer, who was so bitterly opposed to Warwick and the Yorkist pretension that when Henry VI was dethroned he first took up arms on the deposed King's behalf and then went into exile with Margaret of Anjou.

For nearly two years the legal records report only minor matters concerning Sir Thomas. All the time, it appears, he continued in prison. When his pardon was rejected the court sent him to the Marshalsea, and it is mostly to that prison that the documents of the next two years relate.

On June 28 Robert Overton sued for the 60 shillings he had lent the prisoner four years before. Malory came to the King's Bench, overlooked the promissory note, and denied it was his. This suit dragged on for months. Juries could not be assembled, the sheriff forgot to send the writ, postponement followed postponement, and nothing happened. In May, 1457, Thomas Greswold, Malory's old acquaintance the King's Serjeant, sued for a loan of 4 pounds 9 shillings and 8 pence, which Malory had promised to repay the previous Christmas. Despite repeated requests, he said, the money was still owing. Sir Thomas came from the Marshalsea, and after he had examined the bill he declared that he could not deny the debt—the admission may reflect the fact that Greswold, who was a Yorkist, had been helpful to Malory in a number of ways. So judgment was entered against Sir Thomas, with damages of 3 shillings and 4 pence.

Although Malory spent most of his time in the Marshalsea, he must occasionally have been shifted to other prisons. A document of January,

1457, directed to William Edward and Thomas Reyner, the sheriffs of London, and signed by Sir John Fortescue in the King's name, states that Sir Thomas Malory of Fenny Newbold had been kept in the Marshalsea for the security of the Abbey of Combe and various others of the King's lieges, but that for greater security he had been transferred to the charge of the Sheriff of Middlesex and committed to Newgate. The court now ordered, possibly because of Greswold's suit, that he should be committed to the prison at Ludgate. The court made the sheriff responsible for his safe keeping, however, under penalty of £1,000. In less than six months then, Sir Thomas had been in no less than four jails: the Marshalsea in Southwark, which was a general prison; the fortress prison at the Tower, which usually housed political prisoners; Newgate, which took care of criminals and traitors; and the debtors prison of Ludgate.

On Wednesday, October 13, however, Sir Thomas was released until December 28. He himself was put under penalty of £400, and his three guarantors were put under penalty of £20 each. As on the similar occasion in 1454, three years before, the explanation for this ability to put up a very large bail and for the success of his application must be sought in the character of his guarantors. They were Lord Fauconbridge, William Briggeham of Briggeham, esquire, and John Clerkson of Arundel, esquire. The last has defied all enquiry. Brigham however proves to have been a Yorkshireman who was at that time a soldier at Calais: in 1461, when the Yorkists were in power, he was granted an annuity of ten marks from the taxes of a village near Calais. When he went bail for Malory he must have been fairly young, for a Yorkshire pedigree indicates that he did not die until 1494. Fauconbridge's family name was William Neville. He was the Earl of Warwick's uncle, and from July, 1457, until December, 1458, he was in his retinue while the Earl was captain of Calais and while he was plotting the overthrow of Henry VI. Nothing is more likely therefore than that Malory's release was arranged from Calais, on behalf of Warwick the Kingmaker. What Malory did during his two months of freedom is regrettably unreported: he may have gone to Calais; he may have stayed in England. Wherever he was, it is no wild conjecture that he was engaged in activities pleasing to the Kingmaker.

This release was followed by none of the old excitements. On December 28, Malory duly appeared to answer his bail, and just as duly he was recommitted to the Marshalsea. During the next year, however, trustworthy men of the county of Warwick informed the King's Bench that Sir Thomas Malory was out of the custody of the Marshal and had been at large since Easter. To judge by the mildness of the court's response to this information, Malory's freedom may have been amicably arranged. It simply ordered the Marshal to keep Sir Thomas safe and not to let him be at large outside the prison; and, although it imposed a penalty upon the Marshal if Sir Thomas should escape again, the sum was only one hundred pounds, a tenth of the previous penalty.

The last prison record that has been unearthed for Sir Thomas Malory of Newbold Revel was issued in the 1460 Hilary term—the term now ordinarily called Lent. It declares that Sir Thomas was to be committed to the custody of the Sheriff of Middlesex, to be detained safe and secure in the prison of Newgate. It concludes that "ideo dictus Marescallus de eo hic exoneratur," that the said Marshal is hereby released from further responsibility.

As in some of its previous actions concerning Sir Thomas, the court may be guessed to have acted on this occasion from political considerations. The matter is not certain, but there may be significance in the fact that the decision was made only a few weeks before the battle of Northampton, which took place on July 10 of the same year. In that battle, the Yorkists led by Richard Neville, the earl of Warwick, and by William Neville, the Lord Fauconbridge, defeated the Lancastrian forces led by Humphrey Stafford, the duke of Buckingham. Buckingham was killed in the battle: victory set Warwick up on the high horse of power. On March 3 following, he and John Mowbray, the duke of Norfolk, called on the Earl of March at his lodging at Baynard's Castle (a short walk from Newgate) and besought him to take off Henry's crown and wear it as his own as Edward IV.

For the next decade, Sir Thomas Malory, hitherto so prominent in the brief chronicles of crime, drops almost out of sight. There are two interesting records of a person or persons named Thomas Malory (in one of them he is called *miles*) which mention his partaking in the 1462 sieges in the North and his exclusion from pardon in 1468. They are merely mentioned here, because several scholars have expressed doubt (which the present writer shares) that the documents refer to the subject of the present biography. Certainly, they differ from all the documents that we have relied on so far, in that they do not describe their Malory(s) as being of Newbold Revel or Monks Kirby.

Only four more documents clearly relate to our present candidate. The earliest is the general pardon issued at Westminster by the new King on October 24, 1461. As a reader unrolls this great vellum, he may notice among its seemingly endless names a few that are familiar. John Aleyn, *nuper de London*, mercer, comes early. And then, after many an unwinding: "Thomas Mallory miles alias dominus Thomas Mallory de Newbold Ryvell in Com. Warw. miles."

The second document is reported in Nichols' old pedigree of the Warwickshire Malorys. There it is stated that on September 12, 1464, William Fielding conveyed to his son John certain lands at Stormworth, and that among the several worthies who put their hands to the conveyance as witnesses, Sir Thomas Malory was one. This must be our knight of Newbold Revel, who owned land in the same place. The Fieldings were already well established in Newnham-juxta-Monks-Kirby, and there are still many monuments to them in the church—some to the early Fieldings, but more to their descendants, the Earls of Denbigh. What is humanly interesting in this, apart from its evidence that Sir Thomas was then at large, is that William Fielding was a Lancastrian: ". . . a person so well affected to the Lancastrian side," says Dugdale, "that no sooner did Henry VI regain sovereignty, but he constituted himself sheriff of the counties of Cambridge and Huntingdon, being then a knight—in which year, fighting on behalf of the said King in the battle of Tewkesbury, he lost his life and was there buried." If, as seems very likely from so many of his associations, some of Sir Thomas' life and efforts had been applied to Warwick and the cause of York, his presence at the Fieldings' great witnessing party displays a tolerance thoroughly fifteenth century.

The third document is nonpolitical. It implies that in 1466 a son Nicholas was born to Sir Thomas' son Robert, and that not long thereafter, during Sir Thomas' lifetime, his son Robert passed away.

The fourth and last record describes the final act in Sir Thomas Malory's eventful history. On Thursday, March 12, 1471, he died. For him, the comet that not long before had flared in the West was an omen both good and ill. For several years, he had seemingly done the will of Warwick, Mowbray, and Fauconbridge. Now, it was his destiny to die only two months before the battle of Tewkesbury brought death and destruction upon the politicians and causes he had so long served.

On the following Saturday, March 14, Sir Thomas was buried in Greyfriars chapel, within the winter day's shadow of Newgate. Thus his passing was more splendid than anything the records reveal of his living. The glory of Greyfriars was unrivalled. The friary had been founded in 1225. During the next three centuries it was enriched, and as it grew it became the pride of London merchants, and particularly the pride of merchants in the Mediterranean trade. City companies, mayors, aldermen, merchants joined to make it more splendid. In 1471, when Sir Thomas was buried there, it could boast two fine cloisters, each enclosed by several great buildings: a chapterhouse, a dortour, a refectory, an infirmary, a great church, and a very fine library. Among all these splendid structures, the church was the most sumptuous. It was begun in 1279 and completed in 1327; and, judging by its thirty-six windows, it was built in the light, airy style of the new Paris churches: the colors shed by its glass might have resembled the jeweled shadows of Saint-Chapelle. Nine alabaster tombs ennobled the great nave. An elaborate screen, in which the statue of St. Louis was prominent, set off the chapel dedicated to Francis of Assisi.

Such sumptuousness to the glory of God was not to every medieval man's taste. Greyfriars was the pride of the London citizenry. The splendor of its ornaments may also have been the object of a puritan attack in *Pierce the Ploughman's Crede*. For Greyfriars chapel had come to be the most ornate and fashionable place in London to await Judgment Day. Nearly seven hundred persons of eminence rested there: two queens and a king, nobles, goldsmiths, scholars, monks, physicians, judges, and rich merchants from Florence, Genoa, Gascony, Sicily, and Spain.[6]

On March 14, 1471, the mortal part of Sir Thomas Malory was carried along Newgate Street into the splendor of Greyfriars church and borne to the right into the chapel of Saint Francis. There it was laid to rest under the fourth window on the south side between the graves of Thomas Yonge, former Justice of Common Pleas, and Pancius de Coutrone, former physician to Edward III. And when the solemn ceremonies were done, a stone was placed over him. Carved on it was this epitaph:

> HIC IACET DOMINUS THOMAS MALLERE
> VALENS MILES
> OB 14 MAR 1470
> DE PAROCHIA DE MONKENKIRBY IN
> COM WARWICI

Sixty-eight years later, the monastery surrendered to Henry VIII, and for nine years thereafter its church was used as a storehouse. In 1547 it was reopened under the name of Christ Church, and all the great tombs and gravestones were pulled up and sold. The monastic buildings and the church were thereupon turned over to the use of King Edward's new foundation, Christ's Hospital, a refuge and school for children fatherless and motherless. So it remained until the later nineteenth century, and that fact permits a reflection to interest all who are interested in the lives of great English writers. William Camden, Samuel Richardson, Charles Lamb, Samuel Taylor Coleridge, and Leigh Hunt—clad in their long blue gowns, yellow stockings, and broad shoes—must often in their boyhood have strolled or scampered unknowingly over the dust and the bones of the generally accepted author of *Le Morte Darthur*, Sir Thomas Malory of Newbold Revel, *valens miles, chevalier sans peur sinon sans reproche.*

II

PROS AND CONS

The case for the Welsh candidate is mostly priority. John Bale, who first made the proposal, was born in 1495, only ten years after *Le Morte Darthur* was published, and *a priori* he might be thought to have had readier sources of information, to have known more of what he was saying than someone born much later.* But there lies the rub, for there is no evidence at all that Bale had any specific knowledge. He gave no details about his candidate, save that he was *Britannus natione* and that he was born in *Mailoria in finibus Cambriae, Devæ flumini vicina*. No one, however, not even a Welshman, has ever located such a place, either on the Dee or anywhere else. In fact, as Kittredge pointed out, Bale's total suggestion may be a freehand development of a small detail he found in his sources. The note is acknowledgedly based upon the *Syllabus* that John Leland published in 1542. The present writer would add that a phrase in the note, which repeats the title of another book by Leland, shows that Bale also knew the 1544 treatise in which Leland discussed the historicity of King Arthur. In that treatise, Leland spoke of the French and Welsh romances about Arthur and the English collection, *autore Thoma Mailerio*, which derived from them. This statement gives the clue to the begetting of the Welsh candidate, for Leland's own note seems to proceed from a careless reading of a passage in Caxton's Preface to *Le Morte*

---

* Bale's suggestion was first drawn to the attention of modern scholars in Sommer's edition of *Le Morte Darthur*, 1890.

Darthur, the passage in which the printer referred to the fact that although there were many foreign versions of the Arthurian story, there was no complete version in English:

> But in Walsshe ben many, and also in Frensshe, and somme in Englysshe, but nowher nygh alle. Wherefore, suche as have late ben drawen oute bryefly into Englysshe, I have ... enprysed to enprynte ...

The readiest explanation for the Welsh claimant, therefore, is that he was begotten in a loose reading of Caxton.

The most substantial support, in fact, for Malory's possible connection with Wales has been provided by a scholar who regards Bale's theory as untenable. This scholar, Eugène Vinaver, *doyen* of Malory studies, has pointed out that in several places in the *Tristram*, Malory departed from his French sources to bring in Welshmen. Among the knights who come to the tournament of Lonazep, for example, are the unauthorized King of Northgales and King of the best part of Wales. In another adventure, an anonymous *chevalier de Norgales* is replaced by two North Welsh knights whom Malory gave typically Welsh names, Hugh and Madoc. Rather more interestingly, Malory is apparently the only medieval romancer who made Tristram travel to Wales: his hero and Iseult of the White Hands are driven by wind into "the coste of Walys upon the Isle of Servage." There are a few other matters of similar kind, most of them in the book of *Tristram*.

Not everyone who talks about Heaven has been there, however, and it is entirely possible that the Welsh-directed variations in Malory's version of the Tristram story are determined by the simple fact that one of the chief heroes of this romance, in French as well as in *Le Morte Darthur*, is Lamorak of Wales, the only peer of Tristram and Lancelot. Moreover, countervailing any impression that Sir Thomas Malory may have had some special interest in the Wales of reality is the fact that in his version of the Roman War, based on the alliterative poem entitled *Morte Arthure*, he omitted altogether the lively Welsh setting with which that poem begins.

The extreme unlikeliness that a fifteenth-century Welshman would compose a long romance in English, the amorphousness of the case for even the existence of any Welsh Thomas Malory, and certainly the fact that Malory himself thought he was English ("Alas thys ys a greate defaute of us Englysshemen, for there may no thynge please us no terme.") makes the Welsh claim simply a pleasant *jeu d'esprit*. John Bale's Welshman is almost certainly a ghost conceived in error, and *Mailoria* is a ghostly emanation. Professor John Rhys's argument in favor of Bale's thesis is that Sir Thomas' surname is an Anglicized form of *Mailorius*, which in turn is a Latinized derivative from *Maelor*, the name of districts in the counties of Denbigh and Flint. Ingenious as the argument is, it suffers from the ghostliness of its forbear. Until some name is found in the records of Maelor or Mailoria to represent an actual body named Thomas Malory, Bale's and Rhys's conjectured Welshman must, alas, be regarded as an airy nothingness, lacking the substance of either local habitation or name.

Martin's plea for the Papworth Malory as against the Warwickshire Malory is based upon acute interpretation of a detail in *Le Morte Darthur*. Martin wrote before the discovery of the Winchester manuscript, before it became certain that the author was a prisoner, but he shrewdly interpreted the final passage in Caxton's text, the one in which Malory prays for good deliverance, to mean that the author was in captivity. This was a generation before the researches of Cobb, Chambers, Hicks, and Baugh laid bare the prison career of the knight of Newbold Revel, and Martin's information about that candidate contained nothing to hint at such a career. From certain details in the life of the Papworth claimant, however, Martin deduced that he might possibly have been in prison at the end of his life, in 1469. The Papworth man made his will on September 16, 1469, and it was probated the next month. He was only forty-four at the time, and his youngest child was still at breast. Martin guessed from these facts that his candidate made his will in haste and under a sense of compulsion, possibly because he was in prison. His death, in the fall of 1469, possibly while he was in captivity, coincided with the completion of *Le Morte Darthur*, during the ninth year of Edward IV's reign, March 4, 1469, to March 3, 1470, and while its author was a prisoner.

Martin's preference between the two Thomas Malorys was based on a very important criterion, but there are serious weaknesses in his argument. First, the conjecture that the Papworth Malory died in prison is specious, based more upon the book than upon the evidence about the man. Making a will at the age of forty-four and dying soon thereafter is no evidence of imprisonment: it is more likely to be evidence of sudden grave sickness. Nothing in the other details of this claimant's life gives any reason to believe that he was ever in trouble with either the law or the military.

Kittredge, in his footnote concerning Martin's candidate, raises two other objections. The first is that this Thomas Malory was an esquire, whereas the author was a knight. The objection is not nearly so serious as Kittredge believed. Distinctions between the two terms were not nearly so rigid in the fifteenth century as they are now. This Malory's father, for instance, sometimes is called "Sir" in the legal documents and sometimes is not. Whatever he was called, however, he held his lands of the king by knight fee, and so did his son Thomas, even though one document calls him *armiger*. The second objection is that although *Le Morte Darthur* may have been finished early in the ninth year of Edward's reign, it seems unlikely that its author could have died soon after September, 1469. This objection is in no way final, but it has force of a kind.

The Papworth candidate's cause was tenuous from the beginning, and when Hicks began to reveal the prison career of the Warwickshire rival, its tenuousness seemed stretched to breaking. It now seems very doubtful, in fact, that Martin, a judicious and unimpassioned scholar, would ever have supported his own man had he known what is now known of Sir Thomas Malory of Newbold Revel.

To give the quietus to the Papworth cause, two facts may now be added, facts which have emerged from the present writer's restudy of all the claims. First, although Malory introduced into *Le Morte Darthur* many local English place-names that do not occur in his sources—Alnwick, Arundel, Lambeth, St. Albans, and so on—not a single one of them relates to Huntingdon or Cambridge, or even to Shropshire. Second, that although Malory's book, both in the Caxton and the Winchester forms, employs numerous dialect usages, none of them is characteristic of the areas in which Martin's candidate grew up and lived.

In short, the Papworth claimant's case may be dismissed with considerable assurance. Very little can be said for him, and a great deal against. Except for A. W. Pollard, who gave general approval to this identification in his edition of 1900, no scholar has felt warranted in agreeing with Martin.

The case for Sir Thomas Malory of Newbold Revel is considerably more solid, and it seems to have become even more solid since Kittredge first proposed it. It is now so impressive, in fact, so generally accepted, that a skeptical scholar might travel a whole sabbatical journey without finding another Doubting Thomas to comfort him.

Kittredge's essay falls into several divisions. First, he identified the author of *Le Morte Darthur* with the Sir Thomas Malory who is described in Dugdale's *Antiquities of Warwickshire*. Second, he argued that the Warwickshire man's life, as there described, matches the criteria for authorship that may be deduced from the book: that his name was Thomas Malory, that he was a knight, that he was alive in 1469-1470 and of an age to write a book, and that he died before 1485. Kittredge did not mention imprisonment as a criterion, however.

The third section in the essay consists of a lengthy but yet selective list of Malorys, covering three centuries. Its overt purpose is to establish from the various spellings—*Maleore, Mailore, Malorye*, and so on—how the author's name was pronounced. The names were also made to serve a more weighty purpose, for it seems to be on the basis of this list (and probably on the examination that produced it) that Kittredge made his claim on behalf of the Warwickshire knight: "there is absolutely no contestant, and until such a contestant appears, it is not unreasonable to insist on the claims of this Sir Thomas."

Kittredge's apparent procedures, certainly the most extensive and laborious examination of the printed sources of information that had until then been applied to our problem, are described in the following eulogy in a recent study of Scholar-Adventurers:

> But it was not until George Lyman Kittredge of Harvard, early in his illustrious career as a scholar, attacked the problem systematically and with his usual amazing thoroughness that any progress was made. Whereas previous investigators had found but a few Malorys in history, Kittredge began by unearthing the names and habitations of hundreds of persons who lived in England before 1485 and were named Malory, Mallore, Maulore, Mallere, Mallure, Mallery, Maleore, and so forth. Since medieval spelling was always flexible, especially in family names, these records were all possible clues at least to the writer's family. But to qualify as the author of the *Morte Darthur*, any Malory found in the historical records would, according to the evidence deduced from the book itself, have not only to be named Thomas, but to be a knight, alive in the ninth year of Edward IV's reign (March 4, 1469, to March 3, 1470), and old enough at that time to write the book. Any Sir Thomas Malorys aged, say, eleven in 1470, need not apply. From his very large collection of Malorys, Kittredge isolated the sole figure who fitted all these requirements. He was the Sir Thomas Malory of Newbold Revel.

Despite the confidence of his own claim, Kittredge realized that there were dragons to slay. In a trenchant appendix, therefore, he laid low Bale's and Rhys's Welsh claimant, advancing the satisfying reasons we have already credited to him, and also the argument that whereas *Maelor* was pronounced with two syllables, *Malory* was pronounced with three. In a forceful footnote, he also demolished the Papworth claimant as failing to meet some essential criteria.

These elements of Kittredge's case, and especially his apparent proof that there was no possible rival to the Warwickshire knight, formed powerful arguments. But their advocacy was directed toward externals, and they failed to provide the kind of connection that Oskar Sommer seemed to have demanded in the 1890 edition that probably set off Kittredge's inquiries. Sommer seemed to know pretty much the same essential things about the Warwickshire knight as Kittredge knew, and he also knew something about the Welsh candidate and the Papworth Malorys. That he refrained from any identification was because, as he said, he knew nothing to connect these Malorys with the author. It may have been this observation that prompted Kittredge to toy with an interesting parallel between the romantic adventures of *Le Morte Darthur* and an actual event which the Warwickshire Malory may possibly have witnessed. Subsequent critics, notably Vinaver in 1929, focused the comparison upon a particular adventure in the tale of Gareth.

Dugdale, the reader will remember, reported that this Thomas Malory served at Calais under the great Richard Beauchamp, earl of Warwick. In the biography of Beauchamp that was written for his family around 1490 (it is really a biography in drawings), the Earl is depicted in many romantic situations. Among these is a tournament at Calais, where on successive days he fought against three French knights, each time in armor of different color, each time varying his name from Chevalier Vert to Chevalier Attendant. The hero of the tale of Gareth is Gawain's youngest brother, the one untarnished knight among all Malory's *chevaliers terrestriens*. Gareth's nickname, given to him by Sir Kay, is Beaumains. The fact that this nickname is similar to Beauchamp, together with the coincidence that *Le Morte Darthur* describes Gareth-Beaumains fighting in a three-day tournament against Black, Green, and Red knights, led Vinaver to propose that the passage in the tale reflected the Warwickshire Malory's familiarity with Beauchamp's tournament, and that there was therefore internal evidence in the narrative of *Le Morte Darthur* to connect it with the Newbold Revel knight.

This literary parallel proved appealing to many later scholars, taken as cementing the structure of correspondences that Kittredge had revealed. Vinaver's reaction in his 1929 book on Malory is representative: "It is likely that the name Beaumains was added by Malory as a tribute to Richard Beauchamp."

To a later and instructed eye, Kittredge's essay, brilliant as it is, may seem somewhat curious in its judicious arrangements and silences, adroit items in an advocate's technique. But its effect has been overwhelming. His extensive investigations into the medieval records, so he claimed, had turned up no possible rival; his man seemed to fit the criteria that can be deduced from statements in *Le Morte Darthur* and its editorial Preface; and the narrative itself seemed to prove that the Warwickshire man had written into it his own experience.

Nevertheless, there remained one matter for quibbling. The final words of *Le Morte Darthur* contain a prayer for good deliverance. The phrase is ambiguous: it might have a secular meaning, deliverance from prison; it might also have a spiritual meaning, deliverance from the prison of the body.

One firm step toward resolving this ambiguity was achieved in 1928. In that year, Edward Hicks's *Sir Thomas Malory, his Turbulent Career*, proved beyond question that Sir Thomas Malory of Newbold Revel had done time in various London jails.

The core of Hicks's book was provided by legal documents from the Public Record Office that reported several of Sir Thomas' brushes with the law. But Hicks also sought to reinforce the advocacy of Kittredge, by claiming several further parallels between the experience of the Warwickshire knight and details in the narrative of *Le Morte Darthur* which he declared did not appear in the French sources. First, that Sir Hervise de Revel's surname was adapted as a compliment to the Revels, who were the distaff side of Malory's own family. Second, that the introduction of the hermit Sir Baldwin of Britain was a reference to a Baldwin Mountford who turned to a life of religion after a bitter quarrel with his father Sir William Mountford, the Warwickshire sheriff who first took Sir Thomas to captivity in Coleshill Manor. Third, that the names of two knights, Melias de Lile and Neroveus de Lile, and the details of what happened to them, were adapted to constitute a compliment to a certain William de Lile who was captain at Calais when Malory served there with Richard Beauchamp. Fourth, that the famous lament that *Le Morte*

Darthur introduces into the story of Tristram, "For all the while a prisoner may have his health of body, he may endure under the mercy of God and in hope of good deliverance; but when sickness touches a prisoner's body, then may a prisoner say all wealth is him bereft, and then he hath cause to wail and weep," referred to Sir Thomas' own experience as a prisoner. A little earlier, it should here be added, W. H. Schofield had advanced another parallel of similar kind: that Malory's mention of the Duke de la Rouse whom Gareth defeats and sends back to Arthur's court may have been a covert allusion to the John Rous who was chantry-priest at Guy's Cliff at the time that Malory was writing: Rous was in the employ of the earls of Warwick, whose mythical ancestor, Guy of Warwick, was commemorated in the chapel.

Despite all this further evidence of the prison career of the Warwickshire knight, despite the several suggested parallels between added and adapted details in *Le Morte Darthur* and persons with whom the Warwickshire Malory may have been associated, the argument was, to an occasional scholar, still not entirely convincing. "It is open to criticism," wrote Eugène Vinaver in 1929, "in assuming that in 1469-1470 there could exist only one knight of the name of Thomas Malory, who had spent several years in prison. This assumption is highly probable, but it cannot be proved, and until further clues are found to connect Sir Thomas Malory of Warwickshire with the book written by a Sir Thomas Maleore in 1469-1470, our author's identity must be a little less than certain."

Among other matters, the ambiguity of Malory's final prayer for good deliverance still remained. Granted that the Warwickshire Malory had been in earthly prisons, it still was possible that the author was in a spiritual one.

On July 23, 1934, this rivalry between a secular meaning and a religious one was dramatically settled. On that day, W. F. Oakeshott announced in *The Times* his discovery, in a safe in the Warden's bedroom at Winchester College, of a manuscript of Malory's book. How it had not been recognized for so many years is still mysterious, but it proved an exciting find indeed. And for the present book, what is most exciting about it is the prayer at the end of the first main section, that "this was drawyn by a knight presoner Sir Thomas Malleorre." The term that Malory here applied to himself seems void of ambiguity, and when it is employed to clarify the more ambiguous prayers scattered throughout the manuscript at the ends of main sections in the narrative, when it is applied to the final prayer that appears only in the Caxton print, it implies that the author was a prisoner while he was writing much of his book, possibly while he was writing all of it.

Curious matters will need to be reported concerning this parallel, but when it was made it seemed to provide the capstone in the case for the authorship of the Warwickshire knight. Even Eugène Vinaver, cautious in 1929, accepted the identification without question in his edition of 1947.

Ironically, the very discoveries that seemed to have afforded final proof that Kittredge's identification was correct turned out to be double-edged. So far from clinching the identification, they even raised doubts about it.

Some scholars have become perturbed by the contradiction that although the Warwickshire knight was seemingly a Yorkist in politics, the romance he is said to have written is seemingly Lancastrian in its bias. Even more scholars, as evidence was piled on evidence concerning Sir Thomas Malory's imprisonment on charges of cattle theft, extortion, attempted murder, rape, have been made uncomfortable by the moral paradox that is created by allying the alleged perpetrator of these crimes with a book which has always been regarded as the classical exposition of chivalry. Amusing as the paradox may be, it is disturbing to anyone who must deal seriously with Malory. In fact, as C. S. Lewis said just before he died, the issue is a grave one for all readers of *Le Morte Darthur*. Some critics have even been led by it to doubt the identification. So sensible a scholar as the late Sir E. K. Chambers, for example, seems to have had some question, for after acknowledging the *prima facie* reasons for accepting Kittredge's claim, he adds:

> However this may be, it is difficult to resist the feeling that there is a marked spiritual cleavage between the Malory of romance and the Malory whom recent biographical research has revealed.
>
> "What?" seyde sir Launcelot, "is he a theff and a knyht? and a ravyssher of women? He doth shame unto the Order of Knyghthode, and contrary unto his oth. Hit is pyté that he lyvyth."
>
> Surely the Sir Thomas of Monks Kirby could not have written this without a twinge.

Much of Malory commentary during the last thirty years has been occupied with this dilemma. The commentators fall into two groups. A few have argued that the Warwickshire Malory was innocent of the charges brought against him. Many more have assumed that he was guilty, but have lessened the moral gap by reference to Malory's world or by reference to Malory's work.[1]

Critics in the first group have maintained that some of the charges may not have meant what they now seem to mean: first, that *raptus*, for example, might have meant nothing more heinous than that Malory abducted Joan Smyth from her husband, by force perhaps; second, that since it is impossible to regard this Malory as an ordinary freebooter, he must either have had good justification for what he did, or the charges against him must have been malicious. Such defenses carry direct or implicit attacks upon the persons whom Malory was charged with offending. Goodman Smyth was a cuckold, knave, and wifebeater, it has been urged; the several persons whom Malory is said to have threatened and robbed were recalcitrant debtors; the abbot of Combe was unscrupulous; the duke of Buckingham a long-standing oppressor of the people's rights. A subtler variety of the defense is one which wonders whether Sir Thomas may not have been victim of a power-play between two Warwickshire magnates in the political maneuvers that led to the Wars of the Roses: on the one side, the Yorkist Richard Neville, the young man who had recently become earl of Warwick; on the other, his aging Lancastrian rival, Humphrey Stafford, duke of Buckingham.

Among commentators who assume that the charges were well-founded, some seek to lessen the moral paradox by suggesting mitigating circumstances. Thus, one sensitive critic suggests that Malory simply behaved like the landless knights who, once they were done with serving their lords in foreign wars, inevitably turned to violence when loosed upon their native soil. Another excellent scholar maintains that to realize that Malory was not inherently or irreparably evil, we must understand that in his day there was a rising tide of popular resentment against the bloodsucking privileges of the religious houses, a noteworthy product of the shift from a corporate to an individualistic economy.

Still other critics have minimized the paradox by recourse to *Le Morte Darthur* itself. One found it possible to agree with both the criminality of the writer and the chivalric morality of the book by a theory that the writing of *Le Morte Darthur* was something approaching an act of contrition. Quite on the other hand, another argued that it is not nearly so chivalric as it seems to an ordinary eye, for in its first pages King Arthur engages in incest, in Herod-like cruelty to children, and in murderous imperialism against neighboring lands. And in a more subdued vein, a very eminent Malory scholar declared that the association of the book with a doctrine of humanity and gentleness proceeds not from *Le Morte Darthur* itself but from Caxton's Preface. What holiness and gentility the work does contain is mostly taken from the French sources, he maintained, Malory's own attitude being more practical and realistic, based on firm belief in the importance of wealth and an almost pathetic concern with material comforts.

Such attempts to resolve the moral dilemma or dismiss it reflect the seriousness of the paradox, not only for the acceptance of Kittredge's candidate, but even for our attitude to *Le Morte Darthur*. It is therefore appropriate for a while to comment upon these commentaries.

The guilt or innocence of Sir Thomas Malory in all the charges brought against him is something that cannot now be settled for sure. One now-fervent defender has recently claimed that even conviction by jury and judge would not really prove his guilt. And in its own way that may be true, for come Judgment Day there may be revelations to surprise a thousand judges and juries. Nevertheless, short of that day, we must proceed in human fashion, by probability. And in this particular case, or so it seems to the present writer, the probability is overwhelming.

First, to clear up the matter of *raptus*, double-*raptus*, is simple. The documents that A. C. Baugh discovered in 1932 make abundantly plain that in these instances *raptus* did not mean simply abduction by force; the charge is defined only too clearly, *felonice rapuit et cum ea carnaliter concubuit*. This, as Sir Peter Teazle and G. L. Kittredge both affirmed, is a damned wicked world. Whoever brought the charges, the affronted Joan or the affronted Hugh probably, was not maintaining that Malory, like Lancelot, was rescuing a lady, carrying her off from a cuckoldy husband; he was maintaining that Malory had made love in an old-fashioned way, not only in August but also in May.

Whether the Smyths acted from malice, whether the persons whom Malory is said to have threatened and robbed owed him money, are questions that cannot now be answered. But since we know nothing of these people they are possibly questions that should never have been asked. Whether there was a conspiracy against Sir Thomas may be a problem of prepositions, for if there were indeed a conspiracy, it is likely to have been double-sided: for as well as against. From the political elements the present writer has been able to contribute to this Malory's biography, it seems almost certain that he was involved with Warwick the Kingmaker and the Yorkist cause. It is very reasonable to believe that his alleged attempt to assassinate the Duke of Buckingham was politically inspired. Buckingham was a Lancastrian leader, Warwick's rival in both local and national conflict. That might mean that there was a political conspiracy in which Malory was one of the aggressors. The subsequent bringing of Sir Thomas to trial before the inquest at Nuneaton, the fact that three of the four judges on the bench were Lancastrians, may represent a retaliatory conspiracy, one in which Sir Thomas was the victim. The sequels—the attack on Combe Abbey, which followed almost immediately, as soon as Malory had escaped from Coleshill, and Malory's apprehension and commitment to a London jail—bear all the signs of a feud, conspiratorial on both sides.

These may well be the explanations for this series of events. But explanation is not exculpation, and for the many other crimes charged against the knight of Newbold Revel, such explanations do not even seem proper. Rape, cattle stealing, robbery, extortion by threats demand no explanation from politics—especially as one of these crimes is said to have been committed against one of Malory's own political associates.

What is most impressive in the charges is their abundance and variety. Malory is not the only man charged; all in all, nearly thirty men were involved, and in the Essex affairs, Malory was not even the leader. The charges relate to a long stretch of years; they vary in kind, although most of them include robbery; they are charged by people from many ranks in society; the witnesses are extremely numerous; the accusations relate to several places, some of them very far apart. They are moreover charges of a kind common in the fifteenth century. In the Paston Letters, the proceedings of parliament, the Chancery records, and the Coram Rege rolls, there are thousands of similar charges brought against persons of all ranks, many of them men of good education and noble birth, some even men of professional piety. In 1459, for example, the Commons lamented, as they had already so often lamented, the prevalence of robberies, ravishments, extortions, oppressions, riots, unlawful assemblies, wrongful imprisonments. And this time they cited twenty-five notorious offenders. Sir Thomas Malory is not named; but the list relates to every corner of England, and the alleged culprits are all men of high status, esquires, gentlemen, and knights. Heading the list is Henry Bodrugan of Cornwall, a person peculiarly interesting to us, because, in despite of several denunciations of him in the Commons, he became a member of parliament and was in time buried in the Greyfriars chapel, almost side by side with Sir Thomas Malory of Newbold Revel.[2]

The activities charged against these persons are exactly the same as those charged against Sir Thomas. Even their modes of operation, their armory and their bands of associates, are said to be similar. Moreover, the charges brought against Bodrugan, and the charges brought against thousands of other alleged malefactors, were rarely brought to trial or proved in a court. But it is the assumption of all historians that most of the charges must have been well-founded. The fifteenth century, especially in its middle stretches, is believed to have been uncommonly unruly, and the evidence for the belief is mainly such charges as were brought against Malory. To assume that the charges were unjustified would be to convert the Age of Misrule into the Age of Unfounded Charges.

Although four inquests found enough in the charges to commit Malory to prison to await formal trial, he always pleaded innocence and demanded trial before a jury made up of his Warwickshire neighbors. So he never came to trial; he never was found guilty by either judge or a regular jury. These facts may represent normal response in a man charged with serious crime. They may also represent a private mistrust of the judges and juries of London. When Sir Thomas demanded to be tried before a jury of his own neighbors, it might have been because he believed that only so could he get a fair trial. But it might also have been because he knew the normal result of any such demand: that no group of men could ever be persuaded to leave their distant homes and come up to London simply to maintain an Englishman's right of trial before his local peers.

In short, there is now no way of proving whether Sir Thomas was guilty or innocent. But there is strong probability in the matter, and that probability is that he, like so many other minor knights of his day, was a lawless adventurer whom the politicians of his own county turned to at times. Indeed, had he not been identified with the author of *Le Morte Darthur*, it is in the highest degree unlikely that any scholar would ever have doubted the charges proferred against him.

Nor are the sociological and psychological exculpations convincing. Whether there was indeed a rising tide of popular resentment against the bloodsucking privileges of the religious houses, whether landless knights and disbanded soldiers really did play a dominant role in the troubles of the time are matters for learned debate. But Malory was not a landless knight, and he had returned from the wars a long time before.

Nor is there any evidence that he was a rebel in any proletarian cause. Indeed, if he was really the author of *Le Morte Darthur*, the book suggests otherwise:

> Lo, ye all Englysshemen, se ye nat what a myschyff here was? For he that was the moste kynge and nobelyst knyght of the worlde, and moste loved the felyshyp of noble knyghtes, and by hym they all were upholdyn, and yet myght nat thes Englyshemen holde them contente with hym. Lo thus was the olde custom and usayges of thys londe, and men say that we of thys londe have nat yet loste that custom. Alas, thys ys a greate defaughte of us Englysshemen, for there may no thynge us please no terme.

And if the intent of the defenses is to suggest that, in so troubled an age, Malory's crimes would not have seemed so black as they now do, the only answer is that fifteenth-century Englishmen were not so remarkably different from us in their morals. There was much crime and much violence; but whether there was more than at other times is not so certain. Human probability suggests that most Englishmen behaved very much as they always behaved before there was an effective system of law-enforcement. But by the same token, most fifteenth-century Englishmen must have found all this violence and crime alarming, shocking, unchristian. That is the burden of all the bitter complaint in parliament, in courts, and in letters. It is also the burden of every manual of Christian behavior, almost every other sermon, and hundreds of romances, stories, and songs. It is even the burden of Malory himself:

> "What?" seyde sir Launcelot, "is he a theff and a knyght? and a ravyssher of women? He doth shame unto the order of Knyghthode, and contrary unto his oth. Hit is pyté that he lyvyth."

The thesis that *Le Morte Darthur* is an act of contrition, interesting as it is, is an idea only. Nothing in the book refers to Malory's own penitence for either sins or crimes. In his several prayers he does ask for Jesu's mercy, of course; but so must any man, even a saint. And as for assertions that the book is consonant with its alleged author's alleged criminal *penchant*—that it is not so chivalric as it seems, that it lauds cruelty, that its author was a materialistic and practical realist who lacked true understanding of true medieval romance—they surely make molehills outtop the shining mountains.

Assertion that the work is not really moral is, of course, not wholly

new. Four centuries ago, Roger Ascham declared that ". . . the whole
pleasure of this book standeth in two special points, in open manslaughter
and bold bawdry. In which book those be counted the noblest knights that
do kill most men without any quarrel, and commit the foulest adulteries
by subtle shifts." This desolating libel is a puritan's opinion. Recent
assertions that may seem quite similar are not prompted, however, by a
puritan's attitude toward imaginative literature that joins delight with
teaching. Their observation of evil and materialism is prompted simply
by two discordant beliefs: belief that the Warwickshire Malory wrote
the romance, suspicion that the charges against him were true. Yet what
they see in *Le Morte Darthur* is no less *malapropos* than what Ascham
observed. No ordinary reader stresses what they stress. No comparison
of Malory's romance with his sources or with other romances warrants
any assertion that his writing was more materialistic, more violent or
cruel, more bawdy than they. In fact, comparison usually shows the
reverse: that Malory's work is less violent, less concerned with elegance
and civilized comforts, and certainly less erotic than his sources. His
heroes are not innocent of course; but all their sins also appear in the
sources, as traditional and essential elements in the full tragic story.

Malory was a translator who abbreviated and adapted and sometimes
added small details—occasionally even short stories. He is not to be judged
solely by his changes, however; he must be judged by his work as a whole.
He is as responsible for what he chose to translate as for what he chose
to add. He is not to be stripped of what is holy and gentle simply because
he found it in French. Nor is he to be judged by any small gathering of
scattered phrases that may or may not reflect a materialistic outlook. Far
outshining the grey cloud of all such small, unemphasized details is
his reiterated nostalgia for decencies no longer observed, and his idealism
in two lovely tales that are related in none of his known sources: the tale of
Gareth, which is nothing but gentle, and the tale of Sir Urry, which seems
nothing but holy.

It is for such reasons that the judgment of centuries—the judgment
of poets, novelists, and hundreds of thousands of ordinary readers—agrees
that *Le Morte Darthur* is the classic of chivalry. Caxton's opinion is
surely the judgment of almost all men who read the book without knowing
the career of its now supposed author. The book, Caxton observed, contains "noble chyvalrye, curtosye, humanyté, frendlynesse, hardynesse,
love, frendshyp, cowardyse, murdre, hate, vertue, and synne." And in
reference to this admirable catalogue, he made his moral comment and

stated what he believed was the author's intent: ". . . al is wryton for our doctryne" . . . "Doo after the good and leve the evyl, and it shall brynge you to good fame and renomee."

There is no good way of escaping the moral paradox, and what might be the soundest attitude is eloquently expressed by the eminent Malorian who also suggests several others:

> Biographical interpretation has done so much harm to literary criticism that it is a relief to find how very little room there is for it in Malory's case. No one will seriously attempt to read his life into his works or associate these with any phase or aspect of his curious career.

This critical attitude has wide application. One needs to be sheltered indeed to be ignorant that an artist may do great work, even great philanthropic or spiritual work, and yet lead a life far from exemplary: that Leonardo or Michelangelo or Dickens or Dreiser, for example, were no patterns of common propriety. Nor is it any secret that a writer's behavior and outlook may change radically with time. Henry Fielding and John Donne are but two witnesses to that fact. Nor indeed need one restrict such inconsistency to artists: the cloth and the coif have always provided their own specimens of what it is their profession to condemn, and the ordinary man's ordinary injunction is: "Do as I say, not do as I do."

Platitudinous as all this is and true too, it still is not quite satisfying for Malory. His paradox is too absolute: a book that delightfully and apparently convincedly exhorts and exemplifies to an ideal behavior, contrasting with a career that seems to have been substantially devoted to what the ideal specifically condemns. Normal reaction to so naked a conflict of saying and doing is to call the sayer a humbug, and that is now the shocked or delighted response of many of Malory's readers. Moral humbug, however, commonly finds its literary outlet in the sanctimonious phrase, and of this *Le Morte Darthur* has nothing. The paradox is not to be denied: the scholars whom we have reported in this section are witness to the fact. They are all mature, sophisticated critics, in no need of instruction that human behavior is less than consistent and that literary men often say what literary men fail to do. But whereas with Leonardo or Dickens they would not be perturbed, with Malory they are so justly bothered that they cannot leave well and ill alone, but are impelled to explain one or the other away.

There are questions more serious in this problem of identity, however, than the complex matter of Sir Thomas' guilt. It is time now to turn to them, one after one.

Innocent or guilty, Sir Thomas Malory of Newbold Revel was certainly in prison. So was the Sir Thomas Malory the author when he wrote *Le Morte Darthur*. These parallel facts have provided so strong a coincidence in favor of Kittredge's identification, that they have persuaded critics who formerly had doubts. Nevertheless, like so much of the evidence about Malory, close examination shows that the parallel is not quite so parallel as at first glance it seems.

The fact that *Le Morte Darthur* was wholly or partly written in prison has inevitably led critics into comparisons with many other prison books. In all these comparisons, however, one important fact has been overlooked: that *Le Morte Darthur* represents an unusual literary activity. All that was needed for most prison books was literary talent, a good memory, and the simplest means of recording. It would not be easy to think of anything else that is common to such disparate works as, say, St. Paul's *Epistles*, Boethius' *Consolations*, James I of Scotland's *Kingis Quair*, Francois Villon's *Testament*, Charles d'Orléans's lyrics, John Bunyan's *Pilgrim's Progress*, Thomas Paine's *Age of Reason*, and Marco Polo's *Travels*. Quite unlike these, *Le Morte Darthur* could not have been written without the aid of a considerable library. So the question must be asked: how could Malory have been a prisoner and used such a library? Had his incarceration been of the kind that Charles d'Orleans enjoyed a few years before—one spent in various country castles, with freedom enough to carry on a couple of love affairs and to write about them a sequence of virelays and ballades—there might be no problem. But Malory was in Newgate, it is claimed.

No one knows the precise form of Malory's French book, but no one doubts that it was an extensive affair in several large volumes—one for the *Suite du Merlin*, two or three for the *Tristan*, three or four for the *Lancelot, Queste del Saint Graal*, and *Mort Artu*. There may have been still more French romances, such as the *Perlesvaus*, the history of the Grail, and the ordinary *Merlin*. Malory must also have had access to manuscripts that contained two English poems, the alliterative *Morte Arthur* and the stanzaic *Le Morte Arthur*; and possibly he had other English poems besides. Whether all these volumes were simple things like the Winchester manuscript of his own book or the Thornton manuscript of the alliterative poem, written on paper and with no decorations beyond an occasional colored initial; or whether they were bibliophiles' prides like Jacques d'Armagnac's copies, glorious with the gold, reds, blues, and greens in abundant pictures of love and derring-do—we may never know. But penny plain or twopence colored, they were a rare and valuable property indeed.

How Malory could have worked with such a library while in Newgate is something to ponder. He would have had to be one of the privileged prisoners who bought their way to the upper cells by gifts to the governor. Anywhere else in Newgate would have been quite impossible for the protracted deskwork entailed in translation from bulky manuscripts. Unless Malory's finances had improved radically since his arrival, however, privileges of this kind are likely to have been beyond his reach. He was by no means well off; the annual value of his three manors was only £20 or so, and two of the charges brought against him, furthermore, were for small debts unpaid.

Newgate was a small, crowded prison, and even if Malory could have procured conditions suitable for his writing, it is still a problem how he could have got his materials. He surely could not have owned the books and brought them with him to Newgate, for a library of this kind was never owned by any man less than a prince. Even Charles V, Jean de Berry, John of Bedford, Louis de Gruthuyse, Philip le Bon, Ercole d'Este, the Gonzagas, and Jacques d'Armagnac—the greatest collectors of Arthurian romances—did not possess collections quite so extensive as the one Malory used. Nor does it seem likely that any of these would have loaned his precious collection to a prisoner, especially one charged with persistent theft. How reluctant medieval men were to loan such treasures may be judged by the difficulty Caxton says he had in getting an owner to lend him the text for his second edition of the *Canterbury Tales*, and by the fact that even members of the French royal family were made to give receipts for the Arthurian manuscripts they borrowed from their own library.

It has been suggested, however, that Malory may have used a library not far from Newgate. Hicks conjectured that *Le Morte Darthur* was written in the library that Dick Whittington had recently founded at the monastery of the Greyfriars, just down the road from Newgate:

> To Malory, as he reduced into English the many French MSS telling the story of King Arthur and the Knights of the Round Table, the existence of the Library so near at hand must have been a veritable godsend during his long detention.

Regretting that the surviving records do not specify the contents of this library, Hicks reminds his readers that other religious institutions are known to have owned such romances as *Guy of Warwick*, *Lancelot du Lac*, and the *Story of the Graal*, and concludes:

> Sir Thomas Malory was neither the first nor the last inmate of Newgate to indulge in literary activity there. Eleven years before the Warwickshire knight's arrest, Charles, Duke of Orleans, had been released from captivity in various English strongholds extending over a quarter of a century. He had whiled away the dreary hours writing ballads and rondels; but besides confirming himself as a habitual maker of verses, he was a celebrated bibliophile, and had vied with his brother Angoulême in bringing back the library of their grandfather, Charles V, when the Duke of Bedford put it up for sale in London. It is impossible to doubt that he, too, found the proximity of the Grey Friars Library most useful.

Hicks's conjecture is intriguing, but it prompts a variety of practical doubts. For example, Malory could hardly have gone to the Greyfriars without the consent of the governor of Newgate. So it is pertinent to consider what should have affected the governor's decision. His prisoner was said to be a man of parts, charged with offenses remarkable even among what were called "Newgate-birds." The prisoner moreover had shown no small initiative in ensuring that the dust of prisons should lie thin on his boots. As if unresigned to any precept that a quiet mind might make a hermitage of stone walls and iron bars, he twice escaped from jails as substantial as Newgate. Mindful that his prisoners had mutinied and almost torn Newgate apart four years before, that the year Malory came, Sir Thomas Percy had escaped (taking a jailer to boot), and that the environs of the prison, with its market, its butchers' stalls and blood buckets, and its narrow, cluttered lanes running down to the Thames, might be sorely tempting to anyone as inclined to escape as Sir Thomas of Newbold Revel, the governor—one must believe—would have hesitated to license such as he to commute to Greyfriars.

He might have hesitated even longer had he recalled the apparently serious intent of the judiciary to keep this man within limits. Late in 1455, even before his jail break from Colchester, Sir Thomas had been committed to the Marshalsea, and the Marshal had been put under a penalty of £1,000 not to let him escape. When the prisoner was transferred to the Tower, the penalty was increased to £2,000. That is no small sum even now, but to realize what it meant 500 years ago, it is necessary to know what money would then buy. This can be learned aptly from a 1460 reform commission's list of prices that might be charged the prisoners at Newgate. Bed and board for a gentleman was fixed at 3 shillings per week, so the penalty represented the cost of four lifetimes. A gallon of the best beer or ale was set at twopence. Twopence into £2,000 comes to 240,000 gallons, a prospect of loss which should have made the governor's gullet run dry. The governor may not have been perturbed, however. Medieval justice was neither so resolute nor always so savage as it might seem by its words. Even the severest of penalties, the penalty of attainder, could sometimes be settled by bribe or apparently casual pardon.[3]

Had the governor been willing to give his consent, still another permission would have been necessary: that of Friar William Thorpe, famous theologian, *doctor disertissimus*, and provincial of the Greyfriars monastery. Hicks compared Malory with Charles d'Orléans. Even had the great Duke actually used the Greyfriars library, it is unlikely that Thorpe would have remembered him as a man like the new applicant from Newgate. Medieval librarians were certainly no less cautious about their treasures than are their descendants; as anyone knows who has visited Merton and some other old libraries, to deter booklifters they often fastened their books with chains. Unless the learned Franciscan had neglected to check the record of Sir Thomas, who not long before had broken into a famous abbey and made off with property equal in value to a quarter of the whole Greyfriars library, it seems somewhat unlikely that he would have given him welcome and pulled out a bench.

In fact, even if Malory had been given the run of Whittington's library, it is unlikely he could have found much that was useful to either him or Charles d'Orleans. Hicks speaks of the great library, 129 feet long and 31 feet broad, that in 1424 was "filled with books." The dimensions are taken from the monastery's own records. The filling is an unmeasured conjecture, for to line merely the walls of such a room would require about twelve thousand books, six times as many as were owned by the oldest and greatest monastic libraries in all England. The Greyfriars holdings may have increased considerably by 1460, for in 1500 it was reckoned the best library in London; but in 1424, three years after the library had been stocked on Whittington's bounty, its books were valued at no more than 556 pounds 10 shillings. At that time a fair to good manuscript could cost from one to 50 pounds. A conjecture more likely than Hicks's is that in 1460 the great room was furnished sparsely with books, a few hundreds of them: most were in presses, some chained, and the rest laid out, as Leland saw them some seventy years later, on the twenty-eight desks set in the bays and elsewhere.

What the books were may be guessed from the surviving catalogues of similar libraries. In its 1491 catalogue, the library of St. Augustine's Abbey in Canterbury, the greatest library in all England, listed 1,837 books. Nearly all were in Latin, and most of them were Bibles, treatises on theology, philosophy, medicine and science, chronicles, or grammars. The only Latin items that might be called belles lettres are the copies of Ovid, Virgil, Prudentius, Macrobius, Persius, Claudian, and Alanus de Insulis. The only English book is that solemn manual of moral behavior, *Ayenbite of Inwyt*. But there are thirty-one books in French; and although most of these are religious they do include seven romances, three of them Arthurian: *Guy of Warwick*, *Ypomedon*, *The Seven Sages*, *The Knight of the Swan*, a *Lancelot*, a *Graal*, and a *Perceval le Gallois*. These secular French items were the gift of an unusual monk, Thomas Arnold. At the priory of St. Martin at Dover there was a library, which may have been almost the same size as the Greyfriars Library in 1460. It had 450 books and their range was much the same as those at Canterbury. Leavening the serious mass were six lighter works in French: a bestiary, the *Prophecies of Merlin*, a *Roman de la Rose*, a romance of *Charlemagne*, and a romance of *Atys and Prophilas*. Of Arthurian romance or poems in English the catalogue makes no mention at all.

Catalogues of other religious libraries, such as Rievaulx, York, Worcester, Durham, and Bury St. Edmunds, show even fewer romances, usually none at all. The fact is, such libraries were almost strictly professional collections made up of Latin classics, the sacred and religious writings of the early Christian world, medieval commentaries upon that older legacy, and a selection of books on scholastic philosophy, law, medicine, and grammar. Dom David Knowles gives this authoritative word on the matter, one quite at odds with Hicks's declaration that "monastic institutions were well provided with the literature Malory would find essential when compiling the *Morte*":

> No monastic library ever seriously attempted to collect all the Latin Continental books of the later Middle Ages, still less the vernacular literatures of the new Europe. Of the twenty or so books that spring first to the mind of the reader of to-day when he thinks of the Middle Ages—*Beowulf*, the *Chanson de Roland*, the *Romaunt de la Rose*,

the *Monarchia* and the *Divina Commedia*, the *Decameron*, the *Defensor Pacis*, *Piers Plowman* and the *Canterbury Tales*, the *Morte d'Arthur*, the *Chronicles* of Froissart and Commines, the autobiography of Suso, the writings of Ruysbroeck, the *Imitation of Christ* —a few indeed were in a monastic library here and there, but they were there by chance and uncared for.

There is little reason to think that the Greyfriars library was different from the rest. We have evidence, in fact, that it was true to pattern. Early in the 1530's, John Leland examined the collection as part of his antiquarian survey of England. He was the King's Librarian, and like Samuel Pepys he was a man ever with child to see some new book. His habit was to jot down the titles of the more interesting volumes in the places he visited, and at Greyfriars he listed fifty books, all Latin and nearly all concerned with theology, philosophy, and morality. The lion's share consisted of recent works by Franciscan and Dominican scholars. Only six items could possibly be styled nonmonastic: a life of Saint Edward, three chronicles, Alexander Neckham's *De Naturis rerum*, and Walter Map's antifeminist treatise, *Valerius ad Rufinum de non ducenda uxore*, which figures so prominently in the Wife of Bath's delighted crucifixion of five husbands.

The list is not a complete catalogue. Leland's habits were not systematic; usually he noted the titles of such volumes as seemed to him interesting or unusual or represented the particular bent of a monastery or its order. His selection is likely to be typical however. The Greyfriars library had been founded by Richard Whittington—thrice Lord Mayor of London, foe of self-seeking brewers and fishmongers, redeemer of poor prisoners at Newgate, founder of schools, libraries, and a hospital. Dick Whittington (for all his cat) was a man of formidable piety; his reforms and benefices were part of a program of holy living and holy dying. Whether his legacy of £400 to the Greyfriars library included books, it is impossible to say now; but if it did, they were probably like the twenty-four books bequeathed by his friend and trustee, the City Clerk John Carpenter—all Latin, all pious, even the one written by Petrarch. Subsequent acquisitions are likely to have been wholly professional.

If it is extremely unlikely that the Greyfriars library owned a set of the French prose-romances, it is almost inconceivable that it also possessed the alliterative *Morte Arthure*, the stanzaic *Le Morte Arthur*, and the

Suite du Merlin. Copies of the *Suite* must have been extremely rare, for until 1945 only one full copy of it was known to have survived. The alliterative *Morte Arthure* may have been rarer still, especially south of Lincoln. And if by some amazing chance the library did own Arthurian romances and a copy of the alliterative poem, it is astonishing that Leland should have failed to record items so unusual. Not only did he tend to list books by English authors, but the romances and especially the alliterative poem were works that might have particularly appealed to him. He himself was interested enough in King Arthur to do extensive research on the subject, going so far as to examine documents and archaeological remains at Glastonbury. His concern was in the authenticity of Arthur; he was not a little contemptuous of the *fabulae* of romance. The alliterative poem might have been just his meat, for it is essentially a historical poem, shunning almost entirely the supernatural romance to which Leland objected.[4]

Taking one thing with another, therefore, it may be asserted that wherever Malory read his books, it was not in Newgate and not in the Greyfriars library. Just as there is an inescapable moral paradox between *Le Morte Darthur* and the Warwickshire Sir Thomas Malory, so there is a bibliographical paradox between *Le Morte Darthur* and Newgate-cum-Greyfriars.

The foregoing section does not cover all the difficulties inherent in identifying the Warwickshire prisoner with the prisoner who wrote *Le Morte Darthur*.

Malory the author indicates that he was a knight-prisoner while he was writing the first part of his book, and, if his several prayers for good deliverance and for Jesus' help mean the same thing, he was in prison at times in between and when he finished his work in 1469–1470. It is possible, therefore, that he was a prisoner all the time he was writing his work. No one knows how long it took him to write it, but it is in order to guess that he began the work sometime in the second half of the 1460's and he was certainly working at it in 1469.

For the Warwickshire knight's prison record to parallel the author's, therefore, he must have been in prison during the second half of the 1460's. There lies the rub. Recent investigation has produced abundant proof that he was in the Marshalsea, Ludgate, the Tower, and Newgate during the 1450's, but it has produced no evidence whatsoever that he was a prisoner at the time the book was being written. The latest record of his imprisonment is dated 1460. The lack of evidence for later imprisonment is not for lack of searching for it. Albert Baugh and Edward Hicks, who discovered most of the documents relating to Malory's imprisonment, could find nothing for the 1460's in the records that were so profitable for the 1450's. Nor has the present writer's own further search in legal rolls for the 1460's produced any evidence of imprisonment. If only because the records of Malory's previous imprisonments are so numerous, this absence of later records is striking, and especially so if one believes with some scholars that he may have continued the now-in-now-out procedure which proliferated records in his earlier prison years.

Albert Baugh proposed a resolution that would seem to fit all the facts: the absence of records, the fact that the book was written in prison, the locale of Malory's burial. Baugh based this theory upon the closing sentences of a "controlment roll" of 1460 which records Malory's recommitment to Newgate. These sentences read: *predictus Thomas Malory comittitur custodie vicomtis Middlesex pro causis predictis in prisona domini regis de Nugate salvo & secure moraturi quousque &c. Ideo dictus Marescallus de eo hic exoneratur.* Baugh's deduction is this:

> The closing note has an ominous suggestion of finality. Malory is committed to Newgate and the Marshall is released from further responsibility. Ten years later, when Malory died, he was buried across the street from the prison. It is not a violent inference that he died in the prison at Newgate. At all events, after this the Malory entries in the *Controlment Rolls* and the *Coram Rege* series suddenly, and perhaps suggestively, cease.

In short, Baugh suggested—and most critics have agreed—that Malory continued in Newgate prison until his death and that *Le Morte Darthur* was written there.*

We have already given reasons to doubt that *Le Morte Darthur* could have been written in Newgate, and there are also some reasons for questioning whether Sir Thomas Malory could have continued as a prisoner there so long. Vile as medieval prisons were prone to be, Newgate was commonly counted the vilest—a "soore streite and perilous prisone for

---

* The appearance of a Sir Thomas Malory in a 1468 short-list of persons excluded from a general pardon is no valid evidence that the Warwickshire man was then in prison. For one thing, other persons named in the list were not then prisoners; for another, this Malory (not described as of Newbold Revel) may very well be another man.

any man to be in," in the words of the parliamentary rolls. It was a prison for criminals and traitors mainly; it was desperately overcrowded, and all but a few favored inmates were kept in darkness and chains. Food, even water, was inadequate; plague and prison fever decimated the population. Even after Dick Whittington caused the jail to be cleaned and water faucets to be supplied, it continued to be a charnel; of sixty debtors from Ludgate who asked to be transferred there as a way of escaping their debts, forty died, and in one year of the London Coroner's rolls a large part of the deaths recorded took place in this very prison. No one, especially a man getting on in years—in the Middle Ages men were expected to be dead at sixty even in normal surroundings—no one is likely to have lasted in Newgate twelve years and more without break.

A simpler explanation for the long silence in the records from 1460 to 1471 might be sought from the fact that even in the well-documented 1450's Malory's sojourns in prisons were apt to be fitful. Perhaps in the silent sixties he was not in prison at all.

There is some evidence indeed that this may be the simple truth of the matter. The general pardon that the new Yorkist king issued on October 24, 1461 includes this name and address: "Thomas Mallory miles alias dominus Thomas Mallorry de Newbold Ryvell in Com. Warw. miles." Malory of course had been pardoned before, only to have the King's Bench deny him. But now circumstances were changed, for Buckingham was dead, Warwick was riding high, and the judge who had before barred his way to freedom was gone; Sir John Fortescue, the sturdy Lancastrian, was now in exile, fighting his fight in the company of Henry VI and Margaret of Anjou. There is no reason to think that a pardon granted by the new Yorkist king should have been denied implementation to a Sir Thomas Malory who had seemingly done things in that king's behalf.

It is fairly safe to assume then that Sir Thomas was at large at least as early as the end of October, 1461. And the only other evidence is that he continued to be at large, for on September 12, 1464 he joined with several other Warwickshire gentlemen in witnessing a conveyance of land that belonged to his neighbors the Fieldings.

Nor is it a necessary deduction, simply because he was buried at Greyfriars near Newgate, that he was buried from Newgate Jail. That place of burial may even suggest that he was not then in Newgate. Although there is evidence that three or four of its inmates were no paragons, Greyfriars chapel was never a depository for Newgate's dead felons; it had long been the fashionable burial place for the most prosperous and respected citizens of London. Other explanations for this place of burial are possible. Twice in the 1450's Sir Thomas is described as "nuper de London," and there is plenty of evidence that some of his Leicestershire, Northampton, and Huntingdon distant relations lived there too: Edward Malory, who was in the King's household, Robert Malory, who was a lieutenant at the Tower, and Anthony Malory, who was a mercer, are some of them. The burial at Greyfriars might mean simply that in 1471 Malory was living nearby. And if there seems uncommon splendor in the place of burial, it might simply relate to the fact that Richard Neville, the Earl of Warwick for whom Malory may have worked at one time, owned a residence just outside Newgate and usually stayed there when he went to London on business. So too did the Duke of Norfolk, who also was at one time Sir Thomas' patron.

It must be concluded, therefore, that in this matter too, the evidence, so far from supporting Kittredge's hypothesis, bears rather against it. Whichever Sir Thomas Malory wrote *Le Morte Darthur* must have been a prisoner during the second half of the 1460's. There is no evidence at all that the Warwickshire man was in prison at that time, and the little information that we do have about him suggests that he was not.

We must now turn to parallels of a quite different kind, the parallels between details in *Le Morte Darthur* and details in the career of the Warwickshire knight. Seven such parallels have been suggested, and at various times these have been claimed to establish the needed connection between the man and the book. Here again it is a question of how parallel parallels must be.

Kittredge paved the way for a biographical theory that, in giving to Gareth the nickname Beaumains and in describing a three-day tournament in which that admirable knight engaged, Malory was complimenting his splendid and chivalric patron Richard Beauchamp, who at Calais also fought in a three-day tournament. This proposition found ready favor among scholars, and in 1929 Eugène Vinaver inclined to think it proven. Since that time, however, so many objections have been raised against the parallel (particularly by Roger Sherman Loomis) that it has now fallen into entire disfavor: in 1947 Vinaver disclaimed and rejected it.

Among the many objections are these: Gareth's nickname is no compliment; it is an insult applied by Kay when Gareth came to court as a scullion. Beauchamp died thirty years before Malory finished his book.

His fifteenth-century biography is a romantic compilation, and no reliance can be placed upon its depictions of the hero in so many romantic exploits. But if Beauchamp did engage French knights in Arthurian-style tournaments about the time that Agincourt was fought, it by no means follows that his proceedings were the model for Gareth's. The three-day tournament, with its concomitants of different names, different colors, different armor, different opponents, is an ancient cliché in medieval romances. It was quite fashionable to imitate romances in this way. Malory has several examples besides this, and there is no good reason to think that this particular example refers to Richard Beauchamp. In fact, even the resemblances are far from impressive, for most of them are quite general and they are no more numerous than the differences.

Schofield's suggestion that the Duke de la Rouse whom Gareth defeats and sends back to Arthur's court was intended to remind Malory's readers of John Rous, who was chantry priest at Guy's Cliff when Malory was writing, has never found favor. It is hard indeed to agree that there could be any connection between a provincial chantry priest who specialized in antiquarian history and a duke of romance who specialized in bothering young ladies. It is not known what source Malory used for the tale of Gareth, or indeed whether he had any specific source; but in the absence of exact information, it may be guessed that all that he did in this instance was to convert the French adjective *rous* "red" into a proper name, just as he did when he changed *Ladinas le rous* to "Ladinas de la Rouse."

Hicks's additional propositions have also fallen on stony ground. In fact, they have hardly been mentioned since he proposed them. Nevertheless, it is both fair and important to deal with them in this unsparing recital of all the arguments that have been used on behalf of the Warwickshire Malory's candidature.

The first concerns "Sir Hervise de Revel, a noble knight," whom Pellinor nominates as one of four candidates for a Round Table vacancy. Asserting that Malory's French source gives the name as *Rinel* and that it fails to call him "a noble knight," Hicks argued that Malory's variations represent a tribute to the Revels, the distaff side of Malory's family. Serious objections may be raised to the claim. It is true that at this point Gaston Paris's edition of the French book does spell *Rinel*, but its spelling elsewhere is the same as Malory's, and there is no reason to think that Malory's own French manuscript had *Rinel* at this point. Furthermore, that the French book does not apply the same epithet to the knight that Malory does is not really true, for he is included in its compliment to all the four candidates: "il sont preudome et boin chevalier."

Hicks's second parallel relates to Melias de Lile, one of the grail-questers. Hicks maintained that the source from which Malory took the episode where Melias de Lile appears gives the name simply as "Melian" without either the surname or "the fantastic description of *Melias* as the son of the King of Denmark." Although it is true that in the *Queste del Saint Graal*, from which Malory was then translating, the name appears simply as "Melians," it is also true that he is plainly and clearly stated to be "filz au roi de Danemarche." Moreover, it seems very likely that the copy Malory worked from may have had a surname similar to the one he uses, for, in the *Tristan* romance which incorporates the grail-quests, this Danish-born hero is called *Meliant de Lis*. No more need be attributed to Malory than the changing of *Melians de Lis* to *Melias de Lile*. The biographical thesis Hicks advanced in suggesting this parallel is this: since Malory was at Calais and since the deputy-captain there was William de Lisle, the change must have been a compliment to an old colleague. But William is not Melias, and, from all that can be gathered about the real William de Lisle, he was a Warwickshire man and his father was not Danish.

Hicks's third parallel equates this deputy captain at Calais with a quite different Arthurian knight, Neroveus de Lile. Lancelot encounters him at Pendragon's castle and ultimately appoints him his lieutenant. Nothing of this, so Hicks declared, is to be found in Malory's French source. Even apart from the improbability that Malory would equate one acquaintance with two very different Arthurian knights, however, it is hard to agree with Hicks's assertions. The prose *Tristan* was the most popular romance of the Middle Ages; many manuscripts survive and they differ greatly in language and details. None has been printed in full, but in Löseth's analysis of the contents of the various texts, it is reported that "Neroveus de L'Yle" and Lancelot engage in the same adventures at Pendragon's castle as they do in Malory's tale. The only detail in which Malory's version seems to differ is that Lancelot entrusts the castle to Neroveus. This might well be Malory's own change, for it is his habit to round off a tale by bestowing suitable rewards. But there is little reason to think, if he did add this detail, that he added it to suggest a connection between Neroveus de Lile's lieutenancy at Pendragon's castle and William de Lile's captaincy at Calais.

Hicks's fourth parallel has to do with Lancelot's visit to the hermit Sir Baldwin of Britain. In the French *Mort Artu* and the English *Le Morte*

Arthur, both of which Malory was using at this point, the hermit has no name. Hicks argued that Malory's addition is an allusion to Baldwin Mountford of Coleshill, who was cheated of his patrimony by his father, Sir William Mountford, and thereupon "betook himself to a religious course of life, styling himself knight and priest." Sir William Mountford of Coleshill was the Warwickshire sheriff with whom Sir Thomas Malory of Newbold Revel had once served in parliament and from whose custody at Coleshill Manor he later escaped. Hicks suggested that, as he was writing the last part of his book, Malory recalled sympathetically the sorrows of Baldwin and so gave his name to the hermit. To support this conjecture he declared that Sir Baldwin of Britain's hermitage—"under a wood, and a great cliff on the other side, and a fair running water under it"—is exactly like Guy's Cliff near Warwick, where Richard Beauchamp founded a chantry in 1423 in honor of his legendary ancestor Guy.

Fascinating as these equations are, they are scarcely persuading. Coleshill is not Britain; a priest is not a hermit; a chapel is not a hermitage; the cliff at Warwick is not great, it is on the same side of the river as the chapel, and in Malory's day the chantry priest there was named John Rous. Sir Baldwin of Britain, moreover, is the name of a character who was quite popular in northern romance.

Hicks's fifth point concerns the famous lament Malory seems to have added to the story of Tristan:

> So Sir Tristram endured there great pain, for sickness had overtaken him, and that is the greatest pain a prisoner may have. For all the while a prisoner may have his health of body, he may endure under the mercy of God, and in hope of good deliverance; but when sickness touches a prisoner's body, then may a prisoner say all wealth is him bereft, and then he hath cause to wail and weep.

The point is a nice one. It is pleasant, even reasonable, to believe that in adding this sympathetic lament, Malory may have had a mind to his own imprisonment and his own prayers for good deliverance. Nothing in it refers to either Warwickshire or Newgate, however, and all it supports is what we already know from Malory's own statement—that he was a prisoner.[5]

Judging from the inadequacy of all these proposed parallels between the experience of the Warwickshire knight and *Le Morte Darthur*, the situation—at least from the viewpoint of literary connections—is exactly where it was in 1890 when Oskar Sommer declared that there was nothing to connect the author of *Le Morte Darthur* with Sir Thomas Malory of Newbold Revel or any other person who bore his family name. A case cannot always be safely left to its advocates, however, and one task that the present writer set himself was to reexamine *Le Morte Darthur* thoroughly, with the objective of discovering, in the context of our fuller knowledge of all candidates, what more might be said in this matter of correspondence between things in the book and things in the lives of the several candidates. In this reexamination, careful search was made for all possibly significant names, not only the names of persons, but also the names of places.[6]

This reexamination turned up no personal names that unambiguously refer to real people of Malory's day, but it did disclose a good many English place-names: London, Winchester, Bamburgh, Carlisle, Amesbury, Alnwick, Arundel, York, Guildford, Salisbury, Cardigan, Cardiff, Canterbury, Sherwood, Sandwich, Barham Down, Dover, and so on. Some of these Malory took from French or English sources; several others, including the few that indicate genuine local knowledge, may very well be his own contribution to the story.

As has already been reported, none of these names reflects any particular interest in the areas from which the Welsh and the Huntingdon claimants came. Nor, even though these added names relate to small towns and castles in many parts of England, does any of them relate to Warwickshire or the adjoining counties of Northampton and Leicester, where Kittredge's candidate lived. Coventry, Maxstoke, Kenilworth, Stoneleigh, Combe, Nuneaton—none of these names occurs in *Le Morte Darthur*, although they represent castles and abbeys with romantic associations that must have been firm in the mind of the Warwickshire knight. Nor does Warwick, although it was the seat of the Warwickshire Malory's chivalric commander, Richard Beauchamp, and also a castle that is said in Beauchamp's biography to have been Caerleon itself. The names nearest to this Malory's *patria*—Amesbury in Wiltshire and Lambeth in Surrey—are places much too remote to support any Warwickshire identification.

This absence of Warwickshire names means there is no support for Kittredge's identification from this quarter of the evidence. In view of Malory's fondness for introducing the names of English places, it seems to imply as well that the author had no particular interest in the county where this candidate belonged.

In short, none of the attempts to establish connections between persons and places in *Le Morte Darthur* and persons and places in the experience of the Warwickshire Malory has been in any way successful. On the contrary, the general implication of these enquiries is that the author's English connections were non-Warwickshire.

Our next consideration is so vitally important for the identification of the author of *Le Morte Darthur* that it is considerably surprising that it has never been dealt with before. It concerns the dialect in which the romance is written.

In the language of a vernacular medieval text, an editor can usually discern with fair certainty where it may have been copied and where it was originally composed. This certainty depends upon the fact that until the early fifteenth century, vernacular texts were still written by hand and for individual purposes. They were therefore normally written in local dialects, with the dialect varying from copy to copy according to the dialect of the local scribes. An editor's conclusion from such linguistic data is always approximate, but he reckons to be accurate within a third of a century and a radius of thirty miles.

By the 1460's, when Malory was writing, English writing practice had changed a good deal from the practice of a generation or two before. The dialect of London had by then established itself as standard for spelling, grammar, and even vocabulary. Except in Scotland, authors were forsaking the provincial dialects. On the tongue their language must still have been local; in writing, they may seem to an unwatchful eye to be no different from everyone else. Nevertheless, standard language does not submerge local language entirely: in fifteenth-century literary and private writing, it is seldom impossible to find some spellings, grammatical forms, words, and idioms that bear witness to the dialect of the author himself, even though they may be scattered rather thinly among the standard usages.

To apply this to Malory is not altogether easy. The book that Caxton printed is not Malory's original text: Vinaver argues that it is a thrice-removed copy. Somewhere, in copying a copy of a copy, the language has been brought nearer to standard usages. The same things are true of the Winchester text: it too may be thrice-removed from Malory's original, and it has been standardized. Despite all these modifications, it seemed probable to the present writer that the Caxton and Winchester texts were apt to be like other fifteenth-century writings and should retain some vestiges of the writer's own dialect. If Malory were a Warwickshire man, his work should bear linguistic proofs of that fact.

This is the most vital consideration that we have dealt with so far, and the report that follows summarizes one part of an extensive analysis of Malory's language.* As a basis, all words, spellings, and grammatical forms that seemed in any way nonstandard were copied from both texts of *Le Morte Darthur*. These were then compared with authoritative information about the characteristics of Central West-Midland English in Malory's time. As a sharper and more individual control, comparison was also made with the language of documents written in Warwickshire itself during Malory's time. No English writings have survived from Newbold Revel, so two documents were chosen from the town nearest to it. These were the Coventry Leet-Book, which provides nearly three hundred pages of official prose for the period 1440-1480, and the two surviving Corpus Christi plays of the Coventry cycle, which contain some seventy pages of dramatic dialogue. The Leet-Book is a fair copy made late in the fifteenth century; it may well have been standardized linguistically and brought somewhat up to date. The two plays were rewritten by Robert Croo in 1534, and he certainly introduced some pompous words and also some features of early sixteenth-century English. Despite this later tampering, both documents retain many regionalisms known to be characteristic of Warwickshire speech of the time they were first written. And since Coventry is but a short eight miles from Newbold Revel, these are usages that the Warwickshire Malory would have used normally in speech and occasionally in writing.[7]

In Appendix D, a large representation of these dialect usages is set out. Here it is enough to cite a few forms and to report the conclusion that relates to the identity of the author of *Le Morte Darthur*.

In spelling, the two Coventry documents share some striking features. Words like "only," "old," "end," and "earth" are written *wonly, wold, yend, yarth, yorth*. The consonants *v* and *w* are frequently interchanged, especially at the beginning of words: *woise, awoide, veyis* for "ways," and *vast* for "waste." Where standard has *i*, these texts have *u* in certain common words: *hull* "hill," *bruge* "bridge," *furst* "first," *cun* "kind,"

---

* The neglect of this approach by earlier scholars is not quite so strange as it might now seem. Until recently, the only available texts of Malory's work were Caxton's text and editions (most of them modernized) drawn from it. Caxton's text was itself radically standardized, especially in its spelling and grammar.

fure "fire." Initial *h* is dropped from some words, but added to others: *horgans, hy* "I," *hus* "us," *is* "his," *Erod* "Herod." The vowel used in unstressed syllables is commonly *u*: *masturs, waxun, trybus, fasus* "faces." In addition, individual words are often spelled in dialectal fashion, as: *nar* "nearer," *har* "higher," *quost* "quest," *dur* "door," *lone* "lane."

Apart from a dozen or so words like *enderes* "recent," *thee* "prosper," and *looe* "hill," the vocabulary of the two texts is not particularly provincial. But among grammatical forms, these dialect usages are frequent: *yche* "I," *ham* "them," and the "on"-ending which is used for present tense verbs with a plural subject: *aron* "are," *notifion* "notify," *comon* "come."

That these features of the two texts are characteristic of the Warwickshire area is confirmed by standard information on the dialects of Middle English.

Examination of *Le Morte Darthur* for these or similar Warwickshire regionalisms drew an almost complete blank. A very few isolated examples do occur, *yere* "ear" in the Caxton text, and *dud* "did," *looe* "hill," *fryth* "wood" and *untyll* "to" in the Winchester text. Few as these are, they might be significant if they occurred nowhere but in Warwickshire. But these particular examples were also used in other parts of the country —the first two in the London area, for instance, and the others in the North Midlands. The same is true of the one repeated feature in Malory which might be claimed as appropriate to Warwickshire, his practice of replacing normal *a* by *ay* in such words as *laysh* "lash," *daysh* "dash," or *waysshe* "wash." Such spellings were sometimes used in the West-Midlands, but they were used much more frequently in the North of England.

The conclusion that must be drawn from the linguistic analysis is that the language of *Le Morte Darthur* does not support the hypothesis that its author was a Warwickshire man.

Even more forcibly than the literature-life parallels, therefore, the linguistic evidence concerning Malory's book is hostile to the identification that Kittredge proposed. It is no less hostile, moreover, to Martin's less favored proposal that the author came from Papworth and to the proposal that the author was Welsh.

Only one of the supports for Kittredge's identification remains for discussion.* Kittredge maintained—and maintained quite rightly—that

---

* Kittredge's claim that Caxton's preface implies Malory died before 1485 does not demand solemn debate. Even if the implication were there, it would not

any candidate must be of suitable age. Altick put the matter in this form-like way: "Any Sir Thomas Malorys aged, say, eleven in 1470, need not apply." No one would quarrel with that. But there is also the other end. At what point of senescence need a candidate not apply? It is a delicate question. There is considerable evidence that the medieval view was that by sixty a man was bean fodder and forage, ready for nothing but death's pit. Rather than debate medieval theories of life-expectancy, however, it might be best to find out how old the Warwickshire knight really was in 1469.

The crucial item of information is Dugdale's statement that Sir Thomas Malory,

> in *K. H.5* time, was of the retinue to *Ric. Beauchamp*, E. Warw. at the siege of Caleys, and served there with one lance and two archers, receiving for his lance and 1 archer xx. *li. per an.* and their dyet; and for the other archer, x marks and no dyet.

The problem in this is to know what siege Dugdale refers to.

Kittredge, who *en passant* spoke of Malory as an old knight, about seventy, also referred to an attack on Calais in 1436 and pointed out that in Henry V's time there was no siege of Calais. Chambers, and then Vinaver, taking a lead from this, suggested that Dugdale may have made a slip, and that the reign should be Henry VI's. Vinaver pointed out that in 1436 there was a siege of Calais, in which Richard Beauchamp took part, and suggested that this was the occasion to which Dugdale refers. Alas, here again the historical facts are not really so convenient. On June 9, 1436, Philip the Good, duke of Burgundy, set out to lay siege to Calais. By June 29, he and his force of 30,000 were encamped before Oye in English territory. This threat to England's jewel in France raised alarm; and

---

afford any weighty support for an identification with the Sir Thomas Malory who died in 1471. That Caxton's remarks do bear this implication is considerably doubtful, however. His habit in prefaces was to report what he knew of his authors, and at times he was able to do so from acquaintance. In his preface to Malory, the very little that he reports may also be found in the text. This, together with Caxton's statement that he undertook to print the book "after a copye unto me delyverd," suggests to the present writer that he did not meet Malory and knew nothing about him personally. Malory might well have been dead in 1485, but Caxton's Preface does not prove so; for all that he says, his author might still have been alive. Nor, incidentally, is there any evidence from the Preface that Caxton deliberately suppressed embarrassing details in his author's career—as Hicks and Vinaver suggest.

when, on July 3, the fall of Oye was reported, the government turned to the nation. The response was immediate: nearly 7,700 men were soon raised to serve for a month at Calais, as reinforcement for the 6,000 who had been sent already. Among those who brought contingents were Humphrey Stafford and the aging Richard Beauchamp. As it turned out, there was no need for the reinforcements. Calais proved too strong for the Burgundians and Flemings, and before Warwick and the English reinforcements could even sail, Philip disbanded his forces on July 31.[8]

This occurrence near Calais was not a siege, and most fifteenth-century chroniclers do not describe it so. But, if it were in fact the occasion that Dugdale alludes to, then it would give a basis for conjecturing how old Malory might have been when *Le Morte Darthur* was completed. Since it is the event mentioned first in Dugdale's biographical sketch and since Malory's status at the time seems to have been an esquire, it may be assumed that he was a young man. If we guess that he was then twenty-one, it would follow that he was born about 1415 and that when the book was completed he was fifty-four or fifty-five.* For a medieval writer it may be a little old to write *Le Morte Darthur*, but it is not impossible. For a medieval robber and rapist, the dates are very satisfactory; Malory's activities in those roles would reflect the vigor of a man in his forties.

From the point of view of Kittredge's identification, therefore, this rationalization of Dugdale's dating is eminently satisfactory, and it seems even plausible. It does however necessitate some casuistry about the meaning of "siege," and it does demand an assumption that Dugdale made a mistake. The assumption is not unreasonable; the *Antiquities of Warwickshire* is very large and very detailed, and it certainly is marred by some errors. Assumption of error in a crucial detail smacks of special pleading however; and when one examines Dugdale's account of Richard Beauchamp, the impression of special pleading becomes stronger still.

Dugdale's biography of Beauchamp is substantial and circumstantial. But although he tells us a great deal about Beauchamp's activities at Calais in Henry V's time, he says nothing whatsoever about the threatened siege of Calais in 1436. He cites a document that enumerates the forces at Calais during the Agincourt campaign, the number of men-at-arms, mounted archers, foot soldiers, and auxiliaries, with their daily pay. He also states that this document relates to the time when Beauchamp was

---

* Vinaver suggested that in 1450 Malory was over forty. This is a little vague, but it implies that the author was about sixty when the book was done.

made captain of Calais. Thereafter Dugdale moves to happenings of a more romantic kind: ". . . whereupon he hasted to Caleys, and with the more speed, because he heard the French were raising great forces against that place, and there was received with solemn Procession, but when he understood that those forces bent another way, he resolved to practice some new point of Chevalry." The new point of chivalry was the tournament, of which we have already spoken, when Beauchamp engaged three French knights on successive days. Dugdale's authority is the picture book biography that we have mentioned before.

Dugdale does not give exact dates for all these events. Some clarification is available elsewhere, however. The indenture by which Beauchamp served as captain of Calais has survived, and it is dated June 19, 3 H. 5. When Dugdale was writing about Beauchamp and Calais, therefore, the date that seems to have been in his mind was 1414, not 1436. Whether this substantial difference in date should be applied to Sir Thomas Malory's activities at Calais is a grave consideration. Argument alone is fruitless; what is needed is contemporary evidence that would settle the matter. It is therefore very fortunate that Dugdale refers to the document on which he bases his statement that Malory served with Richard Beauchamp at the siege of Calais. The reference is simply, "Rot. in Bibl. *Hatton*," but it gives a direction.

The Hatton papers still survive and they are in public possession. The library was dispersed in the 1870's, most of it going to the British Museum, the rest divided between the Bodleian Library and Delapré Abbey. Repeated searchings by the present writer failed to turn up in any of these places a roll that mentioned Malory's presence at Calais. This disappointment left only one hope. Dugdale, or so it would seem from his *Antiquities*, might temporarily have had some of the Hatton papers in his own possession. If that were the case, then it seemed possible that he might have forgotten to return some of them.* Standard investigations soon disclosed that the Bodleian Library owns a great mass of Dugdale's papers. A quick look at the library's catalogue revealed a volume that might contain what was needed, a volume of Dugdale's documents relating to Warwickshire.

The volume proved to be made up of abstracts and copies of early Warwickshire records, most of them in Dugdale's hand. The most inter-

---

* Hicks thought the document may have been destroyed in the great fire at the Birmingham Public Library in 1879.

esting for our present concern were several documents that relate to Richard Beauchamp and his service at Calais. One is the 1414 indenture between Henry V and Beauchamp relating to the captaincy at Calais. Another is a Latin writ that was sent to thirteen notable men in Warwickshire, such as did bear ancient arms by descent from their ancestors, calling them to bring forces to the defense of the realm. This writ is dated 7 Henry V, and among the persons listed are Willelmus Peyto, Sir Thomas' old enemy, and Johannes Mallory, who must be Sir Thomas' father.

A third document is the one for which we were looking. It is in Dugdale's writing, and it is headed: "Ceste la retenue Monsr. le Counte de Warrewyk des gentz d'armes et des Archers pour la demre a Caleys sur l'enforcement de la ville et les Marches illoeques." A lengthy list of names follows, consisting of five *chivalers*, sixty-nine *escuriers*, and thirty-five *valetz*. Accompanying the name of each of the chevaliers and escuriers is a note about the terms of the indenture under which he served. The five chevaliers are "John Beauchamp, Rauf Bracebrig, Walter Sondes, Baudwyn Straunge, and William Bishopeston." Among the escuriers are "William Mountford, Humphrey Stafford, Ralph de Ardern, John Waldtheve, John Lile, and Thomas Mallory." Malory is listed as follows:

> Mallory   Thomas Mallory est retenuz a j launce et ij archers pr sa launce ouve j archer xx^{li} par an et bouche de court et pour lautre archer x marcs saunz bouche de court.

This note, which is obviously the one that Dugdale translated in his account of Sir Thomas Malory in the *Antiquities of Warwickshire*, employs the formula used in all the other entries. Nearly all the escuriers provided one lance and either one or two archers, and their standard payment was £20 and food. The terms for two of the chevaliers were the same as Malory's; but Beauchamp, Bracebridge, and Sondes provided three, six, and four lances respectively and the corresponding number of archers.

The force Richard Beauchamp gathered was clearly assembled under the indenture system, the method used to recruit forces for the Agincourt campaign. Each captain contracted with the King to provide an agreed number of men-at-arms for a definite period; the King agreed to pay their wages and sustenance. A lance usually meant three or four persons, even though in the indentures only the principal was named. In Malory's case, the lance was probably Malory himself, and his support may have included another man-at-arms or two in addition to the two archers.

The list does not set out the date or the duration of the indentures. But the payment is given as a yearly one, and the occasion is said to be, "pour la demeure a Caleys sur l'enforcement de la ville et les Marches illoeques." For the 1436 expedition the men were recruited for one month's service. For the earlier occasion, however, they were indentured for a lengthy period and as a long-term reinforcement for the garrisons at Calais, Ham, and Guisnes.

As for the word "siege," which has led to so much learned argument among those who support Sir Thomas Malory of Newbold Revel as the author of *Le Morte Darthur*, it does not appear in this list. Dugdale's use of the word in his biographical sketch of Malory is a careless approximation. He uses the same word when—again citing a Hatton roll—he declares that William Mountfort was one of the chief esquires retained with the Earl of Warwick "for the seige of Calais," and that Ralph de Ardern served as an esquire with Warwick at the siege of Calais. In his notices of Sir Ralph Bracebridge and Sir William Bishopeston, however, he is more exact. The former, he writes, was retained "for the strengthening of Calais," and the latter "for the fortifying of Calais."

For dating the list, a terminal date can be deduced from the deaths of some of the persons who are named in it. Nicholas Burdet was slain at Poitiers in 1438, Sir Richard Clodsale's will is dated 1428, Ralph de Ardern of Park Hall in Warwickshire was dead in 1420. This list must therefore be dated before 1420. And since in its heading and details it agrees so closely with the indentures by which Richard Beauchamp was appointed captain of Calais on February 3, 1414, and again on January 19, 1415, it is quite certain that Thomas Malory and his Warwickshire companions were recruited by Richard Beauchamp during the years 1414 and 1415. This was the time when Henry V had decided on the invasion which was to culminate at Agincourt, and as part of his strategy had determined that extra forces must be provided for the defense of Calais.

Thomas Malory was therefore indentured to serve at Calais about a year before the battle of Agincourt. That being so, it is important to decide whether Dugdale was correct in identifying the man in the list with the knight of Newbold Revel who died in 1471. The relevant facts are these. The knights and esquires who appear in the list were almost all Warwickshiremen. There is record of only three Thomas Malorys in Warwickshire during the fifteenth century. One was Sir Thomas Malory of Bramcote, who died in 1412, leaving no heir; the second was Thomas Malory of Tachebroke Malory, who in 1467 is described in a legal roll as a laborer; the third was Thomas Malory of Newbold Revel. The first died too soon; the second was socially unqualified; only the third fits the circumstances. Dugdale's identification must therefore be correct.

This permits us to guess pretty accurately at Malory's life dates. At Calais in 1414-1415 he served as an esquire. The few esquires in Dugdale's list about whom we have exact dates were mostly in their later twenties. But if we guess that Malory was twenty-one, then it would follow that he was born in 1393 or 1394. That would fit in with the apparent age of his father, who was involved in business as early as 1383. And that means, too, that when *Le Morte Darthur* was completed in 1469-70, he must have been at least seventy-five.*

These dates fit well enough the career that has been sketched in our first chapter. Fifty-five or so is a mature age to commit rape and to attempt assassination, but it is by no means prohibitive. But seventy-five is no age at all to be writing *Le Morte Darthur* in prison. Nothing is impossible; but recalling the ages at which medieval authors normally sank into silence, recalling the vitality, energy, and even occasional gaiety of *Le Morte Darthur* and the long, persistent labor that it represents, one needs hardly to be skeptical to doubt that the work was written by an ancient of seventy-five.

In sum, when the hypothesis that Sir Thomas Malory of Newbold Revel was the author of *Le Morte Darthur* is subjected to skeptical examination, almost nothing is left to support it. The man's career seems morally discordant with the book. It is extremely unlikely that he could have written the book in Newgate. The few conjectured allusions to Warwickshire people prove to be no allusions at all. The language gives no evidence of Warwickshire origin, and in fact points elsewhere. It seems likely that the Warwickshire Malory was not in prison at the time the book was written in prison. And even if he were in prison, he was much too old to have written it.

Of Kittredge's criteria and the several other criteria discussed in this chapter, the only one in which the author and the Warwickshire candi-

---

* Hicks, accepting Dugdale's accuracy, deduces the same age. Recognizing that readers might regard this as "scarcely credible," he replies that there were other septuagenarians at the time; for example, John Rous the antiquary who was said to have reached eighty-one. The reply scarcely dispels an incredulousness based, less on any belief that all medieval men died young, than on the nature of *Le Morte Darthur*.

date match is that they were both called Sir Thomas Malory. If there were at the time no other man of that name, this coincidence would be interesting, although in the light of the serious objections to the identity it would be extremely puzzling. There may be a simpler solution. Uncle Remus, when he was discussing the differing accounts of Noah's flood, had a pregnant word on such subjects: "Dere mought a bin two delooges," he said. Kittredge declared that there was only one man of the right name at the right time, and other scholars have accepted his word. It is high time to begin our report on whether the declaration is correct.

III

THE LOCALE OF
LE MORTE DARTHUR

The simple-seeming question referred to in the Preface to this book cropped up while the writer was comparing Malory's version of the Roman War with the version in the alliterative *Morte Arthure*, the poem that Sir Thomas was working from. Many of the variations then noticed were commonplace enough, literary details that other critics had observed already or were to do so soon. One observation, however, was so unorthodox that it touched the spring of this simple-seeming question: Could the author of *Le Morte Darthur* possibly have written like this, and really been from Warwickshire? The basis of doubt was certain peculiarities in dialect, nothing that the literary critic normally concerns himself with. But the question was radical, and if it were to be answered at all, it clearly meant a great deal of work. Furthermore, the present writer, who is not unexperienced in controversy, realized that if he were to set out to destroy one biographical image that was as enduring as it was *mal oret* (= ill-set, ill-framed), he would be expected to raise up another, an image with a frame that might pass a new muster.

The approach Kittredge and his successors used may be described as external. Knowing the author's name and the date of his book, they looked for a person who fitted those details. When Sir Thomas Malory of Newbold Revel was declared to be the only man of suitable name and time, the investigation was turned to finding internal support for that identification in the form of allusions to Warwickshire personages, and to finding out as much as possible about the Warwickshire knight. When an identification is well-founded, such procedures commonly produce enriching confirmations. But with *Le Morte Darthur*, the results were peculiar. The literary allusions proved quite unconvincing. The biographical investigation unearthed nothing that really connected the Warwickshire knight with the book; on the contrary, it created a paradox which made the identification uncomfortable to accept.

Since these approaches had piled up such uncustomary results, it seemed to the present writer that it was high time to attack the authorship problem from the reverse direction: that is, to lay aside for the moment Kittredge's hypothesis and tackle the question by examining the book closely to see whether it gave any indications as to where one might profitably look for a man of the right name and time. If the book did indeed give such leads—and since it is a medieval book it was reasonable to think it might— then the searcher would be very well provided, for we already know some important details. We know that the author's name was Syr Thomas Malorye (with or without the *e*) or Sir Thomas Maleorre (with one *l* or two). The first is the name reported by Caxton and the second is the variation reported in the Winchester text. In the Caxton text the author tells us his book was completed in the ninth year of the reign of Edward IV: 1469–1470. He does not say when he began, but to judge from the pace at which other translators of the time worked it could not be far wrong to conjecture that the book was begun and finished during the later years of the 1460's.

The internal approach is normal in editing anonymous medieval texts. Lacking external information about the authors, editors tackle the authorship problem in these long-approved ways. They scrutinize the contents closely for indications that the writer had special knowledge of particular persons, places, or events, or that he read and borrowed from other authors. They analyze the language of the text in fine detail, to see what dialect the author used and, thereby, where he came from. These are the procedures that will be followed in the present chapter. Since linguistic analysis almost always provides the solidest evidence, it will be there that we shall begin.

The two surviving texts of Malory's work are both thrice-removed copies; and both have been subjected to linguistic standardization, the Caxton text more than the Winchester text. Both contain a scattering of localisms, however. These are not identical, but they are of similar character; and so it is probable that Malory's original text contained more such localisms than either of the surviving texts.

The Locale of Le Morte Darthur

SOME MAJOR DIALECT FEATURES

	Border of N. and N.M.	Central W. Mid.	S.E. Mid. London
Feminine pronoun	sho	ho	she
Their / hir / hor	their	hor / her	hir
Them / hem / hom	them	hom / ham	hem
present-endings: thou	sendys	sendest	sendest
he, she, it	sendys	sendeth	sendeth
we, ye, they	sendys	sendeth	sende
participle ending	drivand	drivind	driving
OE aw	awe, awn	owe, own	owe, own
OE an	man, lane	mon, lone	man, lane
OE eor	erth	(y)orth	erth
ME er	warse	worse	werse
OE y	hill, kin	hull, cun	hill, kin
Unstressed vowel	facys	facus	faces
Shall	sall	shall	shall
Should	solde	sholde	sholde
Final -dge	brig	brudge	bridge
Final -ch	breek	breech	breech
Final -ve	giff	give	give
ON element in lexicon	heavy	light	moderate

Middle English Dialect Areas (*ca.* 1400)

They fall into the usual linguistic categories: spelling, grammar, vocabulary. They are so extensive that the full record of them must be relegated to Appendixes B–E out of regard for the capacity of nonlinguists to tolerate such details. The report presented in this chapter represents the essence of the analysis, supported by a few examples.

The report begins with the language of the main parts of the Winchester text—the parts that Malory translated directly from French and so represent his own language with least contamination from other English usage. Following this comes an analysis of the Roman war tale—forty pages or more—which Malory adapted from an English poem. These pages present a special problem, for their language may be influenced by the poem. The report concludes with a commentary on the language of the Caxton text.[1]

Not to tease the reader too long, we may begin with the observation that set off doubt that a Warwickshireman wrote *Le Morte Darthur*. The localisms scattered throughout those sections of the Winchester text that Malory translated from French are distinctively Northern and North Midland, characteristic of the area that flanks the River Humber in Yorkshire.

There is a light powder of variants from the standard spellings, which taken together form a combination rarely found south of Lincoln. Thus, a great many words that are normally spelt with *i* are here spelt with *e*: *preson, velony, rever, drevyn, gresly,* and so on. This was a practice that may be found in texts from many parts of the country; but it seems to have begun in the North, and it was always more frequent there than elsewhere. The reverse practice, of using *i* for *e*, was more specially northern, and here again Malory has a good many examples, such as *Inglonde, hynge, vinquished, blyssyd.* In words like "clerk," Malory very often used *ar*. This too was a practice that began in the North; and although it gradually affected standard spelling in the fifteenth century, in certain words it is rarely found in any documents except northern ones. It is therefore highly significant that a good proportion of these typical northernisms were used frequently in the Winchester manuscript: *warse* "worse," *warste, warke, warre* "worse," and *warwolf* are the most frequent.

In words that have *a* before *sh* in standard spelling, Malory often used *ay*: *daysshe, wayshen, laysshed* are found very frequently, and *fleysche, freysshe* seem to be similar usages with *e*. As we have noticed already, this spelling is found now and then in texts from the West, but it is found far

A section from Saxton's map of Warwickshire

A section from Saxton's map of Essex

Newgate

Ludgate

Micklegate Bar, York

North view of the Marshalsea, Southwark

*Richard Beauchamp, Earl of Warwick,
in tourney with Sir Hugh Lawney at Calais*

Richard Beauchamp's tomb-effigy

*Humphrey Stafford,
Duke of Buckingham*

Richard Neville, Earl of Warwick

Sir Thomas Malory's parents

Thomas Mallory at Calais

From Eugène Vinaver, Works of Sir Thomas Malory, *Oxford*

Christ's Hospital, from the Cloisters

Hutton Conyers moat and mound

A section from Saxton's map of Yorkshire

The Court of King's Bench

more frequently in works written in the North. The same device of representing "long *e*" as *ei* or *ey*, which Malory used frequently in such words as *teithe* "teeth," *treys* "trees," *feyste* "feast," and *beystys* "beasts," is most typically northern. And although his use of *y* as the vowel in unaccented syllables was not absolutely northern, his marked preference for it over the standard *e* was similar to the preference of northern writers: his *gyfftys* for "gifts," *longyth* "longeth," *castyste* "castest," *sendis* "sends," *bettir* "better," *sadyll* "saddle," and *bakyn* "baken" are a pinch from the myriad examples that give a northern tinge to the Winchester text.

His dealings with consonants were similar—some of them characteristically northern usage, others only so by emphasis. Thus, in "give," "given," "gift," "gate," and "get" he sometimes used the *y* which was usual in the South, but most often he wrote *g*, a spelling that was influenced by the speech of the Viking settlers in the North and more common in the Norse-settled areas than elsewhere. The same social explanation is appropriate to other spellings, also. Some of them, like the following, were used frequently: *mykyll* "much," *lyggyng* "lying," *drawbrygge* "drawbridge," *breke* "breech," *dyked* "ditched," *byghe* "buy."

A further consonantal variant, which was commoner in the North than elsewhere, is what is known technically as metathesis of *r*, or shifting its position in relation to an adjoining vowel; Malory has several examples of this, some of them fairly typical of northern English, such as *gerte* "great," *thirste* "thrust," *shirly* "shrilly," *postren* "postern," and *honderd* "hundred." Another practice characteristic of the North which appears very frequently in *Le Morte Darthur* is the representation of the final consonant in "give," "live," "grieve," "cleave," "prove," and similar words, not with standard *v* or *ve*, but with *f* or *ff*: among Malory's many examples are *gyff, lyff, gryff, olyff, roff*.

A large number of other northern spellings is set out in the Appendix, and here we need only cite a few that anyone familar with Middle English dialects will recognize as particularly northern: *os* "as," *als* "as," *tane* "taken," *awne* "own," *awghe* "owe," *veary* "very," *solde* "should," *senshyp* "shendship" (shame), and *ar* "ere."

The grammatical northernisms in these parts of Malory which were translated from French are not so numerous as the spellings, but they illustrate most of the grammatical features that authorities on Middle English dialects regard as characteristic of northern English.

Them, their, and *scho* are personal pronouns that were seldom used far south of the Humber in Malory's time, and they contrast with the *hem, hir, she* in standard use. It is significant, therefore, that samples of the Winchester text use *them* as often as *hem*, and *their* twice as often as *hir*. Its regular feminine pronoun is standard *she*, but it does have one case of *so*, apparently a northern form.

In verbs, the northernisms of that time were in inflections; for while standard English used *-est, -yth*, and *-e, -en, -eth* when the subject was "thou," "he," or a plural, northern English used *-ys* in all cases. The Winchester text usually follows standard practice in these respects; but scattered throughout are some seventy examples of such northernisms as *she sendis, he dredis*, three like *thou commaundys*, and two like *their shyldys hongys*. In *dryvande* the text also exemplifies the characteristically northern inflection for the present participle, and in certain verbs it frequently uses a typically northern past tense: *leepe* "leaped," *keste* "cast," *swange* "swung," *flange* "flung," and *wrange* are among the most obvious.

There is little in the syntax of these parts of the Winchester text which can be called northern* aside from these two uses of "at" in constructions which would have "that" in southern usage: *so at affter Crystemas* and *lynayge . . . at thyne avision betokenyth*. Northern practice is also reflected in two uses of "althers" in the meaning "of all" and in the use of "to" to mean "until" in this phrase: *but or hit be longe to he shall do me omage*.

The northern element in Malory's vocabulary is more striking, particularly when it is assembled as a whole. Scattered through the several hundred pages of the French-derived parts of the Winchester text are almost two hundred words that, according to the OED and other standard authorities, were either distinctively or by emphasis northern. Most of them are used only once or twice, but some are used often and throughout the book, so that the two hundred words represent almost three times as many usages.

The full list of these words is set out in Appendix A. These are some of the more interesting items: *afonned* "doting," *awke* "crosswise," *bere* "berry," *bere* "impetus," *brym* "fierce," *daffyshe* "foolish," *droupe* "to cower," *dryed* "suffered," *fellys* "hills," *frycke* "bold," *gar* "to cause to," *hete* "reproach," *halse* "to embrace," *kempys* "champions," *layne* "to

---

* Inability to adduce many northernisms in syntax may be due mostly to the fact that they are not easy to recognize. A scholar lacks the necessary spectacles: no general study has been made of dialectal syntax.

hide," *layte* "lightning," *lowse* "to set free," *marys* "marsh," *meaned* "lamented," *mon* "must," *nerehonde* "nearby," *pousté* "power," *rake* "herd," *rosteled* "fell violently," *senshyp* "scandal," *syker* "certain," *skyffte* "to manage," *spere* "to ask," *swap* "to strike violently," *tay* "outer membrane of the brain," *thrange* "crowd," *tyll* "to," *tray* "pain," *umbecaste* "to cast around," *wap* "lapping of water," *mykyll the warre* "much the worse," *wyghtly* "strongly," *wylsom* "dreary."

What is also noteworthy in this list is that so many of the words are of Old Norse origin and reflect the Viking settlements in the North and North Midland regions, and that a good many are poetical words typical of the alliterative poetry that in Malory's day was most popular in the North.

These words are seldom or never used in Midland and southern texts. In all Chaucer's works only twenty per cent of the two hundred words can be found—and some of them are only to be found either in that part of the *Romance of the Rose* which is usually reckoned to be by a northern poet, or in the imitation of northern dialect used by the clerks in the *Reeve's Tale*. It is highly significant that this imitation contains almost as many of the Malory northernisms as the whole of the rest of Chaucer's work.* Other London and standard writers use even fewer: Scrope's *Dictes and Sayings* has only five, and three of Caxton's romances have only sixteen all told. On the other hand, literary works that were written in Yorkshire—the alliterative *Morte Arthure*, *Parlement of the Three Ages*, the Wakefield miracle plays, the poems of Laurence Minot, the writings of Richard Rolle, *Ywain and Gawain*, *Robert of Knaresborough*, and so on—employ a substantial proportion of Malory's northern words. Minot, for example, uses 45 of the same words although his verses total only 900 lines, and the short Oxford selection from Rolle, although his subject is religion, contains about 75. In spelling and grammar, too, these Yorkshire writers all use the forms that have been described as northern in Malory.

When this local vocabulary of *Le Morte Darthur* is compared with modern dialects, its northernism is confirmed and made fairly specific. Wright's *English Dialect Dictionary* shows that many of the words were still used widely in Scotland and the northern counties at the end of the

---

* Somewhat more occur in *Piers Plowman*, which contains much of the old vocabulary found in northern alliterative verse. This is partly a matter of alliterative tradition, and partly, as the present writer suspects, because Langland was influenced by northern alliterative verse.

nineteenth century: the county cited most frequently, and sometimes exclusively, is Yorkshire. The Yorkshire dialect dictionaries confirm that even now most of these words are prevalent in that county, for two-thirds of the whole list of Malory's northernisms are recorded in Pease and Robinson's glossaries of Yorkshire dialect.

This observation that the Winchester text contains northernisms is not entirely new. In a recent volume of essays on Malory, Mrs. Sally Shaw listed a few of the northern forms that have been described in the preceding paragraphs. But her deduction is different from our own. Contrasting these forms with the corresponding forms in the Caxton text, she declared that they show the Winchester text originated "somewhere further north and west than Caxton's London." The locale, she thought, was "certainly not beyond the Midlands, or the variations would have been more numerous and striking." And since Malory "was himself a Warwickshire man," she declared, "it is likely that Winchester does represent rather more closely than Caxton the actual language of the author."

Mrs. Shaw's study of the Caxton and Winchester texts pays more heed to dialect than scholars have paid hitherto, and for that reason alone her recognition that the language of the Winchester text is not solely standard English is a noteworthy contribution toward better understanding of Malory. Nevertheless, her localization is not logical in linguistic terms. The northernisms she cites in her essay are not many, and that may be why she finds them insufficient to justify claiming that the text originated beyond the Midlands. The northernisms listed in the present book are several times more numerous and striking: well over a thousand items, many of which are never found south of the Humber. Numbers, however, are not the whole of the matter. Residual dialect forms do not change their allegiance by numbers: a northern dialect usage does not become West Midland simply because a standardized text retains it but seldom. The overall linguistic texture of the Winchester text would support a view that it was copied in the South Midlands, but the significance of the forms that Mrs. Shaw and the present book cite is that they are dialect variations from that overall pattern. Except for a very few items, such as the spellings *laysh* and *daysh*, which are sometimes found in western texts as well as in northern ones, these variations rarely appear in writings that were composed south of Lincolnshire. They were not Warwickshire localisms in the fifteenth century and they are not now. They do not appear in the Coventry Leet-Book or the Coventry Corpus Christi plays, and only a tiny few of them are listed in modern glossaries of Warwickshire dialect. And, as we have already seen, the recurrent dialect usages that do appear in the fifteenth-century Coventry writings are not to be found in Malory.

Mrs. Shaw may be correct in thinking that the Winchester text represents Malory's own language rather more closely than the Caxton text does, but her thesis that that language is Warwickshire must have been dictated by a prior belief that the author was a Warwickshire man. Purely linguistic considerations indicate that the Winchester variations are northern, and that in a narrower localization they are most likely Yorkshire.

This localization is derived from comparing Malory's localisms with standard studies of Middle English dialect and with Yorkshire literary works and the authoritative books on Yorkshire dialect. A more individual comparison is available, too, in the writings of a group of people who lived at the center of the area to which Malory's dialecticisms seem to point, and who have a personal connection with our subject which will be mentioned in the next chapter. The *Plumpton Correspondence*, consisting of letters written to the Plumptons by their neighbors, tenants, and servants, reflects the English used in and around Knaresborough, a few miles south of Ripon and York. Some sixty pages relate to the period 1460-1480, and so may be used as a control to represent the language used by educated Yorkshire men of Malory's time.

Their writing is predominantly standard, but it is varied with spellings, grammar, and words that are characteristic of Yorkshire. Thus, the writers used *they, thaire, them,* and seldom used *hir* or *hem*. As in their *he has, Horbury sais, he comes,* and *the Kyng and Quene lyes,* they often used the *-s* inflection with verbs that have "he" as the subject; and sometimes they have the same inflection when the subject is plural. Where standard used "that" with the meaning "which," these writers often used *at*. The vowel they used in unaccented syllables was commonly *i* or *y*, as in *plesyde* and *citisins;* and every now and then they wrote *gif* "give," *hafe* "have," *fader* "father," *odur* "other," *hundreth* "hundred," *lyg* "lie," *mickle* "much," *kirke* "church," *beseketh* "beseecheth," *pauper* "paper," *awing,* and *or* "ere." They were not much given to dialect vocabulary, but occasionally they employed such words and locutions as: *gif* "if," *latesum* "latish," *fro* "from," *gar* "cause to," and *kan him thank* "show him thanks."

These Yorkshirisms also appear in the French-derived sections of *Le Morte Darthur,* and the only important usages of the Plumpton correspondents which are not to be found in Malory's book are *gude* "good" and its derivatives. So close is the agreement, in fact, that it would be far from rash to surmise that the text from which the Malory manuscript ultimately derives was linguistically very similar to these letters, which were written in and around Knaresborough at the time that Malory was writing his book.

So far, we have been concerned with northernisms that appear in the general body of Malory's work, the sections briefly drawn from French prose romances. Mrs. Shaw, however, directed most of her attention to comparing the Winchester text of the Roman war section with the Caxton text. The Winchester text, she observed, contains many more northernisms than Caxton, and indeed many more northernisms than any other section of Malory's work. That fact is thoroughly obvious and so is the reason for it. The Roman war section is a prosing of a Yorkshire poem, the alliterative *Morte Arthure*. The Caxton version of this section is rewritten and shortened; but the Winchester text is a fairly direct condensation and paraphrase that takes over many of the poem's words and phrases, and even some complete lines. So although the basic language of the section is standard English, Malory's device of transferring elements from the poem results in a strong northern element, which is so obvious it has been well recognized ever since the Winchester manuscript was discovered.

These localisms in spelling, grammar, and vocabulary of the Roman war episode have usually been considered simply the result of this process. Close examination reveals the matter is more complex, for many of Malory's northernisms do not appear in the poem as it is found in the Thornton manuscript. Since it is common knowledge that Malory transferred northernisms from the poem, it may be enlightening to report the northernisms that appear only in Malory.

Among inflections of verbs in the present tense, these are the differences. With "thou" Malory has five uses of northern *-ys*, four of which are not matched by the corresponding forms in the poem—his *thou lovys*, for example. With a third person singular subject he has 117 cases of northern *-ys*, and sixty-eight of these are not matched in the poem, e.g. his *he settys*; these forms appear in synonyms that he substituted or in passages he added or paraphrased completely. With plural subjects Malory has twenty cases of northern *-ys*, including *knyghtes and lordis longis*, which appears in his added conclusion; but of these twenty cases only four are matched in the poem. Malory has three imperatives with *-ys* inflections, *e.g. herkyns me*, and only one of these appears in the poem. As for the northern *-ande* inflection for present participles, the Winchester text of this section has six such usages and possibly seven; of these, only four are matched in the poem.

In spelling, the following usages in the Roman war section warrant notice. Malory, like the alliterative poem, frequently represented the unstressed vowel as *i* or *y*, but he often used this northernish spelling where the poem has *e*. He spelled *mykyll* "much" three times, and in these cases the poem has standard *myche*. His northern spelling *beseke* "beseech" appears in an added passage. In a few words where the poem employs *e*, he has the northern spelling *ey*: *feyble* "feeble" and *kneis* "knees." In some words that are used frequently, the Winchester version has *ay*, *ey*, *uy*, before *sh*, while the poem has standard *a*, *e*, *u*: *fleysshe*, *abaysshed*, *cruysshed*, and *buyshmente*. Winchester also has a number of northern spellings of isolated words that the poem spells in non-northern style; these are listed in Appendix E.

Comparison reveals the same pattern in lexicographical matters. The Winchester text of this tale transfers from the poem thirty words that may be regarded as northern: these occur at the same place in the two narratives and in the same contexts. Forty-five other northern words, representing sixty-nine uses, also occur in the poem. But they occur at different points in the narrative; and although the separation is commonly only three or four lines, in many other cases it is several hundred lines and the contexts are quite different. Finally, twenty northern words in the Winchester tale do not appear anywhere in the poem. Among these are: *craked* "spoke," *dyndled* "resounded," *glystrand* "shining," *jowked* "struck," *note* "business," *pykys* "goes," *torongeled* "ragged"(?), *sqwatte* "crushed," *thrumbeling* "in a heap," *untyll* "unto," and *umbelyclosed* "surrounded."

The density of the northernisms in this section of *Le Morte Darthur* is patently the effect of its Yorkshire source. Even when Malory used northernisms in different positions, it is possible to think that he may have learned them from the poem; but that would entail his having a remarkable memory for such words and an implausible ease in using them in different contexts. The many words that do not appear in the poem at all cannot be so explained, and they raise a difficult problem. One theory is that Malory worked from a different text of the poem than the one which has survived in the Thornton manuscript. That would be a satisfying explanation if the examples were not so many and were restricted to words. Malory's surplus northern grammatical forms and spellings are more numerous still. A simpler theory might be that these northernisms in the

Roman war section, and also the words that are only remotely matched in the poem, are akin to the northernisms scattered through the rest of the Winchester text, the parts that are translated from French. If that is so, either a northern copyist or Malory himself was responsible for them.

A resolution of this final problem—whether a scribe or the author was responsible for the northern usages—may be sought in the Caxton text. That text is the product of a different line of copying from the line that produced the Winchester copy. If it were free from Winchester's northernisms, it would go a long way to prove that the Winchester usages were the contribution of a northern scribe. If the same northernisms appeared in Caxton, however, it would prove they were Malory's own doing—linguistic localisms that had persisted despite all the standardizing that had been done by copyists on either or both lines of descent.

Caxton's text, as Mrs. Shaw indicated, is substantially standard in its language: even its version of the Roman war is almost consistently standard in spelling, grammar, and vocabulary. That fact, indeed, is a main explanation for what would otherwise seem a strange indifference about the dialect of *Le Morte Darthur*. It is only the many localisms of the Winchester text that prompt any sifting of Caxton for localisms. The present report is therefore restricted to comparing the Winchester northernisms with the corresponding forms in Caxton.

With "their" and "them," which are loan-forms from Old Norse, and with their native equivalents "hir" and "hem," Caxton's usage is not very different from Winchester's except that it uses rather more of the native forms. On the other hand, it quite often has the Norse forms where Winchester has the native ones. From this it is hard to judge whether Malory's original text used the northern *th*-forms more frequently or whether its preference was the more southern *h*-forms.

Caxton's inflections of present tense verbs are almost consistently those found in London and standard English. Nevertheless, a few of its usages confirm northernisms in the Winchester text. With third-person singular subjects, it has four -*s* inflections: *me repentys, what betokenes that noise, myn hede werches*, and *Mellygaunce has*. Few as these northernisms are, they are meaningful. The first three agree with the Winchester forms, and they occur near to one another as though they had been missed by a standardizing copyist in a period of inattentiveness. For the fourth, Winchester employs the standard form *hath*. Similarly, Caxton once uses a northern plural inflection which is lacking in Winchester: its *says his brethirne* matches Winchester's *seyde his bretherne*. There is also one grammatical error in Caxton that seems to confirm a northern form in Winchester: *that me repentest*, where Winchester has *that me repentis*. The northern participial form *dryvande* in Winchester is confirmed as original by Caxton's form *dryuend*.

Caxton's spelling is standard almost consistently. But, although Winchester's northern spelling *mykyll* is usually matched by the standard spelling *much* in Caxton, Caxton twice uses the northern form where Winchester has the standard one. Caxton also twice confirms the northern spelling *lyggyng* "lying"; and it uses the northern spelling *rafe* where Winchester has *rove* (and also *smote*, which is manifestly a standard substitute for a northernism).

Many of the two hundred northern words of the Winchester text are represented by familiar standard words in Caxton. Thus, against Winchester's *afonned* "foolish," *ar* "ere," *bees* "rings," *bone* "gift," *dwere* "doubt," *gart bren* "caused to burn," *mon* "must," *pousté* "power," *romyng* "roaring," *tane* "taken," *tyll* "to," and *warre* "worse, worst," the Caxton text reads: *assoted, ere, bedys, yefte, doubte, brente, maye, power, roarynge, taken, to, werste* or *werse*. There are upwards of a hundred such differences between the two texts. If the northern words were original with Malory, Caxton's forms would intensify its witness that along the line of its transmission there had been extensive standardization; for medieval scribes were not nearly so ready to replace words as to change dialectal spelling and grammar. If Caxton's readings were the original one, however, it would mean the Winchester text had been extensively northernized at some stage or other.

In striking contrast are the cases where the Caxton text has the same northern word as Winchester. These constitute over two thirds of the whole list, and they therefore provide very strong evidence that these northern usages were original with Malory.

Most significant of all are the hundred and more old-fashioned or northern words which Caxton employs in places were Winchester has modern and standard forms. Against Caxton's old-fashioned *heteth, hoved*, and *ungladde*, for example, Winchester uses *is called, stondynge*, and *sad*. And against Caxton's northernisms—*bee* "ring," *be skyfte* "be rid," *garte to* "caused to," *gart sette* "caused to be seated," *kenne God thanke* "show God thanks," *lyth* "joint," *marys* "marsh," *syn* "after," *slake* "valley," *stygh* "road," and *untyl* "unto"—the Winchester text has *bye* (the southern spelling), *be of of, gan, made sette, yelde God thanke, joynte, mores, whan, slad* "slade," *fylde* "field," and *unto*. Since, as we have already seen, the Caxton text is the end product of a line of radical standardizing, these forms cannot have been added by recent scribes: either they were in an early northern copy of Malory's book or they existed in Malory's own writing.

Even in the Caxton version of the Roman war tale, although it is abbreviated to half and radically recast in standard English, there are vestigia of the same kind. Its *stuffed* "provisioned," *graythed* "got ready," *awke* "crosswise," *stale* "position," *conne* "be able to," *stoure* "battle," *lygge* "lie," *stale* "stole," *whomsomeuer* "whoever," and *weltryng and walowynge* do not appear in the Winchester text. Some of them do not appear in the alliterative poem either.*

The only deductions to be drawn from the substantial array of northernisms in Winchester and the confirming and additional northernisms in Caxton are, first, that both texts are standardized and, second, that the text from which they both ultimately derive was considerably more northern than they.

This parent copy must have been very close in time to Malory's own text. How close it was verbally is a matter of probability. One possibility is that it was the work of a northern scribe, who changed Malory's language toward his own. The other possibility is that its language was the same as Malory's or very similar.

Of these alternatives, the first is unlikely for these several reasons: Although medieval scribes were prone to alter their texts towards their own dialects, they seldom altered them to the extent that would be necessary in this case, and they almost always left traces of the language they changed. Although the scribes' tendency in making such changes was to change spelling and morphology rather than vocabulary, the northernisms in Malory are heavily lexicographical. It was certainly no practice of scribes to introduce into prose the diction of poetry; but many of the northernisms in Malory are typical of northern alliterative verse.

The second alternative, that these northernisms existed in Malory's original text, is patently the only reasonable one. And since it is unlikely in the extreme that anyone but a northerner would have fallen into northern usage in the occasional fashion found in *Le Morte Darthur*, the only bio-

---

* These facts are important for the problem of who is responsible for the Caxton form of Book V—a problem I mean to discuss on another occasion.

graphical deduction to be drawn from the linguistic evidence is that Malory was a northerner, probably a Yorkshireman.

The northern element in Malory's language, even in the long passages he translated from French, patently bears some relationship to the fact that at least two of his sources were poems composed in Yorkshire dialect. From linguistic analysis, therefore, we may now turn to the more comfortable topic of Malory's literary connections.

From time to time, Malory characterizes his work as being "breffly drawyn" from what he calls "the Frensshe booke." These terms should be taken with a grain of salt. Malory did considerably more than briefly translate, and he certainly drew from more than one book. In his day, "book" had several meanings: a division within a single work, a complete work within a single set of covers, or a series of separately bound volumes that dealt with the same subject. Malory's references moreover cannot always apply to the same object. The French book referred to in the Death of Arthur section, for instance, cannot be the same entity as the French book referred to in the Tristram section. Some of his references may also be general and loose. When he credits the French book with statements that cannot be found in the particular romance that he was translating at the time, it is hazardous to accuse him of prevarication and inventing sources: he may simply be alluding to something he remembered from some other romance, or reporting his sense of his French reading in general.

Certainly, his sources were far more extensive than his acknowledgment suggests. And among them were English writings that he does not cite at all. Two are well known: the stanzaic *Le Morte Arthur* (there may be significance in the fact that its title shares a grammatical error with Malory's own), and the alliterative *Morte Arthure*. There may have been several others.

For our purpose of localization, the most important fact about these two English poems is that they were both composed in Yorkshire. That fits in generally with the conclusion that emerged from our linguistic analysis. Nothing could be more natural than that a writer who used Yorkshire dialecticisms should have drawn some of his story from romances that were composed and circulated in Yorkshire.

The stanzaic *Le Morte Arthur* deals with the last stage of the Arthurian story, the events that follow the quests of the Holy Grail. After recounting in interlaced style the stories of the poisoning of Sir Pinel and the tragic love of the Lady of Shalott, the poem moves to Mordred's plot against Lancelot and Guenevere, the accidental killing of Gareth, the feud that Gawain assumes, Mordred's seizure of the kingdom during Arthur's absence in France, Arthur's return and the tragedy that ensues when most of the Knights of the Round Table—Gawain, Mordred, and Arthur among them—are killed, and finally the retirement of Lancelot and Guenevere into the religious life and the deaths of the lovers.

It is a simple, pleasant poem in eight-line stanzas, a minstrel's work, to judge by its numerous poetical clichés. Only one medieval copy of it has survived, a late fifteenth-century copy of a late fourteenth-century original. This copy is standardized in language, but its rhymes indicate pretty certainly that the poem was composed in the North Midlands or, in county terms, either in north Lincolnshire or, more probably, in Yorkshire.

Common to Malory's version and the story related in this poem are several important details that do not appear in the French prose-romance, *La Mort Artu*, from which they both derive. The poem describes Gawain's death and burial in a way very similar to Malory's: in the famous scene of the return of Arthur's sword to the lake, the King's assistant in these English versions is Bedevere, although in the French version Bedevere had been killed long before and the assistant is Girflet. They both recount Lancelot's journey to the Amesbury nunnery to which Guenevere had retreated and the last interview of the lovers, although that scene is found in only one of the many manuscripts of *La Mort Artu*.

The verbal resemblances between Malory and this poem are even more striking. These are but a few:

Malory	*The poem*
Than had sir Gawayne suche a grace and gyffte that an holy man had gyvyn hym	Than had syr Gawayne such a grace. An holy man had boddyn that bone.
Now have good day, my lorde the Kynge! For wytte you welle, ye wynne no worshyp at thes wallis nothynge but watirs wap and wawys wanne	But have good day, my lord the kynge Ye wynne no worshyp at thys walle nothynge But watres depe And wawes wanne

Such similarities are now generally agreed to prove that Malory had this stanzaic poem at hand when he was writing Books XX and XXI of his work. Recently it has been further claimed that he also made use of the poem while he was writing Books XVIII and XIX, although the correspondences there are less striking and less poetic in language, and there are considerable differences in construction. For our own biographical purpose, how extensively Malory is indebted to the poem is not particularly important. What is important is that the poem was composed in Yorkshire, that copies of it were therefore most common in that county, and that at the same time he was using this English poem he was also drawing upon *La Mort Artu*, the French version of the same story.[2]

The other English poem that it is generally acknowledged Malory used, the alliterative *Morte Arthure*, is qualitatively far superior to the stanzaic poem and one of the very best literary productions of the whole Middle English period. It is a tragedy on a historical theme, the tragedy of the last years of Arthur. It opens by describing the splendor and power that Arthur had attained after a career of conquest. The challenge from Rome follows, and the campaign in which Arthur defeats the Roman forces in Burgundy. At this height, tragedy begins. Mordred usurps the kingdom during Arthur's absence; the King returns, and in the ensuing civil war the King, the usurper, and most of Arthur's knights are slain. The poem ends solemnly with the burial of the King at Glastonbury.

This poem was a main source and a major inspiration for Malory. Not only did he adapt it directly for his Book V by front-shifting the events to an earlier stage in Arthur's career, thereby excising its tragic conclusion, but he recalled some details when he was closing his work with the piteous tragedy of Arthur and his knights in Book XXI.

Malory's prosing of this poem exists in two very different forms: the Caxton version is radically recast, shortened to half the length, and stated almost entirely in standard language, while the Winchester version is closer to the poem in narrative details and language. For our purpose of localization we need to discuss only the Winchester version.

The only medieval text of the poem as Malory might have used it is the copy made by Robert Thornton around 1430.[3] Thornton may have come from Newton in the North Riding, and since the poem is remarkably consistent in its Yorkshire dialect, it is possible he regulated its language. Most scholars, however, doubt that he changed it very much. Angus McIntosh, the outstanding scholar on Middle English dialects, argued that a few forms indicate Thornton's text was made from a Lincolnshire copy. McIntosh however was concerned only with a copy from which he thought the Thornton copy was made. He judged that the original poem was composed not many miles from York. The same was the opinion of J. L. N. O'Loughlin, who thought it was composed slightly north of York and sustained his opinion with linguistic data as well as the poet's knowledge of the road from Carlisle to York, even to the fine detail of the location of Catterick.

There is little doubt, therefore, that the original copy of the poem and any further copies that led to the Thornton text were made in Yorkshire or nearby. Nor can it be doubted that the copy Malory used came from the same area. We have already discussed his version of the Roman war, showing that its standard language is varied by northern words and forms transferred from a text that may have been much like the Thornton copy in its language. Here is a sample of Malory's version, with the northernisms italicized:

> Than the kynge yode [went] up to the creste of the *cragge*, and than he comforted hymselfe with the colde wynde; and than he yode forth by two welle-strem*ys*, and there he fynd*ys* two fyres flam*and* full hyghe. And at that one fyre he founde a carefull wydow wryng*ande* hir hand*ys*, *syttande* on a grave that was new marked. Than Arthur salued hir and she hym agayne, and asked hir why she sate sorowyng.

These matters are not in dispute: The *Morte Arthure* is a northern poem, probably from Yorkshire. The abundance of northernisms in Malory's version of the Roman war is partly the result of his using that poem. But if we wish to learn something about Malory himself, the matter cannot be left there.

For one thing, from the normal point of view, which accepts the hypothesis that Sir Thomas Malory was the knight of Newbold Revel, there should be something quite astonishing in his use of such a poem. Even in its simpler forms, northern dialect was not easily understood by Englishmen when their own speech was either standard or a southern dialect. John Trevisa, who lived at Berkeley, only sixty miles southwest of Newbold Revel, declared in 1387 that, "... al the longage of the Northhumbres, and specialych at York, ys so scharp, slyttyng, and frotynge, and unschape, that we Southeron men may that longage unnethe [scarcely] undurstonde." For the reverse of the same coin, a northern scribe, who had al-

The Locale of Le Morte Darthur

tered the dialect of a southern sermon for the ease of his readers, justified himself in this way:

> In a writte this ilke I fande
> In other Inglis was it drawin,
> And turnid Ic have it til ur awin
> Language of the Northin lede,
> That can na othir Inglis rede.

If ordinary northern speech and writing was difficult for a southerner, northern alliterative poetry was formidable. Its lexical abundance, which constant alliteration demanded; its many archaisms and verbal formulae, which this kind of verse had inherited even from pre-Conquest days; its numerous dialect words and constructions, particularly usages derived from or influenced by the language of Scandinavian settlers—these made northern alliterative poetry very hard going indeed. Even modern students, equipped with all our dictionaries and guided by editorial elucidations, find it extremely difficult to understand. A medieval reader might not have been troubled by some usages that bother us, but for a great many he would have been in no better case, and he would not have had reference books to help him.

Of all these alliterative poems, *Morte Arthure* is perhaps the most difficult. Certainly it is quite as formidable as *Pearl* or *Sir Gawain*, as this sample of one of its simpler stretches will show:

> Than gliftis the gud kynge and glopyns in herte,
> Gronys fulle grisely with gretande teris;
> Knelis downe to the cors and kaught it in armes,
> Kastys upe his vmbrere and kyssis hyme sone,
> Lokes one his eye-liddis, that lowkkide ware faire,
> His lippis like to the lede, and his lire falowede.

In fact, Oakden, the major authority on the form and language of alliterative poetry, took the *Morte Arthure* as his particular example in declaring that: "It is most unlikely that a London audience would have comprehended such a poem." Sir Thomas Malory of Newbold Revel, although he spent much time in London, was a Warwickshireman. But Warwickshire was no better base than London for cracking the hard nuts of northern verse. The county lay well on the other side of the linguistic fence between north and midlands, and since it had its own localisms, a

Warwickshire way of speaking might even have added difficulties a medieval Londoner was spared.

It should be quite surprising, therefore, that Malory's version of this poem presents a completely intelligible story—one that summarizes very effectively the poem's subject matter and catches much of its heroic spirit. Malory shaped the material to his own plan by adding details that set the episode into the general frame of his own book and by abbreviating and rephrasing the poem so as to bring it toward stylistic and proportional agreement with the rest of his writing. The latter phase of this process entailed omissions of various lengths and a good deal of précis and paraphrase. Some passages are expressed entirely in his own words, although he often carries over words, phrases, and even sentences from the poem. The passages where his version is linguistically closest to the poem are those where the poem is closest to normal English. The long descriptions, which tend to be most dialectal and difficult, are the sections Malory cuts most heavily or subjects to radical précis and paraphrase.

This difference in his procedures could be interpreted to mean that Malory was uncertain about the richly dialectal passages of the poem. It could also mean something more simple: descriptions are the most obvious victims to anyone who is abbreviating a story. The second explanation seems likely, if only because it fits in with Malory's habit elsewhere: he nowhere indulges in extended, set description. That it was not incomprehension which dictated the cutting of these difficult passages may be judged by the fact that his brief précis of them are intelligible and do not falsify either the meaning or the mood of the poetry they represent.

Malory's version as a whole witnesses to a sound grasp of the poem and solid understanding of its intimidating language, which would be astonishing in a Warwickshire man. It may be that paradox that has led some scholars to seek evidence of his misunderstanding the language. Since this approach is a suitable way to refine judgment on the quality of Malory's understanding of northern poetry, a detailed examination was made for the present book. The following report summarizes material which is set out fully in Appendix E. It is based upon specific, apparent misunderstandings by Malory that other scholars have noticed and the further possibilities that were discovered in the special examination.

A good many of Malory's misunderstandings are more apparent than real. Six can be explained as misreadings of *e* as *o*: *foomen* for "feemene" is one example. A difference of opinion about punctuation could explain Malory's substituting *makyng* for "makke." Three differences, such as *langage* for *launde* "langue?" may show him correcting a copyist's slip. Intention is the likeliest explanation for his replacing *belyfe* "quickly" with *blythe*, or *plattes* "places" with *plantys*; there are nine other cases of the same kind.

In some other instances various explanations besides misunderstanding are possible: in several, Malory's difference may have resulted from misreading. His *foomen* and *makyng*, as we have said, are typical of several places where he has misread a letter or a punctuation. In ten other cases misreading of this kind (or deliberate intent) led to divergencies like *kyrtyls* for *kyrnelles* "crenellations." These are the obvious explanations, since the words in the poem were standard ones, known to everybody. The same explanations seem likely for his substitution of *water*, *hateful*, and *freysh* for the poem's *wathe* "path," *hertelyche* "heartily," and *freke* "bold." With the last two it would certainly have been easy for Malory to misread these words in the poem as "wather," "hetelich," and "frick," which not only have the same meanings as his own words, but also appear elsewhere in the poem.

His substitutions for seven words, including *helmys* for *brenes* "corslets," might be held to show only approximate understanding. But it is no less possible that the variations were made deliberately.

Finally, there are the fourteen or so words that have been declared to reveal downright misunderstanding: *elffe*, *bird*, *on bothe sydys*, *brennys* (burns), *deuke*, *dredfull*, *had he none*, *syttande*, *Gotelake*, *noble*, *lugerande lokys*, *stoode*, *creste of the hylle*, *seteled*, which are his substitutes for the poem's *alfyne* "the bishop in chess," *brede* "roast meat," *brothely* "fiercely," *bryttenyd* "destroyed," *derfe* "severe," *on dreghe* "aside," *fangez* "seizes," *gretande* "lamenting," *guyte* "child," *harageous* "violent," *lutterde legges* "sprawling," *stotais* "hesitates," *sowre of the reke* (meaning uncertain), and *styghtylle* "arrange."

Among these there may be genuine cases of misunderstanding, which should not be surprising since the words are rare in the extreme: some of them are unique to this poem. For example, *sowre of the reke*, Malory may have worked out as "soar" and "rig" (the northern form of "ridge"). It may be doubted very seriously that all of these substitutions were prompted by ignorance. Malory's *elffe* for *alphyne* achieves the same innuendo with a word of similar sound. The poem's chess term could scarcely have been strange to a gentleman. His *dredful* seems to be an addition rather than a substitution for *on dreghe*. If he failed to understand *bryttenyd* "destroyed" when he replaced it with *brennys* "burns," it is strange indeed that in three other places he gives highly competent substitutes for the same word. His rendition of *styghtylle* may seem ignorant in this place; but two lines later he translates it quite correctly. And since elsewhere he finds no trouble at all with *greet* "lament," his substitution of *syttande* for *gretande* demands an explanation different from ignorance. That explanation may well be that it is his critics who are in error, for *syttande* does not necessarily mean "sitting": it may be a homonym that means "grieving," as it sometimes did in the north. Elsewhere in this tale Malory knowledgeably translates the corresponding noun *syte* as *sorrow*.

As the full statement of our Appendix shows, very few of the allegations of plain error have been proved. But even if they had all been proved, they would have been of small weight in comparison with Malory's many good translations of unusual words in the poem. It is this competence with the traditional and dialectal vocabulary of the alliterative poem that is most impressive. No one who was coming to northern verse for the first time, no one who was previously unfamiliar with northern dialect, is likely to have been so efficient in simplifying such unusual words as: *birdez* to *maydens*, *cowpez* to *strikes*, *eldes* to *ayges*, *gerte* to *commaunded*, *glopyne* to *greve*, *gome* to *knyght*, *lede* to *good man*, *romyez* to *seyde*, *syte* to *sorrow*, or *worows* to *destroyed*. These are merely samples of his successes. Were the number fewer, it might be reasonable to urge that they were merely intelligent guesses. So many good translations, however, especially when they are backed by abundant evidence of other kinds, must mean that Malory was remarkably well versed in the specialized vocabulary of northern alliterative poetry.

This conclusion may also be supported by one of Malory's stylistic mannerisms—his fondness for alliterative phrases. This habit is not restricted to the Roman war section; it may be observed, more sparsely of course, throughout *Le Morte Darthur*. Some of these phrases are characteristic of alliterative verse in that they employ words rarely found in other kinds of writing. Among many examples, these may be cited: "she wepte as she had bene wood," "double dyked wyth full warly wallys," "brochys and bees," "droupe and dare," "huntyth and hawkyth," "lykynge and luste," "senshyp and shame," "stynte your stryff," "tray and tene," and "worshyp of the worlde." These occur in places where Malory was translating from French; and that there were more of them in Malory's original text is indicated by Caxton's using some that are lacking from the Winchester text: "as wyghte as ever was Wade," "angir and unhap," and "by stygh and by strete."

It is the presence of these phrases which suggests a simpler explanation for Malory's use in the Roman war section of many alliterative phrases that do not appear in the *Morte Arthure*. Some commentators, puzzled by these alliterative additions, have suggested that they are not Malory's own doing—that they were in his copy of the poem, and this copy must therefore have differed considerably from the only version we have, the Thornton manuscript. Malory's inclination to use alliterative phrases and sentences even when he was translating from French weakens this argument. So does a full examination of all his alliterative variations from the poem. Sometimes when he stated the poem's meaning in his own words, he also provided his own alliteration. For example, he substituted for "Our wages are werede owte and thi werre endide," a phrase that has the same sense but an alliteration that does not appear in the poem, "for garneson nother golde have we none resceyued." Sometimes, without changing the poem's meaning, he simply increased the amount of alliteration. Thus, he replaced "Thow has marters made and broghte oute of lyfe" with "Thou haste made many martyrs by mourtheryng of this londis." In this case and in many others, the Thornton text reads so satisfactorily that no editor would have any ground for thinking that it did not represent the original text. Moreover, Malory's procedures with the alliterative *Morte Arthure* are matched exactly—although on a smaller scale—where he drew from the stanzaic *Le Morte Arthur* toward the end of his book. The latter poem uses a good many alliterative phrases, and while Malory sometimes took these over without change, he developed his own alliterative patterns at other times. Sometimes he even incorporated alliterating lines that cannot possibly have existed in the poem—examples of these procedures are set out at the end of Appendix F.

Rather than guess at the existence of a lost text of the alliterative poem which agreed exactly in these details with Malory's tale, it is much simpler to believe that the differences were of Malory's own making. In the full record of the differences set out in Appendix F, there is nothing that undeniably demands Malory used a text different from the Thornton manuscript. As with his added northern words, all that seems necessary to explain the differences is to recognize that Malory was very familiar with northern dialect and northern alliterative verse and that he was not a mechanical translator. In adapting this poem to the design of his own book, he made serious changes in the story, weaving it into the pattern of his whole book of Arthur and the Knights of the Round Table, and converting it from a tragedy by omitting the poem's tragic end and substituting a triumph, which is surely his own.* It is straining at a gnat to assume that he should not also have been willing and able to vary the poem with new words and new alliterations.

This is perhaps as far as one should go with internal evidence about Malory's dealing with the poem and the kind of text he used. But there is an intriguing detail of external evidence which has not been reported before. It will need some preliminary explanation.

Towards the end of his book, when he is dealing with the death and burial of Arthur, Malory makes this statement:

And many men say that there ys wrytten upon the tumbe thys: hic iacet Arthurus, rex quondam rexque futurus.

This famous epitaph, the basis for T. H. White's title *The Once and Future King*, must have been taken from some book.

From the reign of Henry II, when Arthur's body was said to have been unearthed, until late in the sixteenth century, there are several reports on what his epitaph was. The *Mort Artu* gives it as, "Ci gist li rois Artus qui par sa valeur mist en sa subjection .xii. roiaumes." Gerald of Wales records two forms: "Hic iacet sepultus inclytus rex Arthurus cum Wenneveria uxore sua secunda in insula Avallonia," and "hic iacet sepultus inclytus rex Arthurus in insula Avallonia cum uxore sua secunda Wenneveria." Ralph of Coggeshall has, "hic iacet inclitus rex Arturius, in insula Avallonis sepultus." In a later period, Camden's *Brittania* (1610) gives a drawing of a cross, claiming that it was based on a first copy in Glastonbury Abbey, and on the cross are the words, "Hic iacet sepultus inclitus rex Arturius in insula Avalonia." Bishop Usher, quoting Leland

---

* The theory that the text of the poem which Malory used ended just as Malory's tale ended is usually supported by showing that Malory's ending contains alliterating phrases. Malory, as we have shown, was quite capable of inventing his own alliterations. But what speaks more strongly against the theory is that a triumph is an impossible conclusion for the poem, which is structured throughout as a tragedy. Malory's conclusion in this section may not be entirely original, for many late-medieval versions of the Roman war declare that Arthur carried his expedition into Italy and even to Rome; but if he got it from any alliterative poem, it would have been a very different poem indeed from the one we have in Thornton.

as his authority, gives the same epitaph as Camden; but from another source, which claimed to derive from Simon of Abingdon's eyewitness account, he also quotes, "Hic iacet gloriosissimus rex Britonum Arturus."[4]

None of these versions agrees, either in words or wit, with Malory's version. In fact, there are only two known versions of the epitaph that do. One occurs in the short poem called *Arthur*, which Malory is unlikely to have known, but the other occurs in the alliterative *Morte Arthure* and agrees in every detail: "hic iacet Arthurus rex quondam rexque futurus." It is for this and other reasons that Vinaver stated that the epitaph is borrowed from the alliterative poem.

This ascription is as certain as anything can ever be in literary scholarship. But an important detail concerning it has escaped recent notice.* In the Thornton manuscript, the epitaph appears between the last line of the poem and the copyist's colophon, "Here endes Morte Arthure, writene by Robert of Thorntone." The most significant facts however are these: the epitaph is written in a different hand from that of the poem and that of the colophon; it is also written with a thinner and now browner ink. The deduction can only be that the epitaph was not part of the original poem or of the copy that Thornton used: someone unknown had added it to Thornton's manuscript. If that is so, it is peculiar to this copy, and it would be reasonable to think that Malory's copy of the poem was the Thornton manuscript. The manuscript is now in the Lincoln Cathedral library. When it came there is not known, but it may have been early in the nineteenth century. Names scribbled in the margins indicate the manuscript was still in Thornton possession in the seventeenth century. If Malory did use this manuscript, therefore, he probably used it in Yorkshire.†

There is no doubt that Malory read and used two northern poems, and there is good reason to believe that he was at ease with alliterative phrase-

---

* It is partly reported, however, in the introduction to the Camden Society's *Thornton Romances*.

† It is further possible—though arguable—that witness to Malory's use of the Thornton manuscript is afforded by a small set of correspondences. At the end of his work, Malory states, giving the French book as his authority, that the Arthurian survivors—Bors, Hector, Blamour and Bleoberis—went to the Holy Land and there fought for the faith, won victories, and died. As Vinaver pointed out, nothing of this appears in any of the many texts of *La Mort Artu*; the editor asserted that this is another of Malory's inventions, presumably to round off his book. Vinaver may

ology and poetical vocabulary. The first fact may explain the second, but not entirely; for some details in his book suggest that he was familiar with more northern poems than these two.[5]

Among the minor figures in Le Morte Darthur is a knight named Sir Bawdewyn of Bretayne. Arthur, when he first comes to the throne, makes him Constable of England, and in that capacity he fights on the King's behalf. During the preparations for the Roman campaign, he vows to bring ten thousand men to support Arthur's invasion; but instead of going to France he is appointed, with Sir Constantine, as chieftain of Britain during Arthur's absence. In the middle sections of Malory's book he appears only once, as an adviser at court. Towards the end, however, he assumes a role that typifies the moral change that affects Arthur's court in its hour of darkness; he abandons court life and great possessions to devote himself to a hermit's life of poverty, contemplation, and good works. In this capacity, he twice cures Lancelot of serious wounds.

Sir Baldwin does not appear in the French prose romances, and it is an interesting question, therefore, where Malory found him. In *Gawain and the Green Knight*, a Bishop Bawdewyn is mentioned once. In *Sir Gawain and the Carl of Carlisle*, a Bishop Bawdewyn appears twice—once in association with Gawain. He is also mentioned in the *Turk and Sir Gowin*. This Bishop Baldwin, who may not be the same person as Malory's knight-hermit, is apparently unknown to French romances, although he may be the Bishop Bedwin who appears in the Welsh *Mabinogion*.

A knight of the same name, although not labelled as "of Bretayne," ap-

---

be entirely right, but it is also possible that the invention may have been suggested by a peculiarity of the romances collected in the Thornton manuscript. Crusading is a final feature or a theme of several of them. The last stanza of *Sir Perceval de Galles* records that its hero went to the Holy Land, there won victories for the Christian faith, and died. The ending of *Sir Degrevaunt* is the same. (And it may be significant that this extraordinarily virtuous hero is the probable origin of "*Degrave saunze vylony*," a knight who, although he is unknown to French romance, is listed in Malory.) Many of the victories of the hero of *Sir Isumbras* also occur in the Holy Land; and a main motif in the alliterative *Morte Arthure* is Arthur's intent to go to the Holy Land in Christ's cause. From such *données* in the Thornton manuscript, it would have been easy enough for Malory to construct his own conclusion.

In addition, as is shown in the next section of this book, Malory seems to have drawn the names of several non-French knights from two romances, the alliterative *Morte Arthure* and the *Awntyrs of Arthur*, which are found together in only one Middle English manuscript, the one assembled by Robert Thornton.

pears in three catalogues of names in the alliterative *Morte Arthure*. From these it seems that he was an associate of Cador, the knight who succeeded Arthur on the throne under the name Constantine. The one romance in which Sir Bawdewyn of Britain plays an important part, however, is *The Avowynge of Arthur*, a poem in alliterative lines and northern dialect which was composed during Malory's youth, around 1425. The action is set in Carlisle and Cumberland. The threefold vow and adventures of Sir Baudwen, who is drawn as a disillusioned and worldly-wise old man, occupy most of the romance.

Whether Malory learned about him from *The Avowynge of Arthur* or from some other untraced romance is something we cannot know with certainty. Even so, since the only romances in which Sir Baldwin appears are written in northern English and alliterative verse, since his character and his associations in these agree with Malory's view, and since a Yorkshire family named Malory owned a manor in Inglewood Forest, the chief locale of Sir Baldwin's adventures—it seems a reasonable conjecture that Malory learned about this Arthurian from some northern alliterative poem.

Sir Galeron of Galloway too may have been derived from a northern romance. He appears eight times in Malory; the major incidents are: his lending armor to Tristram, a tournament in which he fights on Mordred's side against Lancelot's, another tournament in which he is on Lancelot's side, and his participation in Mordred's attempt to surprise Lancelot in adultery with Guenevere. Galeron figures in some *chansons de geste*, and in *Perceval le Gallois* there is a knight called Galerans dis li Gallois. In English he is found in three poems. In *Gawain and the Carl of Carlisle* and the alliterative *Morte Arthure*, he is simply mentioned. But in the *Awntyrs of Arthur*, a northern alliterative poem written about 1400, he is one of the two chief heroes. In that poem Arthur has alienated his lands, giving them to Gawain. Galeron challenges this injustice, and in tourney with Gawain manages to regain his rights.

In her edition of the first of these poems, Miss Auvo Kurvinen declared, " . . . it seems that the French Arthurian romances connect the name [Galeron] with Wales, the English with Scotland." Malory follows English practice, even though he is at these times translating from French. And since this practice is known only from northern romances, the chief of them written in alliterative verse, it seems possible that he learned of this knight in a northern romance. Here again, the argument may be strengthened by the fact that the first half of *Awntyrs of Arthur* takes place in Inglewood Forest, very near to the place where the Yorkshire Malorys owned their manor.

A further minor figure whom Malory may have taken from northern romance is Gromoresom Erioure—called in the Caxton text, Gromore Somyr Ioure. He is mentioned only once in *Le Morte Darthur*, in the list —with Petipace of Winchylse and Galeron of Galloway—of Mordred's twelve knights who surprise Lancelot and Guenevere together in Carlisle. Vinaver conjectured that Malory here blended the names of two knights, Helynas de Gromoret and Eliors, who appear occasionally (but not in this context) in French romance. The suggestion seems unduly complicated. What is more likely is that Malory took the name from some version of *The Weddynge of Sir Gawen*, a short verse romance on the theme of the loathly lady who was transformed when the correct answer was given to her question: what do women desire the most? The single surviving text of this romance is in East-Midland dialect of about 1450. But that there was a northern original is made probable by the locale of the action and by some close resemblances to other northern poems that Malory seems to have known. The locale is Carlisle, Inglewood Forest, and Tarn Wadling—just as it is in *The Avowynge of Arthur* and *Awntyrs of Arthur*. The narrative plot is the same as the second part of *Awntyrs*: Arthur has bestowed upon Gawain the lands of another knight. In *Awntyrs* the dispossessed knight is Galeron of Galloway; in *The Weddynge*, Gromer Somer Joure. The facts that this strange name is known only from Malory and *The Weddynge* and that there is almost perfect agreement in spelling between the poem and the Caxton text, suggest that Malory took the name from some written text of the poem.

Similarly, the name of Sir Petipace of Winchylse—or according to the Caxton text, "of Wynkelsee"—may have peculiar northern sources. He is mentioned in *Le Morte Darthur* only five times: once in a combat and elsewhere in combat lists, in two of which his name occurs next to Sir Galeron of Galloway's. The name has become a favorite with many of Malory's readers, though nothing very much is said of him: he joins in Mordred's attempt to surprise Lancelot, but elsewhere he always appears on Lancelot's side. Despite his name, Petipace appears in no French romance. But he does appear in the northern poem *Sir Gawain and the Carl of Carlisle*, where he is mentioned as taking part in a hunt near Carlisle in the company of Sir Galeron of Galloway.

This looks as though Malory came across him in a northern poem and liked the name enough to appropriate it for his catalogues. But there is a tantalizing curiosity that may connect Malory and Sir Petipace in a more personal way. Miss Kurvinen suggested that Sir Petipace's locale name is somehow related to Espagnols-sur-Mer, a sea battle in which Edward III fought against the Spaniards off Winchelsea. This is a fancy developed from another editor's suggestion about a battle described in the alliterative *Morte Arthure*. My own note may strike a reader as being no less fanciful. According to the Caxton text, Sir Petipace comes from "Wynkelsee." About a mile from Fountains Abbey is a village called Winksley. In the fifteenth century, its name was spelled in a variety of ways, among them "Wynkylsey." That is essentially Caxton's spelling. But what is really curious is that the same spelling occurs in the will of a fifteenth-century Sir William Malory, who owned property in the village. The manor, however, belonged to a family named Heaviside. It is tempting to think that if the author of *Le Morte Darthur* was connected with Sir William Malory, his interest in Sir Petipace of Wynkylsee may have been whimsical, stemming from an acquaintance with one of the Heavisides of Wynkylsey.

A few small matters of the same kind also indicate Malory had read more English romances than the two poems on the death of Arthur, and that he had read them in northern versions. But enough is enough: let us turn to evidence of a different sort.

If a medieval book displays intimate knowledge of real persons and real places of the author's own time, it is normal to assume by that knowledge that he had something to do with them in his own activities. Malory's Arthurian names afford no evidence about fifteenth-century people. But it is otherwise with places, for every now and then Sir Thomas mentions, apparently with some familiarity, localities and local lore that do not appear in his sources.

Some of these names may confidently be attributed to the English poems he read. Thus, that he located in Amesbury the nunnery to which Guenevere retired in the days of tragedy, and that he seems to have had local knowledge of Kent when he was dealing with Arthur's return to encounter Mordred may be explained by his reading of the stanzaic *Le Morte Arthur*, which has the same details. That toward the end of his work Arthur's court is located in Carlisle, that the love tragedy occurs there, may witness to Malory's northern preoccupation, but may also be because several northern alliterative poems which he knew do the same. His interest in Arundel, however, cannot be matched in his sources, and that may mean that he knew the FitzAlans' castle there.

The same more personal explanation might hold for his introduction of English names into the story of Elaine's tragic love for Lancelot. As in the sources, the tournament which is a central event in that episode is set in Winchester. But Malory adds these local details: Astolat has a castle where King Arthur stays before the tournament; Astolat's English name is Guildford; Elaine's father is Sir Barnard of Astolat, an old baron who lives in a place near the castle; nearby apparently is a hermitage where Lancelot is cured of his wounds; when Elaine dies of love she is carried to the Thames, and the barge with her body floats past Westminster—in the French version it floats past Camelot. In the pages that follow, Malory also added allusions to Windsor Forest as a royal hunting ground, and to Lambeth and Westminster—revealing, incidentally, his very accurate knowledge that the quickest way to get between the two last places is to swim.

Malory apparently had some special interest in the southern counties. He knew something about Arundel Castle apparently; and, as we shall show presently, he seems to have had special knowledge of politics in Surrey and Sussex. His details about Guildford, therefore, fit into a larger pattern, and that they are possibly based upon Malory's personal knowledge might be ascertained from these facts of history. Guildford's now ruined castle is a short walk from Thorp's bookshop. In the fifteenth century it was beginning to fall into ruin, but it was still sound enough for Edward IV to reside occasionally in its palace and for the keep to be used as the county jail. In 1466, the mayor of the town was named Bernard Jenyn, and his manor of Brabeuf faced the castle from just over the River Wey. At the nearby junction of the London and Epsom roads was Saint Thomas' Spital, then maintained by a Dominican friary.[6]

Scholars have taken some of Malory's English names to be passing allusions to events in the Wars of the Roses. There is his description of Mordred's forces in the civil war: "Than sir Mordred araysed muche people aboute London, for they of Kente, Southsex and Surrey, Esax, Suffolke and Northefolke helde the moste party with Sir Mordred," which was thought by Vinaver to refer to the contemporary English situation when Sussex, Kent, Essex, and East Anglia were controlled by the Fitz-Alans, Bourchiers, and Mowbrays—all Yorkists.

More specifically, the following passage may cast its eye upon one of the first great battles of the English civil war:

> So it was done as Merlyn had devysed, and they caryed the King forth in an hors-lyttar with a grete hooste towarde his enemyes, and at Saynt Albons ther mette with the kynge a grete hoost of the North . . . And Kyng Uthers men overcome the northeryn bataylle and slewe many peple and putt the remenaunt to flyght; and thenne the kyng returned unto London.

Stewart, and following him Vinaver, declared that Malory's localization of the battle at St. Albans, which is not in his French source, was an allusion to the first battle of St. Albans, February 23, 1453; for Henry VI, turned mad, was then carried at the head of his host to meet a great rebel army from the North and after the battle fell back on London.

Malory's story of the battles Arthur fought with the northern kings just after he ascended the throne was made more English by the use of names that do not appear in his French source. When the five northern kings invade, Arthur marches to meet them and establishes himself in a castle in the forest of Bedgrayne. In other romances Bedgrayne is located in Cornwall, but Malory identified it with Sherwood and indicated that it lay just beyond the River Trent. The area is enemy territory, and earlier Brastias was made warden to guard it, ". . . the Northe fro Trent forwardes, for it was that tyme the most party the kynges enemyes." Malory's intent in these localizations, so Vinaver urged, was to point to a parallel between his story and some of the outstanding events in the Wars of the Roses.

If the conjecture is well-founded, it may not be overrash to be more specific. A castle in Sherwood just beyond the Trent would probably be Nottingham or Newark, and those are names that have relevance both to the Wars of the Roses and to a person named Malory. When Robin of Redesdale led his great army of rebellious northerners against Edward IV, the King marched to Newark to meet them. Finding them too strong, he first retreated to Nottingham and then to the south. The clash came at Edgecote on July 26, 1469, and among the many eminent northerners who were slain there, a William Mallery esquire was one.

Like the other supposed allusions to the Wars of the Roses, the parallel may strike a critical reader as being more curious than convincing. But if the reader is inclined to take such parallels seriously, he may think with numerous scholars that Malory's sympathies were with Henry VI and Lancaster and that he may have had more than a general observer's concern in the northern revolts that flared up at the time he was writing.

These are speculative matters, and it is fortunate that *Le Morte Darthur* has topographical details which better justify making certain conclusions about the author's locale. For example, when Arthur sends away the Roman emperor's ambassadors, he instructs them in this way: "Loke ye go by Watlynge strete and no way ellys." Arthur is at Carlisle when he says this, and offhand his direction seems a very strange one, since in ordinary usage "Watling Street" was the popular name for the old Roman road that led from London to Chester. But it is not really so strange, for the detail is transferred from the alliterative *Morte Arthure*, where it reflects the northern habit of using "Watling Street" for the road from Carlisle to York via Catterick and Boroughbridge. If Malory was a Warwickshire knight, it was extraordinarily careless of him simply to transfer this name from the poem, for the ordinary Watling Street ran almost by his doorstep in Newbold Revel. If he were a northerner, however, the transference would have been the most natural thing in the world, and especially so if he were one of the Yorkshire Malorys, who owned manors very near to this other Watling Street.

More positive significance may be found in a detail that concerns Carlisle. Late in the Tristram story, when Palomydes, the noble Saracen, finally makes up his mind to become Christian, Tristram takes him to the suffragan of Carlisle, and ". . . the suffrygan let fylle a grete vessell wyth watyr, and whan he had halowed hyt he than confessed clene sir Palomydes. And Trystram and sir Galleron were hys two godfadyrs." In the French *Tristan* the baptism takes place in the *mestre église* of Camelot. Malory's change to Carlisle and his addition of the northern knight, Sir Galeron of Galloway, form interesting witness to his northern preoccupation. But the significant addition is that the baptism was performed by a suffragan, for according to Trevisa, ". . . the Primat of York hath but tweie suffragans in Engelond, that beeth the bisshopis of Caerlile and of Duram." Only an author peculiarly knowledgeable about northern institutions would have been so accurate in so small an addition.

Finally, there is Malory's allusion to a legend about Lancelot's castle of Joyous Garde, where Tristram fled with Isolde and where Lancelot brought Guenevere after Mordred had surprised them together in Carlisle—the same that, in a tragic mood, Lancelot renamed Dolorous Garde. In the French *Tristan* it is located in the north, but vaguely as half a day from the Humber. In Malory it is within comfortable reach of Carlisle, for the Bishop of Rochester, the intermediary between Lancelot and

Arthur, rides to and fro between the two places: it is apparently within a day's ride. In fact, as Malory imagined its situation, it was only sixty miles from Carlisle. Malory did not commit himself to its exact location, cautiously preferring to report the common belief: "somme men say it was Anwyk and somme men say it was Bamborow." Judging from the few details he gives about the castle and the town adjoining it, he himself may have thought it was Alnwick and that Dolorous Garde was the great stronghold that the Percies, the Cocks of the North, had built and strengthened in the hope of holding back the Scots.

The localization is eloquent to Malory's knowledge of the North Country, and so is the folklore he reported. That part of Northumberland is rich in Arthurian associations. It was here, not far from Corbridge, that it is said Arthur fought the great battle of Camlan. Nearby, at Sewingshields, is located a lively legend that Arthur and his court had been found in a cave, apparently awaiting Arthur's return. Dunstanburgh Castle is also a castle with Arthurian associations, for Thomas, earl of Lancaster, who began to build it in 1313, was famed for his foible of taking the role of King Arthur in the pageants at court. As for the legend that Malory reported, it persists in antiquarian histories of the county, though the location may be said to be Berwick as well as Bamburgh, Dunstanburgh, or Alnwick. That the legend was current in Malory's day is witnessed by the comment of William Patten, a Londoner who accompanied the Duke of Somerset to Scotland in 1547. Speaking of Bamburgh Castle, he wrote: "This castle is very ancient, and called in Arthurs days (as I have heard), Joyous Garde." In Malory's time, folklore of this kind was seldom to be picked up from books; normally one had to be on the spot to hear it. It is justifiable therefore to claim that the author of *Le Morte Darthur* must have spent some time in the Border country.

So far, our investigation has been along lines the editor of an anonymous medieval text would follow—the investigations of the language, allusions, and reading of the author. They all point firmly to the probability that the author was a northerner, probably a Yorkshireman.

Le Morte Darthur is not anonymous, however, for both texts indicate that it was written by a Sir Thomas Malorye or Maleorre. It is rare good fortune, therefore, that his name occurs on a medieval version of one of his principal sources. This fact, although it was known to a former owner, did not become public knowledge until the manuscript was bought by the Cambridge University Library in 1945 on advice from Eugène

Vinaver, and its implications have yet to be fully discussed.

The manuscript contains two prose romances in French, an *Estoire del Saint Graal* and a *Merlin*. The former is of no great interest; it is simply another medieval copy of a romance of which we have already many medieval copies. Since it seems Malory made no use of its matter, it need not concern us here. The *Merlin* is vitally important in Malory studies, however, and especially for the problem of Malory's identity.

Its contents may be summarized briefly. It opens with an account of Arthur's war against the northern rebel kings and goes on to events in the early years of his reign: the birth of Mordred, the revelation of Arthur's parentage, his combat with Pellinor, his getting Excalibur, the wars with Rions and Lot, the story of Balin, Arthur's marriage to Guenevere and the founding of the Round Table, quests undertaken by various of its Knights (Gawain, Tor, and Pellinor, particularly), the story of Merlin's infatuation for Viviene, Arthur's wars with the Five Kings, Morgan le Fay's plots to destroy Arthur, and the triple adventures of Gawain, Ywain, and Morholt. Although they do not appear in extant copies, it has been argued that the original romance may also have included a few other episodes: Gahereit's slaying of his mother, the youth of Perceval, Gawain's slaying of Pellinor's sons Lamorat and Drien, and some other episodes relating to the theme of vengeance which runs through the romance.

Now known conveniently as the *Huth-Merlin* or the *Suite du Merlin*, the romance seems to have been written some time after the common *Merlin*, possibly to provide a narrative bridge between that romance and the *Lancelot*. Medieval copies are rare: apart from some short portions embodied in four French manuscripts, the translations in Malory's *Le Morte Darthur*, and the Spanish *Demanda del Sancto Grial*, the only known full or nearly full versions are the newly discovered Cambridge manuscript and a fourteenth-century copy in Picard dialect. The latter copy, until it was bought by Henry Huth and given to the British Museum, was in French ownership.

The Cambridge manuscript, according to Eugène Vinaver, is the work of an early fourteenth-century Anglo-Norman scribe who worked from a Picard original. Late in the fifteenth century, an English copyist must have removed some damaged leaves and replaced them by leaves of the same size, on which he transcribed in his own spelling, but otherwise very accurately, the corresponding portions of the text. Since the last folio is full, it is clear that some closing folios are now lacking from the manuscript. In many details this copy is much closer to Malory's translation than is the Huth copy. It contains, for example, the lengthy story of Arthur's war against the northern kings, which does not appear in either the *Huth-Merlin* or the *Demanda del Sancto Grial* but forms chapters 8 to 18 of Malory's first book. As well, it agrees with Malory against the Huth copy in many details of words, phrases, and names (particularly the long list of names at the beginning of chapter 26 of the first book). Offhand, one might think it was the very text from which Malory worked. Vinaver, however, doubted this, although he admitted that the manuscript must be directly related to Malory's French book, perhaps an immediate copy of it.

Nevertheless, there are external details in the manuscript which connect it with Malory and his work. The most obvious of these is the note, known to Major J. G. Dent, the former owner, but first reported by Vinaver. This note occurs at the top of page 61 (folio 189r) of the romance and reads:

Ci comence le livre que Sir Thomas Malori Chr reduce in Engloys et fuist emprente par Willm̄ Caxton

The note is preceded by a cross which refers to another cross in the margin opposite a section that deals with Ygerne and the proposition made to her on Uther's behalf. The placing is absolutely accurate, for it is with this incident that Malory's translation begins.

Therefore it is obvious that the man who made the note, whose hand seems to be late fifteenth or early sixteenth century, had carefully compared a copy of Caxton's edition of Malory with this manuscript of the *Suite du Merlin*. This might mean merely that the annotator had some literary curiosity, and this may be the reason why Vinaver did nothing but report it. When the note is considered in connection with where it was found, however, it gains remarkably in its implications concerning the locale of *Le Morte Darthur* and its author.

In a letter to H. Eisemann, the dealer who bought the manuscript at Christie's, Major Dent states: "It was found in an old hide trunk, together with all the old deeds and seals relating to the property back to the 12th century, at Ribston Hall, Wetherby, Yorks, by my grandfather, and had presumably always been there." In another letter, Major Dent reports that he had all the deeds, and also a very interesting old cartulary got out for Sir Thomas Mauleverer, who owned Ribston and neighboring lands at that time. "Might Mallory be a confusion with Mauleverer?"

he wondered. The Major also said that he had intended before the War to give the deeds to the Museum at Leeds. He did so in 1947, and they are now in the possession of the Leeds Public Library and the Yorkshire Archaeological and Historical Society.[7]

The earliest deeds belong to the twelfth and thirteenth centuries and relate to the Knights Templar, who from 1224 to 1540 maintained a small house at Ribston on land that had been settled on them by Robert, Lord Roos. In 1338 the community consisted of two chaplain brothers (one of whom served as precentor), a serving brother, two corrody holders, a chaplain, and several officers and servants. By 1498 the community may have been reduced, for its preceptor also officiated at another Yorkshire house.

The rest of the Ribston documents is a cartulary and fifty deeds and documents belonging to the years 1324 to 1794. The earliest relate to the Mauleverers, an eminent Yorkshire family which owned Ribston and a good deal of other property in the immediate neighborhood. The family was connected by marriage with several other important Yorkshire families: the Strangways, the Markenfields, the Crathornes, and, most notably for our own interests, the Conyers and the Tempests. The remainder of the documents relate to the Goodrichs, originally a southern family that acquired Ribston very soon after the dissolution of the monasteries and remained in possession until the nineteenth century. The line of possession of these documents is therefore unbroken—Mauleverers, Goodrichs, Dents, Leeds Public Library, and Yorkshire Archaeological and Historical Society.

Among documents that bear on our own problem, the cartulary is central. This consists of abstracts of deeds relating to the manor of Whixley, an estate of 2,000 acres within the parish of Ribston. The manor belonged to the Mauleverers during the period to which the cartulary relates, but the abstracts also indicate that as a result of gifts there were subsidiary owners of small parcels within the area. Among these, the more interesting are Fountains Abbey and the house of St. Robert of Knaresborough. It is the physical aspects of the cartulary that have most interest for us. Judging by the variety of hands in the document, it was begun early in the fifteenth century and added to at various times until early the next century. Several folios have been inserted at the beginning, and in these appear a brief account of Whixley and a genealogy of the Mauleverers. The hand in which these folios are written is the same as the hand

The Locale of Le Morte Darthur

that added marginal notes in French, Latin, and English to the rest of the volume, occasionally indicating with crosses the abstracts to which the notes refer. The volume is enclosed in oak boards and bound in sheepskin that is now tattered and stained.

The manuscript containing the *Grail* and the *Suite du Merlin*, which Major Dent's grandfather found in the same box as the cartulary, has many of the same physical characteristics. The binding is the same, oak boards covered with tattered and stained sheepskin. It has added marginal indexings in Latin and French, marked by crosses of the same shape as those in the cartulary. And the hand that added the historical and genealogical folios to the cartulary is very similar to the hand that appears in those folios of the *Suite*, which Vinaver declared were inserted during the later fifteenth century as replacement for leaves that had been damaged.

The necessary conclusions are these: The manuscript that contains the *Grail* and the *Suite* was at Ribston when the cartulary was being compiled. Until the 1540's, at least, both manuscripts were owned by the Mauleverers of Ribston. So much seems certain. But the same details and others also give ground for speculation upon certain other matters of importance to us.

The hand that copied the extra folios in the *Suite* and possibly also added pages to the cartulary is that of a formally educated man. The handwriting is professional; the languages are Latin, French, and English. It is a reasonable conjecture that he was a professional scribe in the employ of the Mauleverers. It is permissible to guess that he may have been a member of the community of Knights Templar at Ribston, and a further detail of the manuscript may even supply his name.

The page that precedes the *Suite* carries the last lines of the *Estoire del Saint Graal*. Below those lines, in the right-hand column, is this note, written in a hand different from any other in the manuscript:

> Thomas Jaksone wrete this Bouke; Robertus cōstabyll Wettnes ymeself, wᵗ many mo ther beyng presens that tyme. Also yf it plese yow to rede this Booke, the whych is wrytyn in frenche, ye shall fynd many [one illegible word] therin. Primus, Thomas Rallyns, Thomas Rallinsen, H. Keynes. Robertus cōstabyll scribebat istud, qui vocabatur angelus dei.

The hand is later fifteenth century. The language and the situation that is described smack of a scriptorium. The note presumably refers to the

French book in which it appears, and in that case it must refer to the additions, for the main part of the manuscript is in a fourteenth-century hand.

Thomas Jackson may therefore have been the scribe who added substantially to the *Suite* and to the cartulary. His name and the other names in the note are commonplace: all occur in Yorkshire records, but they also occur everywhere else. Nevertheless, the name of the man who wrote the note, Robertus Constable called *angelus dei* (the Latin suggests the term must apply to a man, not to a book written in French), is intriguing for anyone curious about Sir Thomas Malory. In the later fifteenth century, the Constables were a famous and powerful Yorkshire family, and Robert was one of their favorite Christian names. Moreover, about the very time that the note was written, Joan, daughter of Sir John Constable of Holderness, was the wife of Sir John Malory of Studley, near Fountains Abbey.

The Mauleverers who owned the Ribston documents were related by marriage to the Conyers and the Tempests.[8] The Malorys were related very closely to the Conyers, the Tempests, and the Constables. One of the Ribston documents also bears witness to a close connection between the Malorys and the Mauleverers. This document is a lay-subsidy roll for the wapentake of Claro. The term "wapentake" applies to a large division in the northern counties. Claro Wapentake stretched from Knaresborough to Ripon, and within it Mauleverers and Malorys had lived since about 1300. A "lay-subsidy" is a payment toward public activities which was raised from laymen. Among the persons who appear in the subsidy is a lady named Margareta Mallorye of Clint. More significantly, two of the three people who signed the document and presented it to the commissioners are Sir Richard Mauleverer and Sir William Mallorye. The document is dated September 3, 1594, but it is stretching nothing too far to believe that Malorys and Mauleverers were Yorkshire acquaintances in the days of *Le Morte Darthur*. Indeed, there is ample earlier evidence of such acquaintance. When Henry VII rode into the North in 1485, just after the battle of Bosworth Field, the select gentry of Yorkshire that rode out to greet him included Sir William Malory and Sir Thomas Mauleverer—their names are put side by side in the record. Seven years before, the court rolls of Hutton Conyers, near Ripon, twice refer to both Sir Thomas Mauleverer and William Malory.

These facts give ground for a further conjecture. The hand that wrote the note about Malory and Caxton on the Ribston copy of the

Suite du Merlin—"Ci comence le livre que Sir Thomas Malori chr reduce in Engloys et fuist emprente par Willm̄ Caxton"—is different from any other hand in the manuscript. It is somewhat later and it is more amateur; I would guess that the writer was not a professional scribe. He was obviously much interested in Malory, however, and since the manuscript was probably owned by the Ribston Mauleverers, it may be conjectured that the writer was a Mauleverer too.

The evidence that has been abstracted for this chapter is abundant. Some of it is weighty and adequate in extent; some is incomplete and merely suggestive, so that it can support only cautious conjectures. But taken together, the evidence provides almost certain proof of some basic matters concerning the locale of *Le Morte Darthur* and its author.

The residual northern dialect in both texts establishes almost as a certainty that the author must have lived in the north and probably in Yorkshire. Local names that appear in the book but not in its sources give substantial proof that the author knew the North Country and was acquainted with some of its legends. His familiarity with two Yorkshire poems and his ability to understand the very difficult northern literary dialect of one of them is also certain. Furthermore, it is very probable that he had read other romances from the same area. All this provides weighty evidence, tantamount to proof, that Sir Thomas Malory was a Yorkshireman. The spider web of names and allusions that connects the Ribston *Suite du Merlin* with the Yorkshire Malorys may be some support for this localization.

That there were Malorys in Yorkshire has not escaped notice in scholarly circles; John Leland pointed out the fact as early as the sixteenth century. But the family has never been considered seriously in relation to the authorship of *Le Morte Darthur*. They have been mentioned in the matter, but simply to be dismissed rapidly and out of hand; and the impression that everyone has gained is that there was not a single Thomas in the family. That in fact is what the *Dictionary of National Biography* said, plain and flat, in its first edition of 1893: "none of this family bore the name Thomas." Sidney Lee cites Sommer, and although the German Arthurian had said nothing of the kind, his brevity about the identity of the author and his assertion that there was nothing to connect the book with this or any other known families named Malory had seemingly led Lee to his deduction. Kittredge made wider investigations than anyone else, yet for a reason that must be guessed at, in his advocacy for the Warwickshire knight, he did nothing to dispel the general impression.

This was the impression that the present writer always fell back on whenever he puzzled about the moral paradox between the book and the Warwickshire knight's career: if the only other Thomas were the Papworth man, then despite any moral problem, Kittredge must have been right. It was only when linguistic accumulations, made in another connection, insistently pointed ninety degrees north of Warwickshire, that my second and lamblike question raised its head: "What kind of an English family was it, that it did not have a Thomas somewhere or other?"

Really simple questions demand the simplest of answers. The next chapter will therefore recount what may be garnered from public records and family papers about the Malorys who lived in Yorkshire at the time that *Le Morte Darthur* was being written. The report, the reader should be forewarned, promises *crescendo* but concludes in the quiet of a scholarly *diminuendo*.

IV

ANOTHER MAN
OF THE SAME NAME

The Malorys who were mentioned in our last chapter in connection with the Ribston copy of the *Suite du Merlin* had long been settled in manor houses and estates along the North and West Riding border, within a few minutes' walk of Ripon Minster or Fountains Abbey.[1]

Yorkshire was prosperous in the fifteenth century. The wool trade had fattened the people and the towns, and the sheep that provided the fine fleeces grazed everywhere its moorlands. There were other trades too, enough to sustain thirty and more guilds which supported and performed the miracle plays for which Wakefield, Beverley, and York were famous; they were sometimes performed at Ripon too. Three centuries before, the land had been lonelier; and then its removed and cold beauty was a siren for men who esteemed the life believed to nourish the soul by denying the body. In medieval times, Yorkshire could have called itself the holiest county in all England, and within Yorkshire, the Malory country was not the least pious. Early in English history, Ripon had attracted Wilfrid, Cuthbert, and Willibrod, most famous of Anglo-Saxon saints. In the twelfth century, Saint Robert of Knaresborough and Fountains Abbey witnessed to its continued appeal. Saint Robert set up his hermit hold in a cliff that frowns over the River Nidd, and by Malory's day the saint's miracles had transformed his cave into a pilgrimage shrine and a monastery richly endowed. In 1132, Serlo and his dozen companions laid the foundations of Fountains, when, inspired by St. Bernard of Clairvaux, they abandoned the monastic security of York for the lonely and harsh dale of the Skell, just beyond Ripon. By Malory's day the rigid asceticism that inspired these and many others of Yorkshire's abbeys may have succumbed to prosperity. But there is no doubting the abundance of its following. On each of Ripon's three bridges a hermit had his stand; and in the moors that lay around, holy recluses were as endemic as they are in Malory's Corbenic. Whatever else may be said of the Yorkshire Malorys, this must be true: wherever they walked or rode, the symbols of ascetic piety were always in their view—abbeys, minsters, hermits, friars, and monks in white, black, or gray.

If the Malorys' Yorkshire was a land of minsters, abbeys, and hermit holds, it was also a land of castles: save for Northumberland, no other county had nearly so many. The Northumbrian castles were dominated by military need. Some like Alnwick, Dunstanburgh, Warkworth, and so on were great fortresses, strengthened over the centuries; others were recently built, dotted along the line of the border. The grim command of Anglo-Scottish war and unceasing raids over the Border dictated their placing as well as their structure and use. In Yorkshire, although many of the castles were also strongholds constructed and manned for defense and assault, several were castle-palaces; and, like the scores of fortified manor houses held by the minor nobility—Markenfields, Piggotts, Vavasours, Ughtreds, Plumptons, Conyers, and Malorys—their form and their manning were shaped by the requirements of day-to-day living as well as by the experience of war.

Some of these castles, such as Richmond, Pontefract, and Knaresborough, were held by the Crown. But most were owned by the Yorkshire barony—Hornby by the Conyers, Flamborough by the Constables, Slingsby by the Hastings, Tanfield by the Marmions, Sandal by the Duke of York, Conisborough by Edward the earl of March (who became Edward IV), and Bolton by the Scropes. But the fifteenth century witnessed a tendency for the smaller baronies to be absorbed by the larger, so that the Furnival, Fauconberg, Latimer, and Scrope baronies, for example, were dissolved into the greater power of the Nevilles. By the middle of the century, marriage and alliance had enabled two families to dominate the power and the castles of Yorkshire. Both had their roots in the far North. The Nevilles, earls of Westmoreland, whose power was based on Brancepeth and Raby in Durham, now owned strongholds in the North Riding: among them were the great castles of Middleham and Sheriff Hutton. The Percies, earls of Northumberland and owners of the Border fortresses of Alnwick and Warkworth, were now powerfully seated in

Another Man of the Same Name 117

the North and West Ridings at Seamer, Topcliff, Wressell, Spofforth, and elsewhere.

This Yorkshire land, dedicated so largely to the quest of God's peace, also became deeply embroiled in man's passion and violence. Thus in 1405, while sympathy for the murdered Richard II was still strong, Archbishop Richard Scrope led a northern rebellion against Henry IV. Having received suitable promises from the Earl of Westmoreland, he then dispersed his nine thousand Yorkshire followers, monks as well as knights. Thereupon, he and his leaders were seized, executed, and their heads stuck on the walls of York. Among the trunkless heads that decorated the Micklegate was that of Sir William Plumpton, father-in-law of the chief of the Yorkshire Malorys. In Sir Thomas Malory's day, 1460, when Richard of York, then protector of England, set out to subdue the Lancastrian earls who were mistreating his tenants, he was confronted by a force commanded by Northumberland and Somerset. On December 30, at Wakefield, he fell in battle and his head was stuck on the gate at York, crowned with a paper cap. Only three months later, at Towton twelve miles southwest of York, the Lancastrians were defeated in the bloodiest battle of the Wars of the Roses, in which, or so it would seem, the heir of the Yorkshire Malorys was slain. The Yorkists, led by Edward IV and Richard Neville, the Kingmaker, suffered few losses. The casualties on the Lancaster side—by slaughter, drowning, beheading, and imprisonment—were extreme. Since the severest Lancastrian losses were those of the Percies, the balance of power for a decade lay with those among the Nevilles who supported Edward IV. Henry Percy, third earl of Northumberland, was slain; his heir was imprisoned in the tower. In their stead, John Neville, Warwick's brother, was created earl of Northumberland in a new line.

The Kingmaker's triumph did not bring peace to Yorkshire. Even some Nevilles remained loyal to the deposed Henry VI. The county was heavily committed in attempts to suppress the exiled king and his militant wife Margaret, who established themselves in the Percies' northern castles. In this activity, there is record that a Thomas Malory took part. Within a few years, the county lent much of its strength to Lancastrian revolt. In 1468 it provided the force for Robin of Redesdale's rebellion to restore the Percies to their estates. A Malory died in that rebellion. Also, Robin the leader was probably Sir John Conyers, a neighbor and relation of the Yorkshire Malorys. In the next year, when Sir Humphrey Neville of Brancepeth rose in arms for Lancaster, he drew much of his support from the North Riding. This rebellion was suppressed by Warwick, and on September 29, 1469, while Edward IV looked on, Sir Humphrey and his brother Charles were beheaded at York. Neville's rebellion may tie in directly to the theme of this chapter: in a general pardon issued in the latter part of 1468, Sir Humphrey Neville and a Sir Thomas Malory head a short list of persons excluded from mercy.

Piety, sheep raising, rebellion, violence, weaving, and ordinary immorality were all staples of Yorkshire life in Malory's day; but works of the mind and the imagination had their place too. Six centuries before, in Alcuin's time and Bede's, Yorkshire had been famous for its learning. In later centuries, its artists and artisans were both many and good. Their legacy is with us still: in the ruins of Bolton, Rievaulx, and Fountains; in the architecture, wood carving, sculpture, and painted glass of Beverley, Ripon, and York. In literature the achievement is no less distinguished. If it is justifiable to speak of literary centers in fourteenth- and fifteenth-century England, Yorkshire certainly was the most distinguished among the very few provincial areas to which the term could be applied.

Much of this writing is religious, celebrating the rewards of the contemplative life, as in the prose and the poems of Richard Rolle, Nicholas Love, or the anonymous author of *Saint Robert of Knaresborough*. But it has many other forms besides: drama, history, song, and romance. The miracle plays that were written for Wakefield and York are the best of their kind. In romance, Yorkshire's product is large and at times excellent. It includes both the alliterative *Morte Arthure* and the stanzaic *Le Morte Arthur*, which Sir Thomas Malory read and absorbed into his own great book; there are also sterling versions of the romances of Alexander and Troy, plus romances on other Arthurian themes, including our only early English version of Chrétien de Troyes' masterpiece, *Yvain*. Indeed, Yorkshire preoccupation with Arthur is very remarkable. Even as late as 1486, the burgesses of York deemed it best, when they greeted their new king, Henry VII, with a pageant, to present him with an Arthurian compliment, one in which the long alliterative lines rolled out the nobility of his descent from Brutus of Troy and King Arthur of Britain. The Arthurian myth had its strong political implications, of course, and that may be one reason why Yorkshire's historians, Castleford and Harding, also linger a long time in Logres before they arrive in the England of everyday reality. Yorkshire also had a tradition of Arthurian folklore, which is shown by its legend that York was founded by Ebrauc, King Arthur's ancestor. Certainly the Yorkshire tradition is in this pleasant old tale of Peter Thompson: Peter, while he was groping around the rock on which Richmond Castle was built, stumbled upon a great cavern. Below on a stone table he saw a gigantic sword and a horn, and—around on the floor—Arthur and his knights, all in armor and all gently sleeping. It is to such a legend that Malory refers in his report on the death of Arthur:

> Yet som men say in many partys of Inglonde that kynge Arthur ys nat dede, but had by the wyll of oure Lorde Jesu into another place; and men say that he shall com agayne, and he shall wynn the Holy Crosse.

But this is no place to survey the books and the legends of late medieval Yorkshire. Enough has been mentioned to establish that like Yorkshire's many castles and even more abbeys and churches, the county's literary remains reflect the spirit of both Camelot and Corbenic—that body-soul tension which also lies at the heart of *Le Morte Darthur*: "noble chyvalrye, curtosye, humanyté, frendlynesse, hardynesse, love, frendshyp, cowardyse, murdre, hate, vertue, and synne."

John Leland, reporting on Northallertonshire in 1535, declared that the gentlemen of most name in that wapentake were the Strangways of Harlesey, the Nortons of Norton Conyers, and the Malorys of Studley and Hutton. A century before, a visitor might have added further names. Within twelve miles of Ripon, these also might have seemed families of eminence and power: the Markenfields of Markenfield, the Kendals of Markington, the Staveleys of Ripon Park, the Piggotts of Clotherholme, the Mauleverers of Allerton, the Wyvilles of Masham, the Inglebys of Ripley, the Marmions of Tanfield, the Plumptons of Plumpton Hall, and certainly the Percies of Topcliffe and the Nevilles of Middleham.

The Malory chapel in Ripon Cathedral, just under the library in the southeast transept, witnesses to the eminence of which Leland wrote. Now, unfortunately, it contains no fifteenth-century monuments. Leland speaks of one; but it may have been damaged when the central tower and roof fell in 1450 and removed by the seventeenth-century Malorys, whose monuments now dominate their chapel.

The Malorys' social eminence had the most solid foundation. Walbran thought they may have come originally from the Midlands, and this is supported by their arms, "Or a lion rampant gules collared argent," which are the same as those of the Malorys of Kirby Malory in Leicestershire.[2] By the early fourteenth century, however, they were substantial landowners throughout the North Riding and beyond. At the time *Le Morte Darthur* was being written they owned land and messuages at these places within four miles of Ripon: Woodhouse, Studley, Grantley, Sawley, Aldfield, Mackershaw, and Winksley (Winkelsey as they sometimes called it). Studley and Sawley were manors, and twelve miles west of Ripon they also owned a manor at Linton-in-Craven. In Ripon itself they had several properties, particularly at Westgate; two miles to the northeast there was Malory land in Sharow and Copt Hewick, and a 1,200-acre park and moors with the great manor house nearby at Hutton. A little further northeast from Hutton, not far from the Percy domain at Topcliff, they had property at Dishforth; five miles north was their manor at Sand Hutton; three miles further, they held property in Thornton-le-Street; and beyond that, a mile north of Northallerton, they had interests near Brompton. Eight miles west of Northallerton was their manor at Hackforth; and eleven miles east, near Rievaulx Abbey and not far from Newton—where Robert Thornton may have copied the alliterative *Morte Arthure*—they had a half share in the manor of Upper Helmsley. It is possible they had interests in Lincolnshire too, and they certainly owned property in the far North: a manor at Trafford in Durham and land and a manor near Piercebridge. Most interestingly for our own concerns, up that way they owned a manor at Hylton Floghen, in the parish of Brampton and just south of Penrith by Inglewood Forest—the locale of some of the better Arthurian romances written in the North just before Malory's day, including *Awntyrs of Arthur* and *The Avowyng of Arthur*, which he may well have read. These extensive and widespread tenures, and their marriage alliances with the most important Yorkshire families, establish them as being several rungs higher on the social and economic ladders than their Warwickshire namesakes: the annual rental of Hutton alone was as great as that of all the holdings of Sir Thomas Malory of Newbold Revel.

They had been generous benefactors of religion for a long time. Ripon Cathedral, Fountains Abbey, the shrine of St. Robert of Knaresborough, the Franciscans at Richmond, and all the orders of friars of York were recipients of their bounty, and they established and maintained oratories and chantries at Ripon, Hutton, Studley, and other places. Several members of the family were admitted members of the Corpus Christi guild which was founded at York in 1468, and so may have participated in the great annual procession or even in the cycle of miracle-plays for which the guild was responsible.

Another Man of the Same Name

Politically, there is not much that can be said for certain about them, although the probabilities are all of the same texture. In 1405 their father-in-law, Sir William Plumpton, was a leader in Scrope's rebellion on behalf of the dead Richard II; for his pains, his head was made a decoration for one of York's gates. At the opening of the 1460's, it seems possible that the oldest of the Malory sons gave his life at the battle of Towton. Toward their end, it is almost certain that one of his brothers was slain while fighting in the Lancastrian revolt led by Robin of Redesdale; and a man who may well be another brother took part in the northern guerrilla activities against Edward IV, which were led by Sir Humphrey Neville. Twenty years later, when Henry VII ascended the throne, the family stand was similar but more cautious. In 1487, Sir William Malory stood bail for Sir John Scrope, who had just fought for Richard III at Bosworth Field; but in the same year he was also one of the thirty-eight northern knights who rode out with the Earl of Northumberland, another former rebel, to greet Henry VII into Yorkshire. So far as can be judged, the politics of the family were Lancastrian, and of that fervent Yorkshire minority which adhered to the Percies and the dispropertied branch of the Nevilles.

As John Leland indicated, the Malorys' major holdings were the two great manor houses at Studley Royal and Hutton Conyers. Studley, a mile to the north of Fountains Abbey, was destroyed by fire in 1715—deliberately, according to John Aislabie. Originally owned by the Tempests, in fee to the Percies, the manor came to the Malorys in 1451, as a legacy to Dionisia Tempest, who had married William Malory of Hutton. It remained in the family through the seventeenth century, but early in the eighteenth, John Aislabie took over, and made the estate into the classical *plaisance* that charms some visitors who stroll beyond Fountains and distresses others. The Aislabies' classical residence too went down in fire, while it was occupied by a girls school during World War II. Fortunately, the fire spared the papers the Vyners had acquired when they took over the estate. They are now housed in the Studley Estate Office, and, since they go back to the thirteenth century, they have provided the basis for the account of the medieval Malorys which is given in this chapter.

Hutton Conyers, three miles to the east of Studley, just beyond Ripon, had been Malory property for two centuries before Leland visited the area. It was held in knight's fee of the Bishop of Durham and was feoffed to William and Katherine Malory on May 4, 1333. The manor was originally surrounded by a large park and moors, and it touched at some points the wide sanctuary around Ripon Minster which was known as St. Wilfrid's Mile: the Athelstan Cross and the surviving Sharow Cross were among the nine marks of its bounds, and nearby was the old leper hospital of St. Anthony. The park is now farmland and the manor is gone; the wide and deep moat is dry, save for a spring and one large pond. It is now more than an impressive historical site: it is an exercise ground for hill-climbing motorcyclists. Nearby is a model of what it once was.

At Ripon Minster the Malorys and the Markenfields had been balanced in death for a century and more: Markenfields were borne to the north of the altar, Malorys to the south. When John Leland made his visit, the striking funeral monuments were two tombs to the Markenfields and one to the Malorys. Now the two Markenfield monuments remain but the Malory tomb has gone. It is much the same with their houses. Studley and Hutton have disappeared; but the Markenfield's manor house, balancing Studley a mile to the south of Fountains, is essentially as it was when *Le Morte Darthur* was written. It is set deep in the fields, a gated farm road being the approach. The L-shaped stone house, begun in 1310 by John de Markenfeld, the King's Remembrancer, and adapted to modern living in the fifteenth century, consists of two integrated wings. The first floor houses a chapel in the angle over an undercroft; the hall fills one wing and the chamber the other. The ground floor rooms provided for servants; the upper floor, approached by an outside stone staircase with penthouse, was used by the owners and their guests. The upper hall was warmed by a central hearth; on the east is a solar which was also furnished with a fireplace. There were enough of the square-topped windows to afford ample light. The parapet of the house was embattled and crenellated; but the building, being partly the focus of the farming and grazing that sustained the estate, had rather slight fortifications—principally an *enceinte*, which is now gone, and a moat, which is dry. Studley and Hutton may have been similar, although to judge by the greater size of Hutton's mound and moat, and by the fact that the Malorys and Percies maintained a chantry chapel there, that may have been a house of stronger defense and possibly greater piety.

The owner of Hutton and Studley at the time that *Le Morte Darthur* was written was William Malory, who in some documents is described as armiger but in others is called knight. His family name is found in several spellings: in their own documents the favored form is Malliore, but they also used such variants as Mallorie, Malorye, Malore, Malour, and

Maulere. When exactly William Malory succeeded to the family estates is not recorded, but it must have been before 1438, when he is described as lord of the manor of Hutton: it may have been much earlier, since a William Malory claimed to own Hutton in 1421. He was related to several leading families in the wapentakes of Claro and Allerton: his mother was a Plumpton, his grandmother a Nunwick, and his great-grandmother a Conyers. Sometime in the 1430's, probably, he married Dionisia Tempest, the younger daughter of Sir William Tempest of Studley. When his father-in-law died in 1444, Dionisia became coheir to her family's numerous estates at Studley, Lynton, Trafford, Northallerton, Copt Hewick, Winksley, Woodhouse, Grantley, Aldfield, and Piercebridge; and on the death of her elder sister, Isabella Norton, she succeeded to these estates in 1451.

Not much can be gleaned about their lives. Dionisia was born in 1415. When her husband was born is not recorded, but he may have been older than his wife. In 1451, Dionisia and her sister were parties to the settlement of the manor of Hartforth upon John Norton. That they leased the Studley properties, or had some trouble with Dionisia's inheritance, may be indicated by a letter of attorney of November 23, 1457, which instructs two attorneys to enter into the properties and to deliver full and peaceable possession to William Malory. In 1462, they sold half the manor of upper Helmsley to John and Henry Thwaites, and the next year they sold the manor of Sand Hutton to the same parties. In January, 1462, William Malory together with Sir John Conyers and Richard Pygot was appointed to report to the Abbot of Ripon as arbitrator in a dispute.

The Malorys made two dispositions of their property. The first, signed on April 1, 1462, is a quitclaim, in which Sir William agreed to an ultimate division of his wife's inheritance between their sons and some of his wife's relations. The other is a will dated May 1, 1472, in which Sir William desired to be buried in Ripon Cathedral, bequeathed monies to the four orders of friars in York and the monastery of Saint Robert of Knaresborough, left substantial annuities to his sons and marriage portions to two of his daughters, and bestowed the residue upon two children and his wife. Probate of this will was granted to two of the children on April 25, 1475, so it may be assumed that Sir William died earlier in 1475 and that Dionisia his wife died not long before.

These documents, together with several pedigrees compiled within the next century, show that the Malorys had a large brood of children: six daughters and eight sons. What we can learn about most of them may be left to Appendix A: here we need speak only of three of the sons.

John is mentioned first in all the pedigrees but one, and it is through his son Sir William that the succession was maintained: we may conclude he was the eldest. Nothing definite and exciting can be learned about him, but something may be guessed. His grandson was twenty-six when he succeeded in 1499. Therefore, allowing twenty years for a generation, John might have been born *ca.* 1430. He would then be of age to stand a party to agreements dated 1456 and 1457, and to appear in the records of Fountains Abbey in the 1450's. It is quite surprising, then, that he does not appear in either the quitclaim of 1462 or the will of 1472: in all the genealogies he is described as *Sir* or *dominus*, and his widow Elizabeth was still living in 1487. Clearly he died young, sometime between 1457 and 1462, and he was knighted early. The most plausible explanation, given the political situation in Yorkshire and what we can learn otherwise about the Malorys, is that he might have been one of the legions of Yorkshire Lancastrians who fell in the bloodiest battle of the Wars of the Roses—the Battle of Towton on March 28, 1461.

William, although Walbran thought he may have been the eldest son, is listed second in all the early genealogies. He is mentioned in the deed which his parents made in 1462, in which he is bequeathed half of the manor of Hylton Floghen in Westmoreland, "if he happen that he be upon lyffe." His name does not appear in the 1472 will, however, and Hylton Floghen is bequeathed to his brothers. The wording of the 1462 deed may mean that his parents did not know whether he was then dead or not. In October, 1468, he was apparently alive, for in that year John Birtby made a legal release to William Malory "the elder," but the silence about William in the 1472 will may mean that he was then dead.

This chronology would fit in with a detail that appears in the chronicle of John Warkworth, Master of Peterhouse, who, to judge from his name, language, and interests, was a northerner. Describing Robin of Redesdale's rebellion and the battle at Edgecote on July 29, 1468, Warkworth declared that among the slain in the northern party of Robin of Redesdale were: "Sere Herry Latymere; Sere Roger Pygote, knyghte; James Conyas, sonne and heyre to Sere Jhon Conyas, knyght; Olivere [D]udley, squyere; Thomas Wakes sonne and heyre; William Mallerye, squyere; and many othere comyners." Robin of Redesdale was Sir John Conyers of Hornby; his followers were mostly Yorkshiremen. These details, and the fact that the Piggotts, Conyers, and Wakes were neighbors and relations of the Malorys of Hutton and Studley, make it likely that this William Malory was the son of Sir William and Dionisia Malory.

The remaining son was Thomas. His name does not appear in either the 1462 deed or the 1472 will. It does appear in a Studley document, however, a 1444 amercement which records among receipts from tenants at Raynton and Copt Hewick, "Thomas Maillore vj$d$." It also appears in the Acts of the Chapter of Ripon Cathedral in this entry for 1471: "Willelmus Monkton de Sharow citatus est ad instanciam Thome Malorry: non comparet, ideo suspensus." The nature of this complaint is not stated; but elsewhere Monkton, who owned two bovates of land at Sharow, next door to the Malory estate at Hutton, is cited at various times for withholding legacies, for perjury, and for fornication—for the last offense he was sentenced to walk through the cathedral barefoot and bareheaded, wearing only a shirt and carrying a candle.

These references to Thomas Malory do not state that he is the son of the lord of Hutton. What proves quite certainly that there was a son named Thomas is a long succession of pedigrees that list him as one of Sir William Malory's eight sons. The earliest appears in a Visitation that may have been begun in 1477-1478 by John Writhe when he was Norroy King-of-Arms and continued when he became Garter King-of-Arms. The volume is agreed to be excellently accurate: whenever it can now be checked, its pedigrees prove to be correct. Some go back to remote dates and suggest that documentary research provided their earliest stages. Most of the pedigrees are short, however; and since these occasionally give personal details or record the children of sisters, genealogists now believe that they must have been compiled from information provided by members of the families. The Malory pedigree is of this kind, and it seems probable that the herald was provided with his information about earlier Malorys by Sir William Malory, son of Sir John and nephew of all the thirteen other children of William and Dionisia, some of whom were still living, others not long dead.

In this first pedigree of the Malorys of Hutton and Studley, Thomas is placed sixth among the sons. William Flower's pedigree of 1563-1564 omits William and Robert, and so lists Thomas fourth. A different order is given in the pedigree that was compiled in 1584-1585 by Robert Glover, the Somerset Herald, and was approved and signed by the then Sir William Malory. There Thomas is listed first. In the seventeenth-century pedigree constructed by Robert Dodsworth, the famous Yorkshire antiquary, Thomas is listed third; and this is also the position that Walbran and other later genealogists give.

The heralds and the genealogists do not state their reasons for these different orders. If chronology is their concern, then the pedigree that might carry the most weight is the one Glover made, which was approved and signed by Sir William Malory. The Harleian Society edition of that puts Thomas first.*

Whatever the correct chronological order, it may now be declared firmly that despite the Dictionary of National Biography's flat statement to the contrary, despite the reporting failures of Sommer, Kittredge, and all their followers, there *was* a Yorkshireman named Thomas Malory at the time that *Le Morte Darthur* was written. The fact is made certain by family witness, genealogies made almost contemporaneously, and accounts and records made while the person was alive. Why this Thomas and his brother John do not appear in their parents' wills can only be conjectured. The 1462 deed is largely a quitclaim, and it seems to have been drafted on behalf of Dionisia in connection with her Tempest inheritance. It speaks of, "all our sons of me the said Dyonesse lawfully begotten," and names only William, Henry, Christopher, George, and Richard, without mentioning the daughters—or mentioning Robert, who died as a boy, or John, whose son succeeded, or Thomas. The husband's part in this document was to join his agreement, mostly, to the disposition of the Tempest inheritance. No reference at all is made in this deed to the Hutton inheritance of the Malorys. Nor is any reference made to Hutton property in Sir William's own will: that document also neglects to mention either Sir John or his son William, who succeeded to the estate when Sir William died in 1475. The explanation could be simply that John and Thomas were bastards, or that they were Sir William's sons by an earlier marriage. If that were so, it would admit the possibility that the 1444 amercement may refer to the Thomas Malory who was son of Sir William. If he were Dionisia's son, he could hardly have been born before 1435, when his mother was twenty, and that would make him thirty-four or so when *Le Morte Darthur* was completed. If he were Sir William's

---

* The practice of genealogists since Dodsworth, to make Thomas the third son, is presumably based on these facts: John's son succeeded to Sir William the grandfather, and *William* had for some time been the given name of the eldest son in the family. If these be the reasons, they are contradictory; and the naming tradition lasted for only three generations, and possibly only two.

son by an earlier marriage, he might have been more than ten years older. In either case he could be the Thomas Malory who entered complaint against William Monkton of Sharow in 1471.

The records tell us nothing else about him for certain. Some early genealogies indicate that an Alice Malory, daughter of a Robert or Thomas Malory, married a Yorkshireman named William Vavasour. This might be the alliance indicated in the 1495 will of William Vavasour of Gunby, who asked to be buried at St. Saviour's in York, left forty marks to his wife Alice, and arranged for John Vavasour (a well-known judge) and Thomas Marler to have custody of his wife and two daughters. These identities are uncertain, however, for there was also a William Vavasour of Newton who had a wife named Alice.

More pertinent possibilities than these, however, are suggested by the two documents relating to the 1460's that were referred to toward the end of our first chapter. At that time, discussion of the documents was deferred, because some scholars have doubted that they relate to Sir Thomas Malory of Newbold Revel. The doubts were based on the facts that neither document states where its Thomas Malory lived, that they both suggest he was at large at a time when the Warwickshire knight was believed to be in prison, and that one of them fails to characterize its subject as "Sir." Now that it has been demonstrated that the knight of Newbold Revel was not the only Thomas Malory who was alive in the 1460's, it is time to reconsider carefully these two outstanding and important documents.

The earlier of the two documents is an item in a volume of miscellaneous records now in Lambeth Palace Library.[3] The collection was assembled late in the fifteenth century, probably at the monastery at Ely. Several of its items display intimate knowledge of northern affairs, and their approximately phonetic spelling of some northern names and such phrases as, "Thes tythinges hath my lord of lyncolne," suggest that the information may have been obtained orally. It seems likely that the collection was made while Thomas Alcock was Bishop of Ely, and the facts that he was a Yorkshireman from Beverley and that a John Alcock was prebend at Studley may have something to do with the northern concerns of the collection.

Our item, only three pages long, is headed: "Thes be the namys of dewkes, erlys, barons, and knytes beyng with owre soveryn lord Kyng Edward in hys jorney in to Scotland at the fest of Seynt Andrew in the month of Decembr, Anno Domini 1462." In a subsection that is headed "Milites" the writer lists fifty-seven names, only eleven of them preceded by "Sir." Among the untitled names is *Thomas Malery*.*

The occasion to which this document refers followed Edward's usurpation of the throne and the flight of Henry VI and Queen Margaret to Scotland. Margaret had persuaded the King of France to assist the Lancastrian cause, and on October 25, 1462, she and some eight hundred mercenaries under Pierre de Brezé occupied Bamburgh Castle on the Northumberland coast. Soon after this, Sir Ralph Percy went over to her cause with Dunstanburgh and its garrison, and Alnwick Castle surrendered for want of provisions. By the end of October the Lancastrian forces, headed by the Duke of Somerset, the Earl of Pembroke, Lord Roos, Lord Hungerford, Sir Ralph Percy, and Pierre de Brezé, were in possession of the triad of great Northumbrian fortresses. In face of this alarming turn, Edward IV called for aid from his subjects aged between sixteen and sixty, gathered cannon in London, and set out to lay siege to the three castles. After stopping at York, the King fell sick of measles on the way to Dunstanburgh and, as a result, had to spend all his time in the rear. The command fell to Warwick, who established his headquarters at Warkworth on December 10, and from there directed his large armies in a simultaneous siege of the three fortresses. The heavily-outnumbered Lancastrians did not hold out very long. Bamburgh surrendered on Christmas Eve, and Dunstanburgh three days later. Margaret escaped by sea in a caravel, and Somerset and Percy agreed to do homage to Edward IV. Alnwick held out until near the end of January when Hungerford withdrew with its garrison into Scotland. Sir Ralph Percy, who had turned Yorkist for the second time, was made governor of Bamburgh and Dunstanburgh. Alnwick was entrusted to Sir John Astley and Sir Ralph Grey. Within a very few months, however, Percy and Grey turned the castles back to Lancastrian possession.[4]

A Thomas Malory played some part in these sieges, and the problem is to know which one he was. The list itself fails to say where any of these "milites" came from, but it is possible in the public records to identify all but a few of them. One came from each of these counties: Northumber-

---

* Kittredge reported this document in 1897, but discarded its Thomas Malory from consideration on the score that the document does not specifically call him "Sir," "*miles*," or "knight." He might have been the Papworth man, he thought.

land, Warwick, Gloucester, Leicester, Derby, Cambridge, Oxford, Northampton, Berkshire, and Staffordshire. Two came from Nottingham, Kent, Essex, Lancashire, and Westmoreland. Eight came from Cumberland. And sixteen came from Yorkshire, most of them from the North Riding. In short, two-thirds of the soldiers who can be identified were northerners, and half of them were Yorkshiremen.

Two conclusions might be drawn from these figures: that the man who compiled the list was concerned particularly with northerners who fought in the campaign, and that Warwick's forces at the siege were drawn heavily from the northern counties. The first conclusion is supported by the fact that the writer dates the expedition not from November 3, when the King left London, but from St. Andrew's Day, November 30, when the King and Warwick were gathering men and supplies in Yorkshire. The second conclusion is supported by the political facts. The King called out recruits, raised money in the southern and western counties, and himself marched north with his ordnance from London. But Warwick, who managed the siege, was a Yorkshireman and most of his power lay in the North Riding. During most of the time that Queen Margaret's forces had invaded and occupied the northern castles, he had been in residence at Carlisle, and he had set out for the border campaign in late October.[5]

These facts do not entirely exclude the possibility that the man in this list is Sir Thomas Malory of Newbold Revel. That the list does not call its man "Sir" is unimportant for several reasons, the chief being that only a few of the "milites" in this list are so called, though some of the rest are called "Sir" elsewhere in this document. More serious as an objection is the Warwickshire Malory's age. We have already expressed disbelief that a man of seventy-five or so could have written *Le Morte Darthur*. It seems just as unlikely that a man who was sixty-eight or so in 1462 would have volunteered for a winter siege on the bleak northern border. The King's call was for men from sixteen to sixty. But if the Warwickshire knight were so rash as to volunteer when he was eight years over the limit—and it must be admitted that his record is not one of caution—then he would probably have been by far the oldest man at the siege. We know the ages of nineteen other men in the list. The oldest was fifty-two, two were forty-seven, three more were in their forties, twelve were in the thirties, and one was twenty-nine.

Five Thomas Malorys could be considered as candidates: the Warwickshire laborer, a member of parliament for Bedwin and Wareham, the

Warwickshire knight, the owner of Papworth St. Agnes, and the son of Sir William Malory of Hutton and Studley. Little can be said for the first four, and much could be said against them. But for the last, these circumstances are favorable: the northern disposition of the document itself, the fact that most of its "milites" were northerners, the evidence from other records that many Yorkshiremen were recruited for the siege, the activity of the Earl of Warwick in the north during the months before the siege, and the fact that the list names several persons who were close associates, even relations of the Yorkshire Malorys—Thomas Mountford of Hackford, Roger Danby of York, Ralph Piggott of Clotherholme, John Colville of Coxwold, both John Constable and Sir Robert Constable of Flamborough, both John Conyers and Sir Roger Conyers of Hornby, James Strangways of Harlsey, and Thomas Corwen of Cumberland among them. Finally, there is the agreement in name and the suitable age. One thing taken with another, it is likely that the man in the list was Thomas Malory of Studley and Hutton.

Also, that the man in the list and the author of *Le Morte Darthur* were one and the same seems likely, for in connection with King Arthur's great siege near the Border, the author shows knowledge of the legend that either Alnwick or Bamburgh was Joyous Garde. Again, such details of local folklore were normally learned on the spot. The identification would provide a rationale for the author's peculiar knowledge that there was a suffragan at Carlisle, and a second locale to support his knowledge that the legend of Arthur's return was believed in many parts of England. The same circumstances could even afford an explanation for Malory's assertion that the castle of Magowns, normally located in Tristram's Cornwall, was Arundel Castle in Sussex. This identification smacks of a compliment, and it is therefore not out of the question that it may be a compliment to a magnate who served with Thomas Malory in the northern sieges—the owner of Arundel Castle, William FitzAlan, earl of Arundel.

The second of the documents that mention a Thomas Malory is a general pardon issued by Edward IV in 1468. It survives in at least four copies. One, dated July 16, is addressed to William Paston; the second, dated August 4, is addressed to the executors of the will of Thomas Bekyngton, formerly bishop of Bath and Wells; another, dated November 1, is addressed to the town and burgesses of Nottingham; and the fourth, dated December 1, is addressed to the Dean and Chapter of Wells

Cathedral.* The form and contents of all four copies are the same, the essence being that the King grants a general pardon for offenses, rebellions, and conspiracies committed before the preceding April 15, but excepts certain persons.[6]

The exceptions in their order are: Humfrey Nevyll, knight; Thomas Malarie, knight; Robert Marchal, late of Culneham, Oxon, armiger; Hugh Mulle, late of London, gentleman; Gervase Clyfton, late of London, knight; William Verdon, late of London, scrivener; Peter House, late of London, esquire; Morgan ap Thomas ap Gruffuth, of Carmarthen, gentleman; Henry ap Thomas ap Gruffuth ap Nicholas, late of Carmarthen, armiger; Maurice ap Owen ap Gruffuth, late of Carmarthen, gentleman; Thomas Philipps, late of Rea [or Rye], Gloucestershire, yeoman; Henry VI; Margaret his wife; Edward his son; those with them beyond the realm; and the rebels keeping the castle or town of Harlech in North Wales. Except that Henry VI and his family are omitted from the fourth text, the names and the order of them are the same in all the copies.

These pardons and exceptions manifestly relate to the political troubles of the Yorkist King. William Paston, partly because of his recent marriage to Anne Beaufort, was the most vigorous Lancastrian in his Lancastrian family, and was probably concerned in Buckingham's rebellion; Thomas Bekyngton had been political secretary to Henry VI and very active in Lancastrian politics; Nottingham had witnessed rebellious activity on behalf of the deposed Henry VI: almost all the persons and groups listed in the exceptions are known to have been engaged in military activity against Edward IV or to have been charged with conspiracy.

No less manifestly, the exceptions are set out in groups. Proceeding from end to beginning, these are: The rebels keeping the town and castle of Harlech are the ultimate; these must be Jasper Tudor and the leaders of the mercenaries who landed in Wales in the Spring of 1468, burnt Denbigh, and occupied Harlech Castle in the Lancastrian cause. The next group consists of Henry VI, who was then in the Tower, the Queen and the members of her court in France, together with Thomas Phillips of Rea, who had fought on Queen Margaret's side at Bamburgh and was an active member of the court-in-exile. The third group consists

---

* The Wells copies were reported by T. W. Williams in 1896 and by E. K. Chambers in 1922. The other two are first noted here.

of the three Welshmen from Carmarthen. Though they were allies of
Jasper Tudor, earl of Pembroke, when he had raided Denbigh early in
the summer, the next summer they themselves captured castles in Carmarthen and Cardigan and from them pillaged the neighboring lands in
South Wales. The next group is made up of four men who are all
labelled "nuper de London." They are all known to have been involved
in the London conspiracy that took place in the summer of 1468: together
with other London merchants and citizens, they were charged with being
in treasonable correspondence with Queen Margaret, their accuser being
a certain Cornelius, servant to one of the Queen's companions in exile.

This leaves the three persons who head the list—Sir Humfrey Nevyll,
Sir Thomas Malarie, and Robert Marchal, formerly of Culham, armiger.

Marshall is a puzzle. Although several Robert Marshalls appear in the
contemporary public records, nothing is said about any of them that
clearly identifies him with the man who was excepted from pardon. A
certain Robert Marshall of Normanton, gentleman, who escaped from
Nottingham Jail in July, 1465, may have a slight claim, simply because
one copy of the pardon was sent to Nottingham. This claim is reduced,
however, by the fact that the man in the list is associated with Culham.
The Robert Marshall, citizen and leatherseller of London, who made a
will on July 19, 1468, may be the best candidate.[7] It is true that the records do not associate him with Culham; but that is not quite decisive, for
Hugh Mill, who is associated with London in the exceptions, is associated
in other documents with Bristol, where he was a merchant. What favors
this Robert Marshall is that his will was made so soon after Cornelius' accusations. That he belongs with the Londoners is indicated by the fact
that his name is followed by the "nuper de" formula, which is used with
the London names that follow but not with the two names that precede.*

The patterns and formulae of this list may not constitute the most re-
liable evidence; but for what they are worth, they suggest that Sir
Humphrey Neville and Sir Thomas Malory were a group to themselves.
This suggestion is negatively reinforced by the fact that none of the several other records of the London troubles, the Welsh revolts, and the

---

* The Robert Marshall who is several times referred to in the Chapter Acts of
Ripon Cathedral for 1452-1468 came from Hartlepool, Durham. But despite his
being a North-countryman, nothing in the records associates him with Sir Humphrey Neville—or Culham.

Lancastrian court-in-exile mentions either Sir Humphrey Neville or Sir Thomas Malory.

Why Sir Humphrey Neville was exempted from the pardon is obvious from a long and consistent career. His father was Sir Thomas Neville of Brancepeth in Durham, younger brother of Ralph Neville, the second earl of Westmorland. Humphrey was born at Slingsby in the North Riding in 1439, his brothers being Thomas and Charles. He belonged therefore to the older but disinherited branch of the Nevilles. His great-grandfather Ralph, the first earl, who died in 1425, contrived to leave the greatest part of the Neville properties to his second wife, Joan Beaufort, and through her they were transmitted to the younger branch of the family represented by her son Richard Neville, earl of Salisbury, whose son was Richard Neville, better known as Warwick the Kingmaker. All that went to Humphrey Neville's branch was the title, the lordship of Brancepeth, some manors in Lincolnshire, the Neville residence in London, and some property in Ripon.

This division of fortune between the two branches of the Nevilles was paralleled by the division between their political alliances. In the late 1450's, while Warwick was busy subverting the rule of Henry VI and promoting the cause of young Edward, the earl of March, Humphrey Neville was receiving favors from the Lancastrian regime. In 1457 he was made steward and constable of the castle of Richmond in Yorkshire, then in Henry VI's hands by virtue of the death of the Earl and the minority of the heir. In 1460 he was appointed keeper of Capulbank Park in the county of York, which was then in the King's hands through the forfeiture of Richard Neville, the earl of Salisbury. About the same time he was also made bailiff of Hexham. His subsequent career, however, matches the reversal of Henry VI's fortunes.[8]

Soon after Edward IV's coronation on June 28, 1461, news came from the north that Queen Margaret's friends—Sir John Fortescue, Humphrey Neville, esquire, and Thomas Neville, clerk, with others— had made a dash over the border with Henry VI, gone to Northumberland to raise war, and two days before the coronation had unfurled their banners at Ryton and Brancepeth Castle. During the summer, Humphrey must have been captured and clapped into the Tower, for on November 4, parliament passed an act of attainder against him. Attainder was the most solemn and savage of all civil penalties, entailing severe corporal punishments, loss of all possessions, and legal death of the victim and his family.

But Neville's subsequent career shows, what is shown in so many other affairs, that the fifteenth century's vengeful bark was commonly more terrifying than its bite. Only a week before the attainder, the Prior of Durham sent an anxious letter to the Chancellor which apparently envisaged Humphrey's release. Characterizing him as "a cummerouse man," the prior urged that it should be seen to that he did no harm to the prior and his brethren. Nevertheless, although on December 23 Neville forfeited his lands at Gillyng in Rydale, in February his possessions were restored and a pardon was issued to him on condition he remain in the Tower. Neville paid little heed to the condition. Breaking out of the Tower by the spring of 1463, he was soon stirring up insurrection again in the north. On April 7, 1463, a commission to arrest him was issued to the Mayor of York and four other persons, one being Robert Malorry, who may have been the Earl of Worcester's assistant at the Tower. On June 3, Sir John Neville and Sir James Strangways were instructed to receive him into the King's grace and to offer him letters of pardon. On June 21 a pardon was issued for his treasons and escape, and all his lands were restored except for the manor of Gillyng.

If the Crown could not make up its mind, Humphrey Neville could. Behaving, as it seemed to parliament, "as an unkynde and unnaturall man," he made his way to Bamburgh Castle in the spring of 1464. There Sir Ralph Percy, having once changed to the Yorkist side, had changed back again and was holding the northern strongholds in the Lancastrian cause. By this time Neville had been knighted—possibly by Sir Ralph Percy—and was engaged in guerrilla activity. In July, 1464, he enjoyed a success that was to prove disastrous. With four score spears and the bows thereto, he lay in wait in a wood near Newcastle for Lord Montagu, who was escorting Scottish envoys to York for a proposed truce. Montagu, possibly hearing of this ambush, changed his route. At Hedgeley Moor, eight miles northwest of Alnwick, he encountered the main Lancastrian force under Sir Ralph Percy, Hungerford, Somerset, and Roos; and in the encounter, the Lancastrians were defeated and Sir Ralph was slain. Humphrey Neville must have returned meanwhile to Bamburgh, for when the Yorkists turned their army and their cannon to besiege that fortress, he and Sir Ralph Grey were in command. Warwick demanded surrender, promising pardon to all except Neville and Grey. The great cannon battered down the walls, and on June 30 Neville surrendered, having first obtained pardon for all except Grey, who was carried to Doncaster and there beheaded on July 10.

Thereafter the records have little to report about Neville for almost four years. On August 8, 1465, the Prior of Durham again complained of his intransigence, and in the same year he was attainted once more. The common belief was that during most of this time he was hiding in a Yorkshire cave. But in the early months of 1468 he must have been once more stirring up trouble in the border country, for in the pardon of that year, which was sent to William Paston in July, Malory and Neville are specifically excluded. On July 30 a warrant was issued to pay £2,000 to the Earl of Northumberland for expenses, ". . . in keeping of our great days of truce at our borders, as in subduing and repressing of our rebells and traitors, Sir Humphrey Neville, Archibald Rydley, and other within the county of Northumberland." If we are correct in thinking that the 1468 pardon associates Neville and Malory, that may be the kind of activity in which Sir Thomas Malory was engaged in the spring of the year.

The Kingmaker's devious procedures in 1468 and 1469 might have led almost anyone to believe that he wanted to put Edward off the throne and Henry back again. That may have been Sir Humphrey Neville's reading of the political map, for in the summer of 1469, just after the battle of Edgecote and the capture of Edward IV, he raised an insurrection aimed at restoring the Lancastrian king. What Warwick really wanted, however, was a chastened and obedient Edward, and his response to Sir Humphrey's rebellion was to give somewhat more freedom to the King and to send out a call for troops to put down Sir Humphrey. With this force Warwick moved to the attack, put down the revolt, captured Humphrey and his brother Charles, and sent them to York. There, on September 29, they were executed under the eyes of King Edward, who went up from Pontefract to see the show.

If such were the activities that led to Sir Thomas Malory's being excluded from the pardon of 1468, it is important to know who he was. The candidates are the same Thomas Malorys as we discussed in relation to the 1462 siege of the northern castles. Of these, the owner of Papworth, the Warwickshire laborer, and the member for Wareham may be dismissed out of hand: there is nothing in their records to connect them with such activities. The knight of Newbold Revel, whom we considered to be inappropriate to the 1462 winter siege because of his age, is even less appropriate to insurrection in Northumberland: not only was he seventy-four years old by then, but everything that we know of his political associations makes it difficult to believe that he would have been associated with Sir Humphrey Neville in Lancastrian insurrection.

That leaves Thomas Malory of Studley and Hutton, and here there are circumstances that make the identification plausible. The Malorys and the Nevilles were neighbors; they both owned property in Ripon, and Sir Humphrey's manor and lands at Gillyng were only two miles from the Malory's manor at Helmsley. Their political allegiance was similar: Humphrey Neville was an associate of Sir Thomas Percy and the Malorys owed feudal allegiance to the Percies, the old earls of Northumberland. Moreover, it is likely that Thomas' brother William was killed at Edgecote on July 26, 1469, fighting for the Lancastrian cause in Robin of Redesdale's rebellion, and it is possible that Sir John, the eldest son, died similarly at Towton. Brothers do not necessarily behave alike in politics, but all in all the circumstances are favorable to the Yorkshire Thomas Malory's being the person who is exempted from the 1468 pardon. It is true that he does not appear in the records as "Sir"; but that is scarcely an obstacle, for he could have been knighted in the field by Sir Humphrey, who seems to have been so knighted himself. It is also true that there may seem inconsistency in identifying the soldier who fought against Bamburgh in 1462 with the rebel who was with Humphrey Neville in 1468. But such changes of allegiance were by no means uncommon in the Wars of the Roses, and several of the men who fought in the 1462 campaign changed sides—some of them more than once, as the career of Sir Ralph Percy witnesses.

If this identification is correct, it might make understandable some peculiarities in the legacies of Malory's parents. In 1462 their quitclaim speaks of their son William as though they were uncertain whether he were alive, and in 1472 Sir William's will does not mention him at all. In 1472, as we have seen, he was probably dead, killed in Robin of Redesdale's rebellion. The reason for their doubt in 1462 is unstated; but one may guess that it may have been because even then he was engaged in Lancastrian rebellion. That they had a son named Thomas is certain from his appearance in the fresh and well-authenticated pedigree of the 1480 visitation. But this Thomas appears in neither the 1462 deed nor the 1472 will, and a possible reason is that during much of this period he was occupied in activities of the kind that seem to have engaged his energies in the first half of 1468.

To carry this identification toward what is our own objective, such loyalist activity on the Northumbrian border would give particular point to the northern details in *Le Morte Darthur*: the lack of surprise that the road from Carlisle should be called Watling Street, the knowledge that there was a suffragan at Carlisle, the awareness that in northern legend Alnwick and Bamburgh were believed to be Joyous Garde. And its political commitment lends personal poignancy to the comment, tinged with northern dialect, that Malory the author adds to his account of Mordred's insurrection against Arthur the true King:

> Lo, ye all Englysshemen, se ye nat what a myschyff here was? For he that was the moste kynge and nobelyst knyght of the worlde, and moste loved the felyshyp of noble knyghtes, and by hym they all were upholdyn, and yet myght nat thes Englyshemen holde them contente with hym. Lo thus was the olde custom and usayges of thys londe, and men say that we of thys londe have nat yet loste that custom. Alas! thys ys a greate defaughte of us Englysshemen, for there may no thynge us please no terme. And so fared the peple at that tyme: they were better pleased with sir Mordred than they were with the noble kynge Arthur, and muche people drew unto sir Mordred and seyde they wolde abyde wyth him for bettir and for wars. And so sir Mordred drew with a great oste to Dovir, for there he harde sey that kyng Arthur wolde aryve, and so he thought to beate hys owne fadir fro hys owne londys. And the moste party of all Inglonde hylde wyth Sir Mordred, for the people were so new-fangill.

In the matters of their real world, the world that saw Henry VI pushed off his throne by Warwick, brought back for a time, and then murdered by King Edward, that was how most of the common people of England may have felt: it is certainly what chroniclers report of them.

Before this book moves to its summing-up, two interrelated matters remain for consideration. They are relevant to any candidate whatsoever: the nature of Sir Thomas Malory's imprisonment and the nature of the books that he used in compiling his work, "the hoole book of Kyng Arthur and of his noble knyghtes of the Rounde Table, that whan they were hole togyders there was ever an hondred and forty."

That the author was a prisoner is made certain by the Winchester manuscript of his book. At the end of its first main section, a colophon states that, "this was drawyn by a knyght presoner, Sir Thomas Malleorre, that God sende hym good recover." Elsewhere are statements, some in the first person, which may have the same meaning. At the end of the Tale of Sir Gareth is the prayer: "And I pray you all that redyth this tale to pray for hym that this wrote, that God sende hym good delyveraunce sone and hastely." The *Tristram*, which contains a famous passage in which the author seems to identify himself with the tribulations of a prisoner, ends with a statement that the book was translated by "Sir Thomas Malleorre knyght as Jesu be hys helpe." The *Quest* and the first half of the *Death of Arthur* end with these prayers: "O Blessed Jesu helpe hym thorow hys myght," and "Jesu ayede ly pur voutre bone mercy." And the conclusion to the whole book, which appears only in Caxton's edition, is this familiar entreaty:

> I praye you all jentylmen and jentylwymmen that redeth this book of Arthur and his knyghtes from the begynnyng to the endynge, praye for me whyle I am on lyve that God sende me good delyveraunce. And whan I am deed, I praye you all praye for my soule. For this book was ended the ninth yere of the reygne of King Edward the Fourth by Syr Thomas Maleore knyght, as Jesu helpe hym for his grete myghte, as he is the servaunt of Jesu bothe day and nyght.

While there is only one clear statement that Malory was a prisoner, the rest of these prayers must refer to the same condition. Some readers have continued to believe that they refer merely to sickness, or that they may be a pious Christian's wishes for release from the prison of the body and the world. Such interpretations are not the most obvious ones, especially since Malory contrasts good deliverance while he is alive with prayers for his soul when he is dead. Nor do they altogether fit the normal meaning of "good deliveraunce," for that was a term that was ordinarily applied to release from captivity. The overall implication of Malory's prayers is that he was a prisoner during much of the time that he was writing his book, and perhaps all of it.

How long a captivity this would entail cannot be determined. It may not have been nearly so long as the ten years or so that some scholars, dating their conjectures from the last record of the Warwickshire Malory's commitment to Newgate, seem to think. Malory describes his work as being "breffly drawyn" from his sources, as an activity of abbreviation and translation; and although there was more to his labors than that, recent implications that he worked with the glacial celerity of an introspective novelist seem thoroughly improbable. Other translators of his day worked fast. Geoffrey, knight of the Tour-Landry, states that he selected, translated, and wrote the commentary for his delightful book of tales and advice within a single year; Caxton declares that many of his substantial translations were completed in as little as three or four months;

Gavin Douglas reports that he wrote his splendid and most careful verse translation of the *Aeneid* in a little over a year; William Stewart's gargantuan verse translation of Boece's history of Scotland, 62,000 remorseless lines of it, probably the longest and least-read poem in English, took only three years. Malory's sources were extensive, and they demanded a great deal of reading; but there are many indications of haste in his writing, and it is eminently possible that he might have done the whole job in two years or less. Vinaver, although he seems to envisage a period of several years, puts the bare minimum at a single year. To have finished in two years or one, however, Malory would have needed proper facilities.[9]

Because of the association of Sir Thomas Malory the author with Sir Thomas Malory of Newbold Revel, and so with Newgate, it has usually been assumed that the book was written in a jail for criminals. Such an environment is scarcely suited to writing a book like *Le Morte Darthur*, which demanded that the author have quiet, elbowroom, and a good many books of rare and expensive sort. Nor does it fit very well with the phraseology that Sir Thomas Malory used about himself. The term "knight-prisoner" is the same that he applied to Lionel, Lancelot, and Tristram when the fortunes of war brought them to captivity, and the term "good delyveraunce" is one that he employed when speaking of the pains of Tristram's imprisonment. As Malory uses the term in his text, it is a complimentary term, quite unassociated with crime or criminal law.

This semantic basis is narrow, but it suggests that Malory may have been a prisoner-of-war. And that is a condition which could be appropriate both to the writing of the book and to a blank in the public records. Fifteenth-century records are very extensive about persons who were in prison on charges of murder, theft, debt, or violence; but, except for some leaders who were charged with treason, they do not list prisoners of war. All the extensive search of appropriate collections of documents for the later 1460's—the Chancery, Coram Rege, and Controlment rolls, and also the jail-delivery rolls for York, Knaresborough, and Windsor has elicited no record of any Thomas Malory. That is surprising if he were in prison on criminal charges. But it is not surprising at all if he were a prisoner-of-war: in fact, it would be unusual indeed if any record of such a captivity were ever to be found.

Captivities that resulted from the fortunes of war were sometimes captivities with freedom. Edward, duke of York, may have written his *Master of Game*, a lively adaptation of Gaston de Foix's *Livre de la Chasse*, while he was a political prisoner at Pevensey Castle early in this century. James I of Scotland, so it is believed, wrote his *Kingis Quair* while he was a prisoner at Windsor in the 1420's. Charles d'Orléans, who spent many years as a prisoner in English castles, had leisure enough to write numerous ballades and virelais, and also to conduct two love affairs, it would seem. It is a captivity of this order that seems to be demanded by *Le Morte Darthur*, which could not have been written in the form that it is had Sir Thomas Malory not been in a prison with noncriminal conveniences. It is almost certain, for example, that it must have provided him with facilities for using more than one book at a time. The author's statement at the end of Book XIX, that he will "overlepe grete bookis of sir Launcelot" (a few lines before his prayer, "Jesu, ayede ly pur voutre bone mercy"), must surely refer to the French prose-romance in three large tomes. That Malory places his selections from the *Lancelot* on either side of his much fuller version of the huge *Tristram* romance might mean that he had both romances available at the same time. His story of Arthur's death and the passing of the Round Table so blends the matter of a French *Mort Artu* with the language of the stanzaic *Le Morte Arthur* that they must have been under his eye together. In his last chapters he recalls details from the *Suite du Merlin* and the alliterative *Morte Arthure*, which were his sources for the first part of his book, some of them details which do not appear in his own brief translation of those sources. On the other hand, he incorporates in his earlier books details that are taken from sources that he translates later. His account of the Roman war, for example, which is based on the alliterative poem, contains details about Lancelot, Tristram, and other knights which relate to stories that are not told until considerably later.

Such procedures appear to go beyond the capacity of simply a good memory; they seem to necessitate recourse to books. There are indications moreover that for some of the things that he relates, Malory had access to alternative versions. After he had recounted the death of King Arthur, he declared that, ". . . of Arthur I fynde no more wrytten in bokis that bene auctorysed . . . Now more of the deth of kynge Arthur could I never fynde . . . Yet som men say in many partys of Inglonde that kynge Arthur ys nat dede, but had by the will of our Lorde Jesu into another place: and men say that he shall com agayne, and he shall wyne the Holy Crosse." At this stage in his story he had at least three versions of Arthur's death in mind, the alliterative *Morte Arthure*, the stanzaic *Le Morte Arthur*, and the French *Mort Artu*; but even these three do not provide all the details to which he refers.

The prison must moreover have been such as to afford Sir Thomas some elbowroom and the quiet and the ample writing materials necessary to his unusual literary task. And unless it had a rich library of its own, it must have offered convenient access to libraries that could supply the necessary books. The Yorkshire Thomas Malory is no more likely than any other Thomas Malory to have owned such a library and taken it with him into captivity. He might possibly have owned copies of the two English poems, for they were comparatively small and comparatively cheap. But the great collection of French prose-romances form a bibliophile's rarity that very few men can ever have owned. Nor, given these necessities of Malory's writing and the sparse catalogues of his time, is it at all likely that he would have worked like a research scholar, hunting down new sources wherever they might be found.

It is, therefore, a vital problem where Sir Thomas could have been in prison, or even out of prison, and written the book that he did. In Yorkshire there was a copy of the *Suite du Merlin* at Ribston, and the copy of the alliterative poem that Robert Thornton's family owned. It is likely too that there were in the county copies of the stanzaic *Le Morte Arthur*, since the poem was written in Yorkshire. The Ughtreds of Kexby owned "unum Romaunce quod vocatur Bruyt," which was bequeathed in a will dated 1401; and to judge from the several northern poems on Arthurian subjects, there must have been other such manuscripts from which the English poets could draw. But pitifully few such books are recorded in the many fifteenth-century wills from the north. Nor do they appear in any of the several surviving catalogues of the libraries at northern monasteries.

Nor indeed is there any evidence that anyone in England ever owned such a collection. The most that can be proved is that various people owned a copy of this romance or that: the *Tristan* (or *Palamède*) that Edward I gave to Rusticiano da Pisa when he commissioned him to make his *Compilation*; the fragment of a *Tristan* that was first owned by Richard Duke of Gloucester and later by Henry VII's queen; the great book containing an *Estoire del Saint Graal*, a *Queste*, and a *Mort Artu* which was once Sir Richard Ros's and ultimately came into royal possession; the *Perlesvaus* that was owned in the fifteenth century by the earls of Arundel, which is now in the Bodleian; the *Suite du Merlin* that apparently belonged to the Mauleverers at Ribston and is now at Cambridge; the English book called *Mort Arthur* referred to in a Lincolnshire letter of the early fifteenth century; "A boke cald mort Arthro," which is listed in a short catalogue copied—possibly by John, Viscount Welles—at the end of a religious manuscript; the French *Liber de Roy Arthur* that Sir John Fastolf had in his collection in 1450; *The Death of Arthur beginning at Cassabelaun* that the Pastons owned; and the copy of a *Tristan* that was sold around 1405 for 151 crowns to Richard Courtenay, bishop of Norwich. These are all single manuscripts, however, and apart from the contents of Ros's great book the only collection that appears in any medieval English record is the *Lancelot, Graal,* and *Perceval le Gallois* that are listed in the 1491 catalogue of St. Augustine's Abbey at Canterbury. The Duke of Bedford may at one time have owned that many as part of the library of Charles V of France, which he bought at a great bargain in 1425 and subsequently dispersed, part to Charles d'Orléans and part to Humphrey of Gloucester.

Few Englishmen owned such books in the later Middle Ages. Even among the 7,568 people who were well enough off to leave wills, only one in every twenty-two mentions a book. Those books that are mentioned were moreover almost entirely works of piety and instruction: romances and books of pleasure are recorded very seldom. This evidence is not the whole story of course; we know that some persons who owned books do not mention them in their wills, and the fact that scribes like Robert Thornton could compile anthologies from local materials shows that more people owned books than the wills and the records reveal. But the evidence as a whole does show that except for an occasional monastery that owned a romance or two, usually as the result of some chance gift, the owners of Arthurian romances—particularly Arthurian romances written in French—were almost exclusively noblemen. And even they seldom owned more than one manuscript. Charles d' Orléans, although he was a poet and lists forty-eight books in his collection, names only one book of this kind; and although Jean de Berry, one of the greatest of medieval bibliophiles, owned thirty-eight romances, only two were Arthurian—a *Palamède* and a *Lancelot.* In fact, after the breaking up of Charles V's collection, which included some thirty Arthurian romances, many of them duplicates, the only European collections of the kind that Sir Thomas Malory needed for his own book seem to have been those which belonged to the Gonzaga family, Ercole d'Este, Louis de Gruthuyse, the Dukes of Burgundy, and Jacques d'Armagnac.[10]

Early in the fifteenth century the Gonzagas had a good many works of French literature in their library at Mantua, including several *chansons de geste* and a large part of the chief Arthurian prose romances. Their catalogue lists these titles: *Merlin, Queste del Saint Graal, Lancelot,* the short and the long versions of *Tristan, Guiron le courtois,* and Rusticiano da Pisa's *Compilation.* At Ferrara the library of Ercole d'Este contained more French books of both kinds: the 1476 catalogue lists several *chansons de geste* and also two copies of each of the *Merlin,* the *Saint Graal,* the *Lancelot,* and the *Tristan,* and single copies of *Guiron le courtois* and *La Destruction de la Table Ronde.* These libraries, and particularly the one at Ferrara, were vital sources for some of the most brilliant Italian poetry of the late fifteenth century; Boiardo's *Orlando innamorato* and Ariosto's *Orlando furioso* were both composed on the basis of the Ferrara materials. But they seem to have no relevance to Sir Thomas Malory. Not only is there nothing in his work which refers to Italy in any significant way; but neither of the Italian collections contained all the French romances that he used.

The libraries of Louis de Gruthuyse and Charles the Bold offer better possibilities. They were both located at Bruges, and they were the literary workshops of several of the fifteenth-century Burgundian writers— George Chastellain, Raoul Lefèvre, Antoine de la Salle, and Philippe de Commines among others. They also provided materials for most of William Caxton's earliest work. It was there, under the patronage of Margaret of York, sister to Edward IV and wife of Charles the Bold, that he translated and then published the first book to be printed in English, Lefèvre's *Recuyell of the Histories of Troy.* It was there too that he must have seen "the noble volumes of Saynt Graal, of Lancelot, of Galaad, of Troy, of Perse Forest, of Perceyval, of Gawayn and many mo" to which he referred in his *Order of Chivalry;* many of the same noble volumes he mentioned again in his preface to Malory's *Le Morte Darthur.*

Louis de Gruthuyse (1422-1492), seigneur de la Gruthuyse, was governor of Holland. In 1469 he saved Edward IV from his pursuers, and his reward was to be created count of Winchester in June 1471. Previously he had made visits to England on diplomatic affairs and for the great tournament at Smithfield in which the Bastard of Burgundy and Anthony Wydeville were the main champions. At the Château de Gruthuyse, a mile from Bruges, he maintained a famous library of old and new books. Among the hundred or so manuscripts that he seems to have owned were the works of Raoul Lefèvre from which Caxton translated his *Recuyell* of the *Histories of Troy* and *Book of Jason*, two books on hunting, one the *Des Deduits de la Chasse*, the other the *Livre de Modus et Ratio*, and several Arthurian romances: a *Lancelot*, a *Perceforest*, a *Petit Arthur de Bretagne*, two copies of the *Estoire del Saint Graal*, a *Palamède*, and possibly a *Tristan*. No catalogue of the library has survived, so it is possible that Louis may have owned even more romances.

The library of Charles the Bold (1433-1477), assembled by three generations of book-proud Dukes of Burgundy, was richer still. The inventory made at the death of Philip the Good in 1467 includes a *Queste*, two other manuscripts in which the *Queste* was followed by *La Mort Artu*, three copies of the prose *Tristan*, two copies of the prose *Lancelot*, a copy of *Isaie li Triste*, and one of *Meraugis de Portlesguez*. In addition to these listed romances, he also caused prose versions to be made of Chrétien de Troyes' *Erec* and *Cliges*, and he commanded David Aubert, his scribe, to engross *Perceforest*. Philip le Hardi and Jean sans Peur, his predecessors, acquired other Arthurian romances, which must have remained in Burgundian possession—Chrétien's *Cliges* and *Yvain*, a *Merlin*, and a *Palamède* being the most noteworthy.

Despite his marriage of convenience to Margaret of York, Charles the Bold's sympathies were with Lancaster rather than York. As a result, there were Lancastrian refugees in plenty at the Burgundian court and in the Netherlands. De Commines writes of them graphically: "Some of them were reduced to such extremity of want that no common beggar could have been poorer. I saw one of them, who was Duke of Exeter (but he concealed his name) following the Duke of Burgundy's train bare-foot and bare-legged, begging his food from door to door."

Some seventy years ago, T. W. Williams suggested that Sir Thomas Malory may have gone to Bruges during the 1460's and there met William Caxton and given him a copy of his book. The idea is interesting, but not altogether persuasive. Although Caxton was prone to be anecdotal in his prefaces and to tell what he knew of his authors, his preface to *Le Morte Darthur* does not suggest that he knew anything about Sir Thomas Malory other than what he could have learned from the manuscript. He also stated that the publication was in answer to a demand prompted by his printing *Godfrey of Boloyne* the previous year; and his habit of putting his manuscripts into print rapidly makes it unlikely that the "copye unto me delyverd" had been on his shelf for sixteen years or so. Nor is there any evidence in Malory's text that he may have done his work in the libraries of Bruges or Flanders. The Caxton text of Book V does contain two Flemish references: in one it adds "in Flaundres" after "arrived at Barflete"; in the other it gives Arthur's route as "entred into Lorayne braban and Flaunders," where Winchester has "into Lushburne and so thorowe Flaundirs and than to Lorrayne." But the first is topographically incorrect; and although the second provides a more logical route than that through Luxembourg, it does not display any great *expertise* about Flanders. Finally, the Bruges libraries, for all their Arthurian richness, seem to have had no copy of the *Suite du Merlin*, which Malory used for his first four Books.

The fifth great Arthurian collection belonged to Jacques d'Armagnac (1433-1477), the stormy but magnificent feudal recalcitrant who became duke of Nemours. He inherited parts of the libraries of Jean de Berry and Jacques de Bourbon, and he extended his collection by having his several scribes make copies, some of them duplicates, for his castles at Carlat and Castres. No catalogue of his library survives, but nearly a hundred of his manuscripts, identifiable by signatures, arms, and ownership notes, are now housed in the Bibliothèque Nationale and other libraries in Paris and elsewhere. Among these are many Arthurian romances: three copies of the complete Vulgate Cycle, containing the *Estoire del Saint Graal, Merlin, Lancelot, Queste del Saint Graal*, and *Mort Artu*; four copies of the prose *Tristan*; two copies of *Palamède*; a *Little Arthur of Britain*. There is also good evidence that he owned other romances which cannot now be traced, among them the *Suite du Merlin*. Except for the English poems, therefore, the library possessed, sometimes in multiple copies, the romances that are comprehended within Malory's term "the French book." It must also have contained a book that is intriguing because of Malory's fondness for adding long catalogues of Arthurian names: *La Devise des Armes*, which contains a heraldically annotated list of all the Knights of the Round Table, a kind of onomasticon or name-index to Arthurian romance.* The work declares it was written in the French of Carlat, and there is reason to believe it may have been compiled by Jacques d'Armagnac himself. The library also owned Gaston de Foix's *Livre de la Chasse* and other books on hunting of the kind which Malory may have had in mind when he spoke of the book of venery, hawking, and hunting that is called the book of Sir Tristram.

* It is just possible too that Malory's added code of chivalry (p. 120) may be related to the chivalric rules that introduce the *Devise*. They share points not included in earlier reports on chivalric ideals.

It was from this collection that Michel Gonnot of Crozant, Jacques d'Armagnac's scribe, compiled the great manuscript, now known as Bibliothèque nationale fr. 112, which is the nearest parallel to Malory's book among all the manuscripts of medieval Arthurian romance. Gonnot copied and edited several large books for the Duke during the years 1460-1470, some of them conflations of different texts of single Arthurian prose romances. He seems to have completed this particular job of editing and copying in July 1470, only a few months after Malory finished, for the last section of the manuscript is dated "Au jourduy llle jour de juillet l'an mil cccc soixante diz a esté escript ce darnier livre." The book was very large, totalling some 1,100 folios, and its objective was to encompass the whole body of Arthurian romance within one frame which had its own individuality. This was achieved by completeness of coverage of the material represented in Arthurian and Tristan prose romances, and by a procedure of copying large excerpts taken from different texts of the individual romances and arranging them in sequence. In large measure, it was a procedure of conflating, anthologizing, and arranging; but it also involved some shortening of the excerpts, a good deal of condensation, some concentration on individual heroes, and a fair amount of disentangling and clarifying the narrative *entrelacement* of complicated sections. In its conflationary aspects, it represents an editorial procedure comparable with that which produced those versions of the prose *Tristan* which blend Tristan's adventures with the adventures of Lancelot and the quests of the Grail. In its comprehensive, unifying, condensing, and clarifying aspects it is akin to Sir Thomas Malory's *Le Morte Darthur*, which in considerably shorter compass contrives to cover most of the Arthurian ground by more drastic use of these same means.

The first quarter of Gonnot's book has been lost; but it may be judged to have been extracted mainly from the *Estoire del Saint Graal*, the ordinary *Merlin*, and the first part of the *Suite du Merlin*. The three-quarters that survives, 870 folios in all, is based upon the last part of the *Suite du Merlin*, at least one copy of *Palamède*, and more than one text of the prose *Tristan* and of the complete prose *Lancelot*, including the *Queste del Saint Graal* and *La Mort Artu*.

Gonnot's objective and procedure, and the Arthurian items in the Armagnac library, are remarkably similar to the objective and procedures of Sir Thomas Malory and the kind of Arthurian collection that he must have drawn from. There are moreover some intriguing resemblances between the texts from which Gonnot worked and those that Malory must have used. Thus, Gonnot's extracts from the *Suite du Merlin* include one substantial episode that has been found nowhere else but at the end of Malory's translation of the *Suite*. And apart from Malory's version of the tale of Alexander the Orphan, which he must have taken from some fifteenth-century text of the prose *Tristan*, the only medieval text in which this engaging story is narrated as a single unit is Gonnot's compilation. Moreover, of the three manuscripts of the prose *Tristan* in which this tale is related as scattered episodes laced into other narratives, two were made for Jacques d'Armagnac in the 1460's. These manuscripts, Bibliothèque nationale fr. 99 and Chantilly 316, must have been made from the same original, and they are both in the three-volume form that Malory must have read. Just as Malory concluded, "Here endyth the secunde boke off syr Tristram de Lyones . . . But here ys no rehersall of the thirde boke. But here folowyth the noble tale of the Sankgreall;" so the division in the two Armagnac manuscripts reads, "Cy finist le secont livre de Tristan Cy apres s'ensuit le tiers livre de Tristan." Their *Tristan*, moreover, is followed by the *Queste*. Finally, these Armagnac manuscripts resemble Malory's narrative more closely than any other known French manuscripts. The text of the *Queste* which Vinaver judged to be nearest to Malory's French book is Bibliothèque nationale fr. 120; the texts of the *Tristan* that the same editor declared to be essential even for the understanding of Malory's version, particularly in its second half, are Bibliothèque nationale fr. 99 and Chantilly 316. All three were Armagnac copies.[11]

So fragmentary is our knowledge of medieval copies of the Arthurian texts and their transmission—so many must have been lost or destroyed— that these resemblances between Malory's translation and the romances that Jacques d'Armagnac owned, this seeming fact that the Armagnac library was the only one that contained all the French books Malory used, might seem merely extraordinary coincidences, were it not for some unprecedented names that Malory added to his story. These are the place-names from southwestern France which occur in a cluster near the end of Book XX.

After his quarrel with Arthur, Lancelot sailed to his own land of Benwyke: "som men calle hit Bayan and som men calle hit Beawme, where the wyne of Beawme ys," added Malory in his characteristic fashion (*Beawme* may be a copyist's error for Béarn, which was a major center of the Anglo-French wine trade). There Lancelot furnished and garnished all his castles and distributed among his chief followers these fiefs that he owned: Benoic, Guienne, Limousin, Poitiers, Auvergne, Saintonge, Perigord, Rouerge, Béarn, Comminges, Armagnac, Astarac, Pardiac, Marsan, Foix, Tursan, Landes, Provence, Languedoc, Agen, Sarlat, Anjou, and Normandy.*

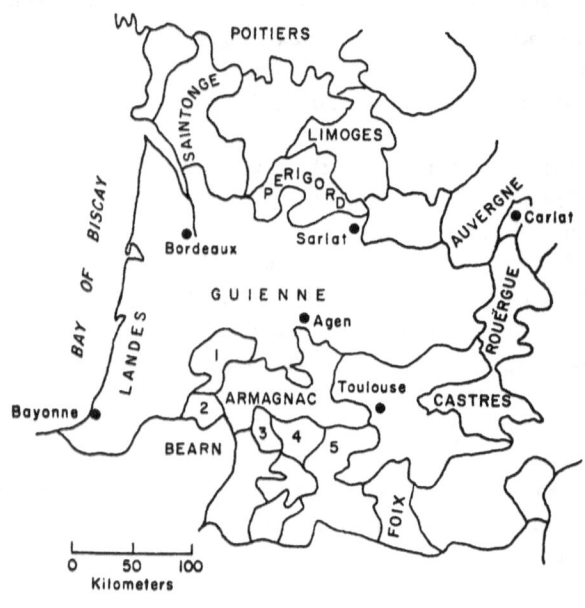

1. MARSAN   2. TURSAN   3. PARDIAC
4. ASTARAC   5. COMMINGES

Southwestern France (*ca.* 1450)

The stanzaic *Le Morte Arthur* and the French *Mort Artu*, which Malory was using at this point, have almost nothing of these details. The French romance records only that Lancelot gave Bors "l'enneur de

---

* To these should perhaps be added a few personal names that appear quite early in *Le Morte Darthur*. Malory's knight Sentrayle de Lushon (pp. 432, 1150) is renamed from the *Nicorant le pauvre* of the French source: Sentrayle was the name of a notorious French freebooter, and Lushon is in Comminges, one of the places mentioned in Malory's list of Southwestern names. Two other knights who are unnamed in the *Suite du Merlin* were also given by Malory names that associate them with southwestern France: Phelot of Langeduke (Languedoc) (p. 109), and Mylis of the Laundis (p. 119). Both locale-names occur in Malory's southwestern list.

Benoic" and Lionel that of Gaunes: the English poem says only that Lionel was made king of France; Bors, king of Gaunes; and Hector, king of his father's land. Normally, the French romances, so far as they are specific, associate Benoic with Brittany. Malory's change of the locale to southwestern France may be explained by his associating Gaunes with Guienne and Benoic (*Benwyke*) with Bayonne (*Bayan*); one of his spellings of the name of Lancelot's father Ban is *Bayan*. It is his filling-in of the details of this association that is most striking, however. There can be little doubt that they are his own additions; and it seems almost certain that they must derive from some special knowledge of southwestern France, possibly acquired from experience.

Vinaver hinted that since several of the smaller fiefs—Armagnac, Astarac, Comminges, Marsan, Pardiac, Tursan—are situated in the area in which the French conducted the campaign by which they reconquered Guienne, the additions raise a possibility that Malory served in that area at that time. That may be so. But it is no less significant that Armagnac is at the center of the whole southwestern area to which these names belong, and that its Duke's extensive estates included castles and fiefs in several of the particular areas of Gascony, Auvergne, and Agenais to which Malory refers. The 1453 campaign was not the only occasion on which an Englishman might have visited Armagnac. Indeed, there are records that at the time that *Le Morte Darthur* was being written, not a few Englishmen were prisoners there. In 1460 Thomas Philip complained of the cost of being ransomed from the Count of Armagnac's castle at Castlenau. In July, 1462, a safe-conduct was granted to John Waleys and Thomas Brown, who were then prisoners *in manibus Countis Armaynak*. And on April 30, 1469, the Duke of Milan's ambassador at Tours reported that an English fleet had sailed toward Bordeaux and landed men on the coast. Two thousand of them, he reports, had been captured between Bordeaux and Bayonne, and "they will be kept prisoners and well guarded." Unfortunately, the ambassador had no reason to name any of the prisoners. Even more unfortunately, the archives of Jacques d'Armagnac have been lost. As a result, any notion that Sir Thomas Malory may have been one of these prisoners and that he worked in the Armagnac library must be something merely to play with. But if any young scholar-adventurer should be inspired to pursue this quest into the wilderness of French archives,* he may sustain himself with the knowledge that the best candidate

---

* The present writer's own scanning of the available *Inventaires Sommaires* for departments within medieval Armagnac has turned up nothing that looks like a prison record.

for the authorship had very good reasons for being out of England by the early summer of 1468 (the English régime was seemingly hot on his neck) and that the timing was suitable for finishing the book before March, 1470.[12]

When provable facts are sparse in a problem of identity, conjecture, special pleading, even tendentiousness are hard to avoid. The second chapter of this book has paraded defects in the arguments on behalf of three previous candidates for authorship of *Le Morte Darthur*. It would be absurd to claim that the data and the arguments set out in the third and fourth chapters provide unassailable proof that Thomas Malory of Studley and Hutton was the author. All that has been proved is that the author was probably a northerner, a Yorkshireman, that there was a Yorkshireman named Thomas Malory who was alive at the time *Le Morte Darthur* was being written, and that this Thomas Malory would fit vital characteristics of the book much better than any other known person of his name.

The criteria by which the candidates must be judged are these facts concerning *Le Morte Darthur*: 1. It was written by Sir Thomas Malory. 2. It was completed in 1469-1470. 3. It exemplifies medieval chivalry in both the secular and the religious aspects of the code. 4. Its principal source was a so-called French Book, which in fact consisted of several large prose romances. 5. It draws heavily from two English poems that were written in Yorkshire, one of which is very difficult in its language. 6. It also shows the author's knowledge of other northern English romances. 7. Its language is mainly standard English, but northern dialect words and forms are scattered throughout the two surviving texts, and they were almost certainly present in the original form of the book. 8. Malory's prosing of the alliterative poem contains northern words and forms that do not appear in the poem. 9. Local English references that Malory adds to his story indicate he may have had some knowledge of Surrey and Sussex, and that he was certainly familiar with some places, institutions, and legends of the North of England. 10. The author was a knight-prisoner while he wrote some or all of his book. 11. The author seems to have had Lancastrian sympathies.

Fifteenth-century public and private records yield these possible candidates: 1. Thomas Malory of Tachebroke Malory in Warwickshire, a laborer. 2. Sir Thomas Malory of Newbold Revel in Warwickshire, knight. 3. Thomas Malory of Papworth St. Agnes in Huntingdonshire, armiger. 4. Thomas Malory of Hutton and Studley in Yorkshire. There may be even a fifth. A Thomas Malory served in the parliaments of 1449-1450 and 1450-1451 as member for Bedwin in Wiltshire and Wareham in Dorset; the former borough was controlled by the Duke of Buckingham, and the latter by the Duke of York.*

Three of these candidates cannot be regarded at all seriously. The Tachebroke man is disqualified by being unsuitable in both occupation and status. The Papworth man died just too soon—in late September, or early October, 1469—and nothing that we can learn about him suggests that he would have used northern dialect, made northern allusions, or been able to read difficult northern alliterative poetry. The member of parliament for Bedwin and Wareham is a puzzle, since there is no record of Malorys in either Dorset or Wiltshire; he may not be a fifth candidate at all, but the same person as one of the others. If he were a southerner, however, he would be disqualified for the same reasons as the Papworth Malory.

The candidate who has been favored by almost all writers ever since Kittredge first proposed him also fails to meet almost all the criteria. He has the right name and he was living at the right time, but those seem to be his only qualifications. Nothing in his life suggests that he would have known or been able to read difficult northern poetry. His own Warwickshire dialect is not represented in the book, and it is unbelievable that he would have employed northern dialect when he was translating from French. There is no evidence that he was ever in the north, and little likelihood that he is the man referred to in the 1462 and 1468 records. None of the local English allusions that the author added to the story relates to Warwickshire, and nothing that we know of the Warwickshire knight would explain why he should have added allusions to the towns, institutions, and legends of the North Country. He was in jail on criminal charges during the 1450's, but there is no evidence at all that he was in jail when *Le Morte Darthur* was written and substantial indications that he was not. His career indicates a Yorkist alliance rather than a Lancastrian one. Lastly, when the book was composed, he was at the thoroughly disqualifying age of at least seventy-five. Unless some extraordinary things in his career and character have yet to be uncovered—that he lived long enough in the north to adopt its dialect and to become thoroughly familiar

---

* The Thomas Malory of Kent whom Hicks mentions *en passant* is apparently the Papworth man whose will is in the Canterbury registry.

with northern literature and life, and that he had physical and intellectual youthfulness far beyond that of any ordinary medieval man—the conclusion must be that he was not the author of *Le Morte Darthur*.

Although we know almost nothing for certain about the career of Thomas Malory of Studley and Hutton, some things make him the only candidate who can be considered seriously. His name is right. The eminence of his family makes it possible that he could read French and have access to literature. Their location near Ripon and Fountains ensures that he would have spoken northern dialect of the kind that is scattered throughout *Le Morte Darthur*. The same factors would make it possible for him to have been familiar with northern alliterative poetry and able to read it with understanding. The family estates stretched into Durham, and so give a basis for the interest in northern poetry, legends, institutions, and places that is displayed in the book. His apparent age in 1469 is eminently suitable.

Lending some support to these facts and probabilities are also these further circumstances. Some families with whom the Yorkshire Malorys were acquainted owned Arthurian romances. A neighbor at Ribston who is certain to have known the Studley Malorys was prompted to write a precise note about *Le Morte Darthur* and its author on a copy of a French romance that was the source for the first four books of Malory's work. The William Malory who was killed at Edgecote while fighting with Robin of Redesdale was probably this Thomas Malory's brother. The Thomas Malory who appears in the 1462 list of knights who served at the siege of the northern fortresses may well have been this Thomas Malory, and so may the Sir Thomas Malory who was excluded from the general pardon of 1468. These factors raise the probability that his political sympathies were of the Lancastrian kind that most scholars discern in *Le Morte Darthur*.

The weaknesses in the case are that he is not described as a knight or a chevalier, as the author is, and that there is no record of his having been a prisoner.

The first weakness is not really very serious.* This Malory's family was an eminent one, and any reader of fifteenth-century documents knows that the terms *armiger*, *esquire*, *knight*, *chevalier*, and *miles* are

---

* Kittredge, who must have known of this Thomas Malory, presumably ignored him because of the absence of title.

used very loosely, and that often they are not used even when they were appropriate. Many men who were qualified to be knights never formally laid claim to the title, partly because *esquire* was coming to be a term of greater social status. Men could be dubbed knights simply by other knights. And scribes would label a gentleman with different titles in seemingly indiscriminate fashion. To instance this loose practice simply in Malory affairs: the father of the Newbold Revel Malory is not always called *Sir John*; the father of the Papworth Malory is sometimes called *knight* and at other times *armiger*; the father of the Yorkshire Malory is labelled as *armiger* in his will but as *miles* in the direction to the escheator after his death; his grandson William is called *miles* in a 1481 perambulation of Ripon, although he was not actually knighted until the next year; his great-grandson John is represented as *armiger* in a document of 1510, but as *miles* in documents dated five and eight years before; in the 1462 list of *milites* in which Thomas Malory appears, many names besides his lack *Sir* or *miles*, even though some are given the title elsewhere in the same document.[13]

Nor is the lack of evidence about imprisonment an effective estop. Many men were prisoners in the fifteenth century, and yet do not appear in the records of imprisonment. Much depends upon what kind of prisoners they were and where they were imprisoned. If they were prisoners-of-war, as Sir Thomas Malory may have been, it is very unlikely that their captivity will ever be found in a record. It was not a fifteenth-century custom to keep records of prisoners-of-war.

Yet, although the circumstances make it plausible, perhaps even likely, that the Yorkshire Thomas Malory was the author, there is no certain proof. All that seems certain is that the man who wrote *Le Morte Darthur* was so remarkably familiar with northern dialect, northern literature, and northern affairs, that he must have been a northerner himself—probably a Yorkshireman. The case for Thomas Malory of Studley and Hutton is that he is the only Yorkshireman of appropriate name and age who has been found in documents at the appropriate time. There had been Malorys in Yorkshire for many generations, however, and it is not inconceivable that among junior branches of the family in and around Ripon and York, or even in the Malory family that was established in the county of Durham, there may have been an unrecorded Thomas whose claims, if we knew them, would seem more substantial than those of his Studley namesake. In default of evidence to this effect, however, it may fairly be urged that the only known candidate who has any serious claim to being considered the author is Thomas Malory, son of Sir William and Dionisia Malory of Studley and Hutton in the county of Yorkshire.

APPENDIXES

APPENDIX A
Pedigrees

1. MALORY OF NEWBOLD REVEL, WARW.

Sir Stephen Malory = Margaret Revel
of Winwick   of Newbold

Sir John Malory = Agnes

(Sir) John Malory = Philippa

Sir Thomas Malory = Elizabeth   Helen = Robert
of Winwick, New-   d. 1479   Vincent of Bar-
bold and Swinford   nack, Northants
d. 1471

Robert Malory, d. in
father's lifetime[1]

Nicholas, b. 1466;
high sheriff 1502

Authorities: Burton's *Leicestershire*, Nichols' *Leicester*, Dugdale's *Antiquities of Warwickshire*, Bridges' *Northamptonshire*, "Escheator Rolls."

Appendix A

Notes: 1. The statement as to Robert's death is based upon Dugdale and Bridges. Kittredge questions its accuracy, on the score that a Northampton Inquisition of 1479 reports the death of a Thomas Malory and says that his heir is Robert Malory, aged twenty-three. Vinaver's guess that this Thomas Malory may be a different person is likely, for although the Papworth Thomas Malory's will does not name a son Robert, several public records indicate that Robert succeeded to the Papworth estates and could have been about twenty-three in 1479 (cf. pedigree of Malory of Papworth).

2. Camden's visitation of Warwick, 1619, records the marriage of Eustace Burnaby to Phillippa, daughter of Thomas Malory. This may mean that Sir Thomas had a second child, named after his mother.

2. MALORY OF PAPWORTH ST. AGNES, HUNTS.

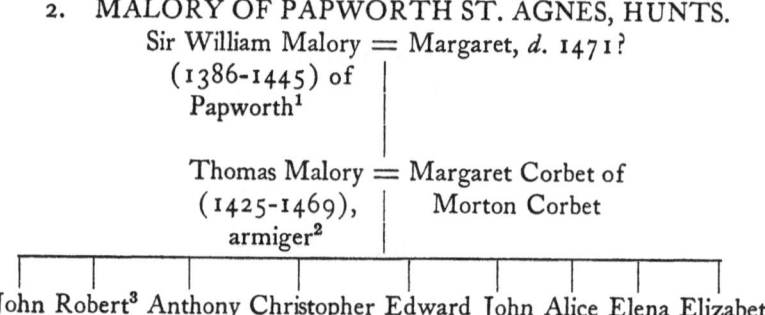

Sir William Malory = Margaret, d. 1471?
(1386-1445) of
Papworth[1]

Thomas Malory = Margaret Corbet of
(1425-1469),   Morton Corbet
armiger[2]

John Robert[3] Anthony Christopher Edward John Alice Elena Elizabeth

Authorities: Blaydes, *Visitations of Bedfordshire*; idem, *Genealogia Bedfordiensis*; Walbran's *Memorials of Fountains Abbey*; *Victoria County History, Bedfordshire*, III; Martin's article in *Archaeologia*, 1898; *Calendar of Fine Rolls, Calendar of Patent Rolls, Feet of Fines, Calendar of Close Rolls*.

Notes: 1. At his death in 1445, Sir William, who had been Knight of the Shire for Cambs. in 1433, held the manor of Shelton in Beds., the manor of Papworth in Hunts., and lands in Cambs., Hunts., Salop, and the adjoining march of Wales (Cal. Pat. Rolls, Oct. 28, 1445; VCH, II, 162, *Inq.p.m.* 23 H.6 No.10): his heir was Thomas, not yet of age.

2. Thomas' will (Godyn fo.28, reported by Martin in *Athenaeum*, 1897) is dated September 16, 1469, at Papworth; probated October 27, 1469, at Lambeth: it does not state his rank; but in *Calendar of Fine Rolls*, 1461-1471, he is called esquire (Nov. 18, 1469) when Thomas Basse and John Stokker, drapers of London, are appointed as trustees. On

Appendix A 159

December 5, 1459, he was granted a commission *de kidellis* in rivers of the Ouse from Huntingdon to Halywell, and this was repeated June 16, 1460 (Cal. Pat. Rolls 1452-61, 556, 612); on July 1, 1463, he was appointed assessor in Hunts. (Cal. Fine Rolls, XX, 98). His threats to Parson Richard Kyd are recorded in "Early Chancery Proceedings," (C.1, bdl.26, su.619), and further details relating to his property appear in *Calendar of Fine Rolls* (XV, 98, 246, 277).

3. Thomas' will mentions all the children in the above pedigree except Robert. John (1453-1469) was the eldest; the youngest was also named John, and the will says he was still at nurse. All the children were under age, and the will provides for their education. Robert presented the living of Shelton—while he was still a minor—to John Philip in 1471 (Cal. Pat. Rolls, 274); succeeded in 1479 (Cal. Close Rolls, Jan. 15, 1479), having proved his age. He did homage for his lands in 1482, and died without issue. Anthony, who had become a mercer in London, succeeded to the estates.

3. MALORY OF KIRBY MALORY, LEICS.

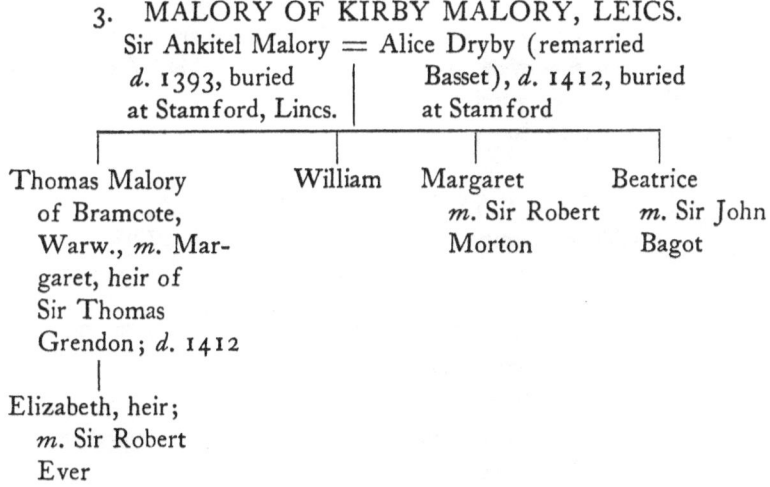

Authorities: Gibbons, *Early Lincoln Wills*, 49, 57, 110; Nichols' *Leicester*, p. 761; Burtons' *Leicestershire*, pp. 139-140.

Note: A William and Alice Malory are listed in 1462 as members of the Guild of Knowle at Hampden-in-Arden, Warwickshire, in Bickley's *Register of the Guild of Knowle*, 1894, and a suit of about the same date (Early Chancery Proc., bdl.33, su.225) mentions the same pair as owning land in Corby, Lincs. They may belong to this branch.

Appendix A

4. MALORY OF WELTON, NORTHANTS.

Sir John Malory owned Welton in 1421. His heir was Ellen, wife of Sir John Bernard of Iselham, Cambridgeshire. She died July 10, 1468. Baker's *Northamptonshire* records no Thomas in this branch, nor do the public records.

5. MALORY OF LICHBOROUGH, NORTHANTS.

The manor of Lichborough was granted in 1376 to Sir John Malory of Winwick and his wife Agnes (cp. pedigree of Malory of Newbold Revel). The property reverted to and continued in the line of Peter Malory. In 1471 it was owned by Robert Malory, who was attainted in connection with the Lambert Simnel plot. Baker's *Northamptonshire*, p. 406, records no Thomas Malory in this branch except for a man who died in 1552; nor do *Visitations of Northants*, Phillimore's *Northampton and Rutland Wills*, nor the public records.

6. MALORY OF WALTON-ON-THE-WOLD, LEICS.

This manor was owned in 1442 by John Malory and his wife Anne (Habard). Their sons were Anthony and John. Nichols' *Leicestershire* and Baker's *Northamptonshire* record no Thomas Malory in this branch, nor do the public records.

7. TEMPEST OF STUDLEY, YORKS.

Sir William Tempest (1391-1444) of Studley	=	Alienor, heir of Sir William Washington; d. Jan. 2, 1451 at Piercebridge		

Isabella, d. 1450?, m. Richard Norton, coheir	Dionisia b. 1415, m. Sir William Malory of Hutton; coheir, heir 1451	Roland, inher. Piercebridge	John, (1442-1444)

Sir John Norton, *als* Conyers, *m.* daughter of Roger Ward

Authorities: Surtees' *Durham*; Foster, *Yorkshire Pedigrees*; documents at Studley Royal.

Note: Surtees inserts another William after Sir William Tempest and makes Roland his brother.

8. MALORY OF HUTTON AND STUDLEY, YORKS.[1]

[2]Sir Christopher Malory lord of Hutton Conyers (cal. 1340, d. 1374) = Joan, heiress of Robert Conyers

[3]Sir William Malory d. 1412 = Katherine, coheir of Sir Ralph Nunwick

[4]William Malory, succ. 1412 = Joan, daughter of Sir William Plumpton[4]

[5]Sir William Malory, d. April, 1475 = Dionisia Tempest (1415-1473?) heiress of Sir William Tempest of Studley[5]

[6]Sir John [7]William [8]Thomas [9]Christopher [10]George [11]Richard [12]Henry

[13]Robert [14]Margaret [16]Isabel [15]Elizabeth [17]Joan [15]Elinor

[18]Sir William d. 1499

John, d. as a boy

Joan, d. as a girl

Isabel

[19]Sir John (1472-1528)

Authorities: *Visitation of 1480-1500*; Flower's *Visitation, 1563-4*; Glover's *Visitation, 1584*; pedigrees in Harley 1487 (Walbran's copy, York Minster); John Hopkinson's, Thomas Wilson of Leeds, and Thomas Beckwith's pedigrees (all MSS in York Minster; all three were Yorkshire antiquaries, Hopkinson one of Dugdale's assistants); Walbran's genealogy of the Studley Malorys; Surtees' *Durham*; *Victoria County History, Yorkshire* (section on Hutton Conyers and *passim*); wills in the Borthwick Institute, York; papers relating to Ripon Cathedral and Fountains Abbey (in MSS and in Surtees Society editions); Malory family papers in Leeds Public Library, Yorkshire Historical Society at Leeds, and the Vyners' Estate Office, Studley Royal. (In the following notes, the Studley Royal papers are characterized by "ST" and the numbers by which they are pigeonholed.)

Notes and Sources: 1. The Malory arms, according to Thomas Wilson, were: "Or a lion rampant gules collared argent." The 1480 visitation (p. 148 in Surtees Soc. edition) characterizes them as "Les Armes Malory toupace a une lion Ruby a une colier perle. Et sus son heaulme la teste dung cheval Ruby assisse en ung torche perle et dyamond." Powell's Roll of Edward III and Willament's Roll of Richard II have them "blazoned but with a double tail and without the collar" (*ibid.*, p. 169). The Malory shield in Ripon cathedral is: "Or a lion gules with a forked tail collared with a crown argent."

2. Sir Christopher's marriage to Joan Conyers may have settled the Malorys at Hutton. ST 51/51 refers to a deed of 1347 by which Sir Roger Conyers and Sir Christopher Mallore, as lord of Hutton, granted lands at Lynton to Fountains Abbey, and its confirmation for tenements in Melverbie, Balderwick, Dishforth, and Rainton in 1536 by Sir William Malory.

3. Sir William, as son of Christopher, miles, is granted Hutton Conyers in 1374 (ST 304/4). He and his wife are referred to, under the year 1375, in relation to Hutton Conyers in an Inspeximus of 1461 (Leeds Public Library, M28). In 1388 he witnessed a feoffment of Studley by Sir Richard Tempest to the Duke of Northumberland (ST 51/18). In 1408 the Bishop of Durham granted tenure of Hutton to William Maylorre, who held by *fermeté de chevalier* (ST 51/58). His will, dated November 1, 1412, described him as chevalier de Hoton, requests he be buried in the Collegiate Church at Ripon, makes his wife executor, and leaves gifts to the Friars Minors, Carmelites, Dominicans, and Augustines at York, and the Friars Minor at Richmond (ST T/60).

4. Except that the early visitations record his place in the pedigree and his marriage to Joan, daughter of Sir William Plumpton (*d.* 1405, Beckwith) of Knaresborough, no information is available about this William Malory. According to an award of 1422 (ST T/61), his widow was then alive and held the mill at Hutton. Joan Plumpton can be fitted into the Plumpton pedigree (see *Plumpton Correspondence*, xxi-xxvi) as daughter of the Sir William Plumpton who was one of the leaders in Archbishop Scrope's Yorkshire rebellion against Henry IV and was executed at York in June, 1405, his head being stuck on Micklegate.

i. An award of 1422 (ST T/61) refers to both Denise, daughter of Sir William Tempest, and William Malory, grandson of Wil-

Appendix A

liam and Joanna Malory: by it, Christopher Malory granted William Malory the manor of Hutton for sixteen years (i.e. until 1438), with the proviso that if he die in that period, Christopher was to grant Denise an annual rent of 100 shillings.

ii. The will of William Mallore, squire, son of Sir John Mallorie ST T/63), dated October 1423, makes his wife Jane executor (together with Richard Norton and John Carver, priest), and Sir John Mallore my father supervisor of my will. This Sir John is likely to be brother of Sir William (3).

iii. The *VCH* fits in between William (4) and Sir William (5) a Christopher Malory whose will (York Reg. II, 527) was probated 11 July, 1427: it leaves the residue of his estate to his widow Isabel (who remarried to William Vincent). Christopher Malory was party to the award of 1422 (ST T/61): cp. note i above; William and Isabel Vincent settled a property dispute in 1438 by quitclaim to William Malory, who is probably William Malory (5). The activities of the last, however, and the sheer number of successions at this period that the VCH suggestion would entail, make it improbable that Christopher should be fitted into the line of succession.

5. This William Malory is recorded as lord of Hutton in 1438 (Feet of Fines, H.6, 18; VCH, I, 403). In his will he is called *armiger*, but in the direction to the escheator of York in 1476 he is called *knight*. He acquired Studley and other Tempest properties by right of his wife in 1451.

Dionisia, the wife, was daughter of Sir William Tempest of Studley and Alienor, daughter of Sir William Washington. Sir William Tempest died in January, 1444, leaving Dionisia and her elder sister Isabel as coheirs (Surtees, Durham, II, 327). Isabel married Richard Norton of Norton Conyers and died before 1451, leaving her son, Sir John, as her heir. (This Sir John married Jane, daughter of Sir Ralph Piggott.) Thereupon, Dionisia came into the full inheritance of Studley, Linton, and Trafford, and many smaller properties; although the manor of Hartforth was settled on Sir John Norton, then aged twenty-six. A demise of September 4, 1452 (ST 51/25)—by Ralph Piggott, Roger Danby, *et al.*, to Dionisia Malory—lists the manors of Lynton, Trafford, and Studley, and messuages in Studley, Lynton, Trafford, Northallerton, Copt Hewick, Aldfield, Winkesley, Woodhouse, and Grantley.

In September, 1452, William and Dionisia Malory, *et al.*, made a set-

Appendix A

tlement (ST T/69) of property at Denton, near Piercebridge, upon Roland Tempest; this was confirmed by John Norton in 1453 (ST T/70); and on October 18, 1452, John Dernton granted Dionisia a quitclaim of any right he had in the manors of Studley and Lynton, etc. (ST 51/32).

Sir William witnessed a Ripon Fabric Roll for 1453/1457 (Mems. Fountains, III, 164). On October 3, 1457, John Birtby (a chaplain) quitclaimed the manor of Hutton to Sir William Maillore *senior* (ST 51/8). On November 23, 1457, letters of attorney (ST 304/23) were granted to Richard Proctor and John Welles to enter into the manors of Studley and Lynton and to deliver to William Malory, John Birtby, and John Hoton—both chapel clerks. On October 25, 1458, the Archbishop of York gave permission to Dionise and William Malory for an oratory at Studley (Mems. Fountains, II, 315). In 1467 William Malory brought suit at the King's Bench against John Wythes (Coram Rege Rolls, 7 E.4, Easter, m.20; Trinity m.28v).

A deed (ST 51/27) signed by William and Dyonesse Maillory makes a grant to three priests at Ripon—Christopher Kendal, John Byrtby, and Thomas Easeby—of the manor of Lynton together with seventeen messuages and two hundred acres, lands in Grantley, Winkesley, Copt Hewick, Brampton, Skell, Woodhouse, and half the manor of Hylton Floghen, to perform "our last will." Hylton Floghen was to go to William Malory the younger, "our son, ... if he happen that he be uppon lyffe." The rest was to be divided between "all our sons of me the said Dyonesse lawfully begotten"—viz. Henry, Christopher, George, and Richard. If William were dead when they died, the premises were to be divided "by our feffes, Randolph Pygot and John Whyxlay": the latter was seneschal at Fountains. If any die, his part was to remainder to the eldest of any of the sons who happen to be alive; in default, to remainder to John Norton esquire; and for default to John Norton's sister, Isabell Barton; and for default, to the right heirs of Sir William Tempest, and Hylton Floghen to the heirs of Alienor Tempest, late wife of Sir William Tempest. These bequests were made by, "the said William and Dyonese by the assent and agreement of the said William"; and no mention is made of Hutton properties, the inheritance of the husband. This deed is dated April 1, 1462.

In 1463 they sold the manor of Sand Hutton to John and Henry Thwaites, and in 1462 they had sold half of the manor of Upper Helmsley to the same parties (Feet of Fines, 3 Ed.4, 163; *VCH*, II, 94). On

Appendix A   165

October 3, 1468 (ST T/72), John Birtby signed a release to William Malory the elder, armiger, of rights in Hutton, Holme, etc.

The Will of William Malliore senior (York Reg., IV, f. 125v) is dated May 1, 1472, and was probated by Johanna and Christopher Malory on April 25, 1475. He is referred to as *armiger*, and desires to be buried in the church of St. Peter and St. Wilfrid, Ripon, near the altar of the BVM. Apart from small bequests for mortuary and burial, chaplains and clerk at the funeral, the five orders of friars at York, the monastery of St. Robert, Richard Proktore (the house in which he lived for life), he leaves to his sons—Henry, Christopher, George, and Richard—lands, tenements, revenues, etc., for their lives to the value of 40 marks, in Linton, Brampton, Copt Hewick, Grantley, *Winkelsey*, Woodhouse, and Hylton Floghen; to Joanna "filie mee" 100 marks for her marriage from rents of the manors of Hutton and Over-Dodynsall; to Margaret, his daughter, a similar sum for the same purpose (and if either dies, the survivor to have 200 marks); the residue to go to his wife Dionisia, Christopher Mallorie and his sister Johanna, who were also to serve as executors. The witnesses include: Godfrey Plumpton, John Hoton chaplain, George Malliore, Richard Proktor, and others.

The pedigrees in the early visitations differ from these wills in the number and order of the Malorys' sons (William, Henry, Christopher, George, Richard). The 1480-1500 visitation (Surtees edition) has: John, William, Henry, Christopher, Robert, Thomas, Richard, George; though the College of Arms copy, which is earlier, gives the pedigree in the crane's foot form and shows this order: John, William, Henry, Christopher, Robert, Thomas, Gregory, Richard. In Sir Anthony Wagner's manuscript, the order is the same as in the College of Arms copy, but lacks Thomas and George. (Its reliability is challenged by the fact that George appears in both of his parents' wills.) Flower's visitation, 1563-1564, omits William and Robert and gives this order: Sir John, Christopher, Henry, Thomas, George, Richard (the College of Arms copy, MS D.2, mentions only Sir John, "sonne and heire"). Glover's visitation, 1584-1585, has: Thomas, George, Richard, William, Robert, Christopher, Henry, Sir John (the College of Arms copy, MS 2nd, D.5, puts Thomas sixth, though without numbering). Harley 1487—and this is followed by the seventeenth- and eighteenth-century antiquaries and Walbran—has: Sir John, William, Thomas, Christopher, George, Richard, Henry. There is enough confirmation in Studley and other documents to support the sons listed in these pedigrees, and it may be assumed that their absence from the wills means either that they were dead or otherwise ineligible.

6. Sir John died during his father's lifetime (1480 visitation and others). His dates are nowhere given, and he is not mentioned in either of his parents' wills. Flower's visitation says he married Isabel, daughter of Christopher Corwen (of Cumberland) or Sir William Hamerton (the College of Arms copy, however, gives the husband's name simply as "Carvan"). In his honor, his widow Elizabeth founded a perpetual chantry chapel at Hutton by April, 1487, and was dead in 1487 (Ripon Chapter Acts, 282). A John Malour (Malore) *senior* is mentioned several times in the Bursar's books for Fountains Abbey in 1456-1457, in relation to Aynderby, Parva Usburn, etc. (Mems. Fountains, III, 24, 33, 64, 113, 114). An agreement of June 4, 1457 (ST 51/37) recites a bond of £200 between John Malory, William Plompton, Roger Warde, and William Malory and William and Dionisia Malory and their heirs (John is not mentioned among them).

His son William (18) succeeded to the Hutton and Studley inheritances in 1475 upon the death of Sir William (5). Sir John's other children, according to the 1480 visitation and Walbran's *Yorkshire Genealogies* (MS, York Minster) were: Robert, John (*ob. puer.*, but presumably living in 1456-1457, when the Fountains Bursar refers to John Malour, *senior*), and Joan (*ob. virgo*).

The date of Sir John's death is not recorded, nor the date of his knighthood. The rank is recorded only in the 1480 visitation and pedigrees and in the 1487 reference to the foundation of the chantry chapel at Hutton (Chapter Acts, 282); it does not appear in the several references during his lifetime. This fact and his absence from the 1462 and 1472 wills suggest that he died *ca.* 1460-1461, and that his death and his knighthood may have come very near to one another (for the possible implication, see the text). The fact that his grandson, Sir John, was born in 1472, implies that this Sir John must have been born no later than 1430. This would make it most unlikely that he could have been Sir William's son by Dionisia, who was born 1415 (for a suggestion about this, see the text).

7. Walbran suggests that this William may have been the oldest son, presumably because of the naming tradition in the family (though this was a short tradition). He witnesses a fabric roll of 1453-1457 and is mentioned in the 1462 deed (ST 51/27) but not in the 1472 will, which makes other disposition of the property at Hylton Floghen bequeathed to

him earlier. He was apparently alive in 1468, when John Birtby made a release to William Malory *the elder* (ST T/72): the same man's quitclaim of 1475 does not use this qualification. William Malory is mentioned with Thomas Malory in a 1444 amercement (ST 51/39). On January 17, 1464, Sir John Conyers, Richard Pygot, and William Maleore, esquire, were appointed arbiters in a dispute by the Abbot of Fountains (Vyner Papers 5383, Leeds Public Library). A note in the hand of the Abbot of Fountains (Mems. Fountains, I, 148) mentions William Maleore, squire, January 12, 1469. (The last three notes might, of course, refer to the father rather than the son.)

Warkworth's Chronicle records the death of a William Mallerye, esquire, at Edgcote, July 26, 1469, as one of the northern party that fought under Robin of Redesdale and was killed. Walbran questions whether this refers to this William Malory, on the score that in 1475 William is referred to as son and heir of Sir William Malory. As *Victoria County History* proposes, however, the 1475 reference is likely to be a simple mistake for grandson and heir, for the successor was in fact Sir William (18), son of Sir John. The 1480 visitation says that he died *sine liberis*.

8. Thomas Malory is not mentioned in either will. He appears in the 1480 visitation, however (except in Sir Anthony Wagner's copy), and all the later pedigrees. The name occurs in an amercement of 1444 (ST 51/39) next to William Malory, and in the "Acts of the Ripon Chapter" for 1471 (p. 15, fol. 63, following an item dated 13 May 1471): "Willelmus Monkton de Sharow citatus est ad instanciam Thome Malorry, Non comparet ideo suspensus." If these all refer to the same man, he may have been born by the 1430's and died after 1471. This would fit in with the probable dates of his brother Sir John (*ca.* 1430-1461). In the early pedigrees, Thomas' place differs among the sons of Sir William (5); in the 1480 visitation he is sixth son; in the Harleian Society edition of Flower's visitation, fourth (in the College of Arms MS only John is named); in Glover's visitation, first or sixth; in Harley 1487, third. Later genealogists have settled on third; but Glover's visitation, which is signed by the then Sir William Malory, may have most weight.

A Thomas Malory appears in the list of *milites* who fought in the 1462 campaign against Alnwick; and in the 1468 pardon, a Sir Thomas Malory follows Sir Humphrey Neville in heading the short list of persons excluded from pardon. (For the significance of these, see text.)

9. Christopher is mentioned in both wills and all pedigrees. He was

present at the reading of John Kendal's will in 1469 (Chapter Acts, 227); held a messuage in Blossomgate, Ripon, in 1478-1479, at Annesgate, 1502, a grange and garden in Prest Lane, 1503-1504 (Chapter Acts, Mems. Ripon, III, 166, 257, 264); admitted *generosus* to the Corpus Christi Guild at York, 1473 (Register, 87); made executor of his father's will and probated it in 1475; was licensed to marry Isabel Malthouse on January 15, 1486 (Test. Ebor., IV, 350); and as *armiger* probated his brother Richard's will (Chapter Acts, III, 329).

10. George is mentioned in both wills and all pedigrees (except in Sir Anthony Wagner's copy of the 1480 visitation). As *armiger*, he probated the will of his brother Richard in 1506-1507 (Chapter Acts, III, 329); in 1498 he was appointed administrator of the estate of his sister, Margaret Constable (Test. Ebor., IV, 28n); was admitted to the Corpus Christi Guild in York; gave two shillings for spiritual purposes to Ripon Minster in 1511-1512 (Chamberlain's Rolls).

11. Richard is mentioned in both wills and all pedigrees. As *armiger*, he oversaw the execution of Lawrence Lancaster's will, March 21, 1504 (Chapter Acts, 293) and in 1498 was made administrator of Margaret Constable's estate (Test. Ebor., IV, 28n). He was admitted to the York Corpus Christi Guild in 1474. His will was probated in 1506-1507 (Chapter Acts, 329).

12. Henry is mentioned in both wills and all pedigrees.

13. Robert is mentioned in neither will, but he appears in the early pedigrees, where he said to have *ob. puer*. A Robert Malory is mentioned —relative to Aldfield, where these Malorys owned property—in 1446-1448 (Mems. Fountains, III, 96).

14. Margaret was bequeathed 100 marks for her marriage in the 1472 will, but is not mentioned in the 1462 one; the genealogies indicate that she married Sir John Constable. The *inq. p.m.* of her nephew Sir William (18) indicates that she survived her husband, who died in 1498.

15. Elizabeth (*ob. puer*) and Elinor (*ob. virgo*) are mentioned in the 1480 visitation, but do not appear in either will, nor in any public or family documents.

16. Isabel is not mentioned in her parents' wills, but appears in the early pedigrees. In 1475 she paid a sixpenny tithe for the villat de Monkton (Dodsworth MS 50, Bodleian), and an Isabel Malory of Clint is mentioned in the Whixley Cartulary (Yorkshire Hist. Soc., Leeds). The 1480 visitation says she *ob. virgo*.

17. Joan is mentioned in the early pedigrees; and although she is not

mentioned in the 1462 deed, she was bequeathed 100 marks for her marriage in the 1472 will and, with Dionise and Christopher, the residue; she was also made executor, and with her brother Christopher she probated the will in 1475.

18. Sir William, the grandson, is not mentioned in the 1462 or 1472 wills. A William Malory, *armiger*, paid tithes in 1475 for properties in Winkesley, Studley Roger, Grauntley, Westgate in Ripon (Dodsworth MS 50, Bodleian). A William Malory, son of Elizabeth, was admitted to the Corpus Christi Guild at York in 1470 (Register, 75). His name heads the Hutton manor court roll for 1477-1478 (ST 51/42). On August 22, 1482, he was knighted by the Earl of Northumberland. On August 26, 1487, he mainprized for Sir John Scrope of Bolton under penalty of £2000, and in the same year he founded a chantry chapel at Ripon for John and Elizabeth his parents (Chapter Acts, 282, 320). He was among the Yorkshire gentry who greeted Henry VII into Yorkshire in 1487, according to Leland's *Collectanea* (IV, 185). He witnessed accounts for the repair of Ripon Cathedral in 1493-1497 (Chapter Acts, III, 164). According to the *inq. p.m.*, he died July 2, 1499; his manor of Hutton was worth 20 pounds and that of Studley 20 marks. His heir was John, aged twenty-six and more. His wife was Joan, daughter of Sir John Constable (Reg. Corpus Christi, 143n; *inq. p.m.* Ser. 2, XIV, 61).

19. According to his father's *inq. p.m.*, this John was twenty-six and more in 1499; and so he was born *ca.* 1472. On July 11, 1502, he perambulated with the Sheriff of Yorkshire as one of twelve Yorkshire knights; in Memorials of Fountains (III, 198) he is entitled *miles*, but in 1509-1510 he is called *armiger* (*ibid.*, 173). The early pedigrees indicate he had three wives before he died in 1528; Margaret Thwaites, Margaret the daughter of Sir Hugh Hastings of Fenwick, and Ann York (College of Arms MS D.2/95 has a fourth, a daughter of Reade in Borstal, Oxon.).

20. A William Mailore of York quitclaimed for lands in Lincolnshire to John Talbot, earl of Shrewsbury, on April 3, 1449 (Bodleian Charter 34, dated at Ingleby, Lincs.).

21. The will of John Mallour of Westgate, Ripon—probated September 28, 1462—refers to his wife Alice (survivor); children, Joan (Mawer) and Richard; and to Thomas Thwaites, a relative. These must belong to a closely related branch of the Studley Malorys.

APPENDIX B
The 1462 List of "Milites"

The list of milites who served at the siege of the northern castles in December, 1462, appears in Lambeth Palace MS 448, fo. 146v. The spelling in the document is erratically phonetic, and so presents some problems in identification. The names are here set out in alphabetical order, and annotated with such identifications as seem to be probable.

1. John Acheton. The Aketons were lords of Aketon and Allerton, Yorks, but there is some possibility of the Lancashire Ashtons.

2. John Apylton: not identified.

3. John Aschley: most likely Sir John Astley, K.G., of Astley, Warw., who served at Bordeaux in 1447 and had charge of Alnwick after the 1462 siege.

4. Ewrard of Bedoun. Probably Sir Edward Bethom (1415-1472) of Bethom Manor, Westmorland.

5. Moreys of Berkley: Sir Maurice Berkeley (1429-1472) of Beverstone, Glocs., Knight of the Body of the King's Chamber.

6. Henry of Bolde. The Bolde family came from Bold, Lancs.

7. William Bothe. The Booths were a Durham family (Robert Booth was Dean of York in the 1480's).

8. John Boteler (1429-1463) of Warmington, Lancs.; Constable of Beaumaris Castle; beheaded at York.

9. Piers Glyfton. The Cliftons came from Clifton, Notts., and Eresby, Lincs.

10. John Colvyle. The Colville family came from Coxwold in the North Riding.

Appendix B

11. John Constabyl. The Constables were the great Yorkshire family whose chief seat was at Flamborough, and were related by marriage to the Malorys.

12. Robert Constabyl (1423-1488) of Flamborough, Yorks.

13. Christopher Coneres. Second brother to Lord Conyers of Hornby; his own seat was at Kirkby, Yorks. The Conyers were related to the Malorys by marriage.

14. John Conyas. John Conyers of Hornby was "Robin of Redesdale," who led a revolt in 1469 (in which a William Malory was killed fighting on Conyers' side); attainted for treason at Blore Heath.

15. Roger Conyers. Presumably another member of the Hornby family.

16. Christopher of Carowen. The Corwens were a Cumberland family, to whom the Malorys of Studley may have been related by marriage.

17. Thomas Crowen. Sir Thomas Corwen of Cumberland; member of the commission for Peace and Army in Cumberland, 1461-1467.

18. John Grakyngthorp. Sir John Crakenthorp of Holgill and Newbiggin, Westmoreland; commissioner of the peace for Westmoreland.

19. Roger Danby. Mercer and alderman of York; M.P. for York 1453-1454. His name appears in a Malory document of 1452 (see genealogy).

20. Richard Dokette: attainted for treason, November, 1461.

21. William Everyngham. The Everinghams came from Beverley, Yorks. This one was Lord of Birkin, near Pontefract; a Lancastrian.

22. Thomas Feryr: no information.

23. John Fogg: of Ashford, Kent, but of a Yorkshire family; knighted before the coronation of Edward IV.

24. Thomas Fyndhorne (1420-1464) of Carlton, Cambs.; captain of Guisnes 1452-1456; helped Queen Margaret to capture Alnwick, 1462. Beheaded at York.

25. Jafery Gate: of Beauchamp Roding, Essex; later Custodian of Calais.

26. Piers of Grethorn: a member of a family seated at Crathorne, Yorks.; Sir Ralph Crathorn was one of those (with Sir William Malory) who greeted Henry VII into Yorkshire in 1487.

27. Thomas Gararde: Sir Thomas Gerard of Bryan, Staffs., but himself a Yorkshireman.

28. John Grysseley: Sir John Gresley (1418-1487) of Brinklow, Derby, and Colton, Staffs.; his principal seat was at Slingsby, Yorks.

29. Ralph Grey (1427-1464) of Wark and Heaton, Northumber-

land; held extensive holdings in county, including at Alnwick; executed for treason.

30. John Gryffon: not identified.

31. Leonard Hastings: possibly a member of the Leicestershire and Warwick family. But Sir John Hastings and Sir Hugh Hastings came from Fenwick, Yorks., and were related by marriage to the Malorys.

32. William Harrington (1430-1488): a Cumberland man; attainted for treason.

33. William, Lord Hastings (1431-1483): Northamptonshire family; King's chamberlain.

34. John Hevingham; Suffolk family.

35. John Howard (1430-1485) of Stoke Neyland, Suff.; Duke of Norfolk, 1483.

36. John Hodyliston (1425-1492): the Huddlestones came from Millom, Cumb.; constable of Cockermouth, 1462; sheriff.

37. Thomas Lampole: Sir Thomas Lamplough of Cockermouth, Cumb.

38. Per Ale: see following.

39. William Ale: William Legh (A-Lee) of Isell, Cumb.; Lancastrian; attainted for treason at parliament at Westminster, 1461.

40. Thomas Malery: see discussion in text.

41. William Marcham Dale: Sir William Martindale (1410-1470) of Newton, Cumb.

42. Thomas Mownforth: Thomas Mountforth (1425-1463) of Hackford, Yorks.

43. Thomas Montgomery (1430-1495) of Faulkborn, Essex; knighted at Towton, 1461; King's Carver.

44. Thomas Nocston: not identified.

45. William Norys (1433-1506) of Yattenden, Berks.; Edward IV's cupbearer and carver; supported Henry VI on return in 1470.

46. Herry of Osey: Sir Martin of the See was with the Yorkshire gentry (including Sir William Malory) who greeted Henry VII in 1487. An Edward de la Mare was executed at York, 1463.

47. Piers Padolyse: not identified.

48. Ralph Pigot. Sir Randolph Piggott of Melmerby and Clotherholme, North Riding; associate of Yorkshire Malorys, and a close neighbor.

49. William Reyner: not identified.

50. George St. Gorge: there was a Sir William St. George in Cambridge.

Appendix B

51. John Savey: Sir John Saville (1415-1482) of Thornhill and Bewbiggin, Yorks., sheriff of Yorks.; Steward of Wakefield 1461-1482; Yorkist.

52. John Scot (1423-1485), of Brabourne, Kent., M.P. for Kent 1461-1462.

53. John Stanley: of Clifton, Staffs., Lancastrian but fought for Yorkists at Blore Heath.

54. William Stanley, of Holt, Notts.; met Henry VI in Nottingham, 1470.

55. James Stanyewysshe: Sir James Strangways; on commission with Warwick to arrest rebels in North Riding in 1461; with Sir William Malory and other Yorks. gentry who greeted Henry VII in 1487.

56. John Swan: not identified.

57. John Wyngfeld: John Wingfield (1428-1481) of Letheringham, Suff.

Notes: 1. R. Davies, *Municipal Records of City of York*, 1843, prints a compotus-roll of December, 1462, which makes provision for men living in the wapentake of Ansty who went riding with Edward IV to the castles of Alnwick, Dunstanburgh, and Bamburgh in the month of December.

2. The document of which the list is part is headed: "Thes be the namys of dewkes, erlys, barons, and knytes beyng with owre soveryn lord Kyng Edward in hys jorney in to Scotlond at the fest of Seynt Andrew in þe month of Decembyr, Anno Domini 1462." That this does not envisage the beginning of the journey from London, but the expedition in its northern phase, is indicated by the date, November 30, and by the fact that the Earl of Warwick is listed, although he was then in the North Country.

3. Several of these names also occur in the list of Yorkshire gentry whom the Earl of Northumberland led out to greet Henry VII in Barnsdale, a little beyond Robin Hood Stone, in 1487: Leland's list (*Collectanea*, IV, 185) is: Sir [Robert] Multon, Sir William Gascon, Sir Robert Constable, Sir Hugh Hastings, Sir William Evers, Sir John Pikering, Sir Robert Plompton, Sir Pers of Medilton, Sir Cristofer Warde, Sir William Malary, Sir Thomas Malyvera, Sir William Engleby, Sir James Strangways, Sir Rauf Rabthorp, Sir Thomas Normanvile, Sir Martyn of the See, Sir Robert Hilliart, Sir Rauf Crathorn, Sir William Bekwith, Sir Robert Utreyte, Sir Thomas Metham, Sir Richard Counyers, Sir William Darcy, Sir Stephen Hamerton, Sir William Stapleton.

APPENDIX C
Extract from Warkworth's Chronicle
(Camden Society, London, 1839, pp. 6-7)

The relevant sections in Warkworth's report on the battle of Edgecote, 1469, are these: "And anone aftere that [the marriage of Warwick's daughter to the Duke of Clarence, with the Archbishop of York, Warwick's brother, officiating], by ther assignment, there was a grete insurreccyon in Yorkeschyre, of dyvers knyghtes, squyres, and comeners, to the nowmbere of 20,000; and Sere William Conyars knyghte was therre capteyne, whiche callede hym self Robyne of Riddesdale. . . . And of the north party ther was slayne Sere Herry Latymere, sonne and heyre to the Lorde Latymere; sere Rogere Pygot, knyghte; James Conyas, sonne and heyre to Sere Jhon Conyas, knyght; Olivere [D]udley, squyere; Thomas Wakes sonne and heyre; William Mallerye, squyere; and many othere comyners, &c." The Latimers were a branch of the Neville clan: in fact the Sir Henry Latimer and Oliver Dudley (incorrectly reported as Audley by Warkworth) were both sons of Lady Elizabeth Latimer, wife of George, Baron Latimer, uncle of Warwick the Kingmaker. The Latimers held property in the North, so these facts do not lessen the northern quality in Robin of Redesdale's forces; but it certainly does support the opinion that Robin of Redesdale's rebellion had the support of the Kingmaker during the desperate period when he turned against Edward IV, even to the extent of seeming to embrace the Lancastrian cause which he had formerly fought against. The rebellion was probably mixed in its motivations: some rebels were inspired by Warwick's own political intents; others were old-style Lancastrians.

Appendix C

Lady Latimer's will (see Swallow, *De Nova Villa*, 149) directs that her body be interred in the chapel of Richard Beauchamp in the Collegial church of Warwick (Richard Beauchamp, earl of Warwick, was her father) "betwene my naturaly borne sonne Harry Latymer and Olyver Dudley late my sonne in the lawe. And I ordeygne and wulle that there be iiii severall stones of faire marbull with images uppon theym of coper and gilted convenable . . . for myne astate and their degreez with the epitaffez of oure burthez decesses and other metely thyngez . . ." These may still be seen in the great Beauchamp chapel in St. Mary's at Warwick.

APPENDIX D

Linguistic Analysis of Le Morte Darthur: Winchester Text Excluding Roman War

This present appendix does not contain a complete account of the language of Malory's work. It is concentrated on the Winchester text, it ignores Book V, and the Caxton text is cited only in relation to details in Winchester. The reasons for these limitations are that Winchester and Caxton are both predominantly written in fifteenth-century standard English. Winchester, however, has a considerable number of variations, almost all of them northern (sampling reveals no significant differences in the work of the two copyists). Most of these are represented by standard forms or words in Caxton, but with some very significant variations, in which Caxton has northern forms which are represented by standard forms in Winchester. The analysis is therefore directed toward the northern element in both texts, and to their bearing upon the linguistic texture of Malory's original text.

Analysis of Book V is deferred to Appendix E because it presents the special problem of an episode derived from a northern poem.

I. *Morphology*. 1. The ON *th*-forms of the third-person plural personal pronouns (*they, their, them*) are predominant in Malory. *They* is regular in both texts; in W, *their/there* are about twice as frequent as the native forms *hir/her*. Between *them* and *hem* there is approximately even distribution. On pages 21-36, for example, the figures are: *their* 28 occurrences, *hir* 13; *them* 21 occurrences, *hem* 21. Caxton agrees broadly; although it has rather more *h*-forms, it sometimes has the *th*-forms where W has *h*-forms. The neuter pronoun is normally the Midland *hit/hyt* in W, occasionally *yt/it*: in Caxton the proportions are roughly the reverse. The feminine pronoun is normally *she* in both texts. In pronouns, therefore, the usage is standard, such as might be found in a document from almost any area at this time. There is however one possible example of a distinctively northern form: *so holdith* 948 (C. *she*), which probably represents the northern form *sho*.

2. The inflections of present indicative verbs are generally standard, but in W there are a good many northern inflections.

a) The regular inflection of the second person singular is the standard one: *-yst* in W, *-est* in C. But W has two examples of the characteristic northern inflection *-ys*: *thou besymys* 264, *thou commaundys* 274 (also *has thou* 717 in 1-vol. ed.). C confirms the second example, but uses *-st* in the other cases.

b) The inflection for the third person singular is normally the standard one: *-yth* in W, *-eth* in C. Scattered throughout W, however, are a good many *-ys* inflections: thirty-three examples of *me repentys*, e.g. 1164, 1219; eight of *methynkes* 1162, etc.; and also *me semys* 501, *repentis me* 119, *mervaylles me* 303, *me forthynkes* 429, *me wantis* 116, *us thynkis* 1172. This inflection predominates in impersonal constructions, but there are some twenty personal ones, e.g. *she gretys* 140, *he gretys* 268, *lyggys* 402, *what ayles* 1128, *she sendis* 142, *repentys* 1128, *hauntys* 269, *dystresses* 269, *growys* 255, *hongys* 255, *longis* 174, *worchys* 1238, *rydys* 1127, *lovys* 1136, *betokyns* 1237, *she shrekys and wepys* 324, *regnys* 545, etc. Although this inflection may occasionally be found in East-Anglian writings in Malory's time and in London documents a little later, it was originally northern; and in Malory's day it was still essentially a North-Midland and northern usage, although less markedly so than the same inflection for the second-person singular and the plural. In the C text all but three of these constructions are replaced by the standard *-eth*. It is significant, however, that the three exceptions occur close together: *me repentis* 1219, *betokyns* 1237, *worchys* 1238. No less significant is it that C once uses an *-s* inflection where W has *-th*: *has* 1135 (W *hath*); and that a grammatical error in C: *that me repentest* 258 (W *repentis*), confirms the W reading.

c) In the plural, the usual inflection is *-th* in W (varied by *-e* or *-en*), and *e/en* in C (varied by *-th*): this reflects standard usage. In two instances, however, W employs the distinctively northern *-ys*: *soddeyn adventures befallys* 147, *their shyldys hongys* 268. Although C uses *-en*

Appendix D

in these cases, it nevertheless once uses an *-s* that is lacking in W: *says his bretheren* 269, where W has *seyde*.

3. The present participial inflection in both texts is the standard *-ing* (in its various spellings). W, however, once uses the characteristic northern *-ande*: *dryvande* 305; and this is confirmed by C's *dryuend*. In contrast with this northern detail, there are perhaps a score of past participles in which W uses the *y*-prefix, which is found most commonly in southern and western texts but was also used quite often in standard: C sometimes confirms and sometimes varies from W. Thus: *ipurveyed* 22, *yfared* 28, *ityed* 481 also appear in C; in *i-armed* 20, *ibrought* 552, *ygyffyn* 363, *ihorsed* 29, *isette* 1196, C lacks the prefix; in *y-hurte* 1072, *y-barryd* 1130, the prefix appears only in C.*

4. In W, the second-person singular forms of preterites (especially the auxiliaries *was*, *were*, and *had*) are often uninflected. This is a northernism.

5. In W, *ar* "are" and *ben* provide the normal usage, *beth* being a rare variant. In C, *ben* usually replaces the *beth*-forms and occasionally the *ar*-forms as well. Here again, a mixture of standard and northernish or North-Midland forms in W is matched largely by predominantly London forms in C.

6. In the past tenses of verbs, W frequently employs forms which are predominantly northern or North-Midland. Some of these also appear in C, but others are represented by standard forms. Examples of those used most often are these: *faught* (C *fought*) 751, *flange* 263 (C same), *hylde* 296 (C *helde*), *hynge* 158 (C *henge*), *lepe* 1049 (C *lepte*), *stake* 48 (C *stack*), *stange* 1235 (C *stonge*), *stale* 1243 (C same), *strake* 112 (C *stroke*), *swall* 1049 (C *swalle*), *swange* 395 (C same) *sware* 274 (C *swore*), *thanke* 142 (C *thanked*), *thrange* 351 (C same), *throoff* 263 (C *throfe*), *trade* 1134 (C same), *wan* 314 (C *wanne*), *wysshe* 755 (C *wasshe*), *wrange* 528 (C same).

7. The plural inflection of nouns in W is normally *-ys/-is*; C also uses this inflection, although it frequently spells *-es*. Thus, except for the standard *-en* plurals in *brethern, chyldyrn, eyen*, "eyes" and a single use of *kyne* "cows," both texts are remarkably free of the *-en* inflection which is commonly found in southern and western texts and is quite frequent in London ones.

* From these *y*-prefixes (and other evidence), Angus McIntosh thinks the Winchester MS was copied in the South Midlands (possibly southwest Northants.), and that this would explain the southerly overlay of the language of this MS.

Appendix D

II. *Syntax*. There is little that can be characterized as noticeably regional in the syntax of either text. In W, however, there are at least two instances of the northern use of "at" as a conjunction in constructions that employ "that" elsewhere: *so at affter Crystemas* 1103, and *lynayge ... at thyne avision betokenyth* 929 (Vinaver unnecessarily amends the second example). There are also two uses of *alther(s)* "of all" in a construction that the OED characterizes as northern: *our allther* 147, *youre althers* 1173. The conjunctive use of "to" in the meaning "until," which occurs in W 55, is recorded by the OED solely in northern documents. In all these cases, C has a standard usage.

III. *Spelling*. W uses a great many spellings that are much commoner in northern and North-Midland documents than in standard ones; these are commonly represented by standard spellings in C. The following groups comprehend a large part of the examples.

1. In W, the characteristic vowel in inflections is *i/y*: *gyfftys, yevith, flemyd, drevyn, ygyffen, strengyst, repentys, sendis, semys, yatis, betokenyth, bettir, sustir, castyste, longyth, mykyll, stakir, tydingis, sadyll, lopyn, foughtyn, bakyn* are samples of many hundreds of examples. C often uses the same vowel, but it frequently has *e* instead. This spelling practice is not regional in any absolute sense, but it is more prevalent in northern documents.

2. In words like "give," "gave," "given," "gift," "gate," "get," the *g*-forms—which are due to the influence of ON cognates, and are found most often in northern and North-Midland documents—are much more frequent than the native *y*-forms in W. In C the reverse is true. Neither text is consistent in the matter, however; either spelling may appear even in close proximity to the other.

3. W has several examples of the northern and North-Midland spelling *mykyl* where C has *much*, e.g. 1015; C sometimes confirms the northern form, however, e.g. 905; and it sometimes has *mykel* 502, 931, where W has the southern form. The following spellings in W are similar, predominantly northern or North-Midland and influenced by ON: *brygge* 91 (twice), *drawbrygge* 327, 353, *lyggyng(e)* "lying" 170 (three times), *lyghest* 864, *lyggys* "lies" 402, *to lyghe* 926, *to byghe* "buy" 1227, *egged* 580; *dyked* "ditched" 255, 308, *beseke* "beseech" 931, *breke* "trouser" 817. In most of these cases, C has standard forms: *brydge, lyeth, lie, bye, breche, edgyd*; but for two of the instances on page 170 it confirms W's form *lyggyng*.

4. In words like "cleave," "clave," "give," "gave," "grieve," "prove,"

Appendix D

W very often represents the final consonant as *f/ff*: *claffe* 270, *gaff* 143, *gyff* 23, *yeff* 272, *gryff* 463, *olyff* 1196, *preff*, *roff*, *roofe*, *stroof*, *lyff*, *sauff* "protect." These spellings, which are found most often in northern documents, are numerous in W although they are varied by *v*-forms. C normally uses the standard *v*-spelling; but it sometimes confirms the W spellings, and it twice uses *rafe* where W has *rove* 821 and *smote* 821.

5. Metathesis of *r*, a practice more prevalent in the North than elsewhere, is occasionally found in W: *shirly* 1090, *gerte* 263 (glossary), *worought* 1146, *chyldyr* 373, *postren* 387, *thirste* "thrust" 390, and frequently in *honderd*. C has the unmetathesized form in these cases.

6. The northern form of "should" is used twice in W: *sulde* 982, *solde* 1137. In these cases, C has the standard *sh*-spellings. Similar differences between the two texts is represented by: *same* "shame" 526, *sawe* "shaw" 548, *samefully* 1173, *senshyp* 843, *seeth* "sheath" 995.

7. Before a consonant, *or* is often written *our/ur* in W: *floure* "floor" 255, *bourde* 375, *fourde* 255, *fourme* 147, *furthe* 36, *furthewith* 1004. These spellings, which are found most commonly in northern and North-Midland texts, are matched by *o*-spellings in C.

8. Before *sh*, *a* is commonly written in W as *ay*, a practice found most commonly in northern documents: *bedaysshed* 1122, *daysshe* 531, *laysshed* 602, *waysshen* 22 are examples. Similar in character are: *freysshed* 532, *freysshly* 31, *fleysshe* 602. These spellings, although they are occasionally found in western documents, are more typically northern. The C text has *a*-spellings in these cases.

9. W very often uses *e* in words which are spelled with *i* in standard; among the words often so spelt are: *preson*, *presoner*, *presonment*, *levynge*, *shevird*, *velony*, *rever*, *wete*, *wetyng*, *gresly*, *speretes*, *leve*, *levith*, *glemeryng*, *menyver*, *peteous*, *wetting*, *drevyn*, *fenysshe*, *hedeous*, *gresyled*, *bede*, *chevilry*, *prevy*, *strekyn*, *redyn*, *wretyn*, *smeten*, *lettir*, *spette*, *prevayly*, *previte*, *kechyn*, *suspeccion*, *whether*, *setthen*. The C text sometimes uses these spellings, but often has *i*-spellings. The *e*-spellings may at this time be found in texts from most regions, but they are most common in northern texts.

10. The following words are sometimes given what is predominantly a northern spelling in W: *tyll* "tell," *togidirs*, *rydy*, *kyst* "cast," *blyssyd*, *hynge* (*heng* "hung"), *byry*, *Inglonde*, *vinquished*, *dynte*. The standard *e*-spellings are also used, however, and in C they are normal.

11. Also very frequent in W, and often repeated, are such spellings as:

Appendix D

jarfaucon, sparde (sperred) "shut," *harte, start, starke, gwardon, clarke, parfyte, harborow, harde* (heard), *sparde (sperred)* "asked," *warse, warste, parelous, arraunte, dwarffe, arred, garlonde, warne, swarved, armyte, warke, warre* "war," *warre* "worse," *carved, disparbeld, farme, warne, farr, warlowe, warwolf, jarmayne, Marlyon, armytage.* Some of these words are also spelled with standard *er,* and "dark" and "stars" are also spelled *durk* and *sturres.* Although C also uses some of these *ar*-spellings, it frequently uses *er* instead. The *ar*-forms are commoner in northern texts at this time than in London texts, and in some words, notably *sparde, warre* "worse," *warse, warste, warke, warwolf,* the spelling seems to have been unusual outside the North.

12. W's usual spellings *owe* and *owne* represent standard usage; but it has four examples of the northern *awne* "own" (425, 757, 763, etc.) and also *awghe* "owe" 610. C has *o*-spellings in these cases.

13. In W, "ere" is normally written *or,* but there are seven instances of *ar*: 168, 982, 1200, etc. C sometimes has *ere* instead of *or* and always has this standard spelling instead of W's *ar*-forms. Similarly, W. occasionally has *ware* instead of standard *were,* e.g. 159, 945, while C has *were* consistently. These *ar*-forms are found commonly in northern and North-Midland documents, where they are influenced by ON cognates.

14. The northern spelling *ey/ei* for long *e* is used frequently in W in several words: *freynship, treys, beystys, fleymed, feyste, creyme, teith,* In almost all cases, C has the standard *e/ee*-spelling.

15. The following are isolated words in which W and C usually vary, with W sometimes having a predominantly northern variant and C the standard form: (a) W very often spells *ony, onything*; C usually has *a* in these cases. (b) W has three examples of *tane* "taken" (70, 282), against C's *taken.* (c) W usually spells *whother, whotherwarde,* where C has standard *i/e*-spellings. (d) The normal spellings for "or" and "nor" in W are *other, nother*; while C usually has *or, nor.* (e) W sometimes has northern *hundreth* against C's standard *hondred, hundred.* (f) W once spells *veary* 527, where C has *very.* (g) W has *alther* "of all," 235, 1173, and *elther* "elder" 104, where C has *alder* or *elder.* (h) W sometimes spells *sunner* against C's *sooner.* (i) W several times has *os* "as" (160, 897, etc.) and once, *als* 225, where C has standard *as, also.* (j) W's usual spelling *nat* contrasts with C's normal *not.* (k) W has *every,* where C often has *everych*; and W normally has *sye* "saw," against C's *saw(e)*.

16. There are a number of other fairly consistent differences between

Appendix D 183

the two texts which are not dialectally significant—e.g. W's usual *a* and C's usual *o* in "hand," "land," "stand," etc.; C's habit of using *oo* against W's *o* in *soo, doo, goo*, etc.

The grammatical and orthographical forms set out in this analysis are not systematic nor extraordinarily striking in the context of the whole of *Le Morte Darthur*, but they represent the kind of sprinkling of localisms which commonly occurs in later fifteenth-century texts. Most of the forms are northern or North Midland, either distinctively or by frequency of use. They justify these conclusions: (1) That since Caxton's, despite its being the more standardized text, confirms some of the regional details in W and also has some that are lacking from W, the original text from which W and C derive must have contained more such northernisms; (2) that both texts have been standardized somewhere along the line of transmission—C much more so than W; (3) that since these forms probably existed in the head text, it is very probable that that text was northern and very improbable that it was Warwickshire in its language.

IV. *Vocabulary*. The following words that appear in the Winchester text of *Le Morte Darthur* (excluding Book V) seem to have been northernisms either absolutely or comparatively. Except for their use by Malory, many are recorded mainly—even solely—in northern alliterative poems. The evidence for their status is provided by specific statements in Rolf Kaiser's study of Middle English dialect vocabulary and in the *Oxford English Dictionary* (OED) and the Michigan *Middle English Dictionary* (MED), by the locales of the Middle English documents cited by the dictionaries, and by the distribution in modern dialects recorded in Wright's *English Dialect Dictionary* (EDD).

AFONNED, doting, madly in love, 647.8: OED *fond*, these senses only in Nthn documents; MED slightly wider usage; EDD, Nthn, NMid. ANGRE, anger, 8.8: OED, mainly Nthn citations; MED, somewhat wider; EDD, Sc. Nthn, Dev. AR, ere, 168.10 and six other usages (against normal *or*): OED, Nthn use from ON *ar*, Sthn use from unstressing of OE *ær*; MED, similar; EDD, Sc. *air*. AWKE, crosswise, perverse, 415.7: OED, prob. from ON, rare and most examples Nthn; MED, same; EDD, Yks, eAng. SCys.

BANDYS, BONDYS, limits, 88.16, 1132.18: OED, mainly Nthn quotations; EDD, Sc. and NCys. BANKE, hillside, 842.17: OED, ON and still common in Nth; MED, similar; EDD, shows wider use. BEDAYSSHED, adorned, 1122.2: this form not in OED; MED, only other quotation Yks; not in EDD. BEE, ring, 1238.2: OED gives *bee* as

Appendix D

Nthn type against Sthn *bye* (which appears in 360.24, although Caxton there has *bee*); EDD, Sc, Irel, Yks. BERE, berry 910.5, 915.35 (cp. *byry* 962.28): not in OED, MED, EDD; but possibly from ON *ber*, *baer*. BERE, force, impetus, 323.13: OED has no ME citations; MED, only Nthn citations; Kaiser, Nthn (ON *bir*). BYGLY, strongly, 1153.6: OED, possibly ON, Nthn citations; MED, same; EDD, obs. Sc. BOUNDE, ready, 8.35; OED, ON *buinn*, Nthn (also Chaucer, Langland); MED, mostly Nthn citations; EDD, Sc. Nthn, NMid. BRETHE, power, anger, 1217.17: OED records mostly in Nthn documents. BRYM, fierce, 1193.6: OED, Nthn in ME; MED, Nthn and NMid citations; EDD, Sc, NCys, Yks, Der. BRYMME, sea, 912.4: MED, ON source, in ME chiefly Nthn. BURBELY, BURBELYGNE, BURBLE, bubbl-ing, 683.17, 563.3, 1104.2: OED, Nthn citations; MED, somewhat wider; EDD, Sc, eAngl.

CAN, did, 665.2: OED characterizes this form as Nthn, in contrast with Sthn *gan*. CARLE, churl, 271.9, 271.11: OED, ON *karl*; only Nthn citations; MED, same (also Chaucer, Capgrave); EDD, Sc, NCys, Der. CHAFFLET, scaffold, 518.25: OED records only this example and *chaselette* (possibly an error) in *Awntyrs of Arthure*. CRAGGYS, rocks, 432.11: OED, Nthn dialect before 1300, Sc, and Nthn citations; MED, Nthn citations, also Nthn place-name element; EDD, Sc, NCys, Yks.

DAFFYSSHE, foolish, 555.25: OED, obs. except Nthn, related to *daft*, which is chiefly Sc and Nthn; MED, only this quotation; EDD, daffish, MidCys. DAWED, awoke, 808.18, dawned 984.2: OED, obs. except Sc; MED, wider use; EDD, Sc, NCys. DEDE, death, 9.27, 1260.24; DEDELY, deathly, 880.31, 999.31, 1074.14, 1192.7: OED and Kaiser indicate that these ME forms are predominantly Nthn. DERE, to injure, 37.10: OED, Sc, Nthn and NMid (also Chaucer, Caxton); MED, wider use; EDD, Sc. DYKED, moated, ditched, 255.2, 308.27, 320.25: OED, largely Nthn; MED, same; EDD, mostly Sc, NCys, NMid. DONE, gift, 374.18, 571.35, 1148.25: OED, rare, only citation 1524; EDD, Sc. DRYED, suffered, 1257.3 (in alliterative phrase *dryed and dwyned*): OED citations for ME, mainly Nthn, now Sc and Nthn dialect; MED, wider but Nthn emphasis; EDD *dree*, Sc, NCys, Yks, Chesh. Der. DROUPE, cower, 482.3, 1212.5: OED, Sc, Nthn; MED, same; EDD, Sc, Yks, Shr, Hrf. DWERE, doubt, 579.12, 685.24: OED citations, Nthn and eAngl; MED, similar. DWYNED, pined, 1257.3 (in alliterative phrase *dryed and dwyned*): OED, now Sc, ME citations Sc and Nthn; MED, same; EDD, shows wider use but emphasis Sc and Nthn.

EME, uncle, 378.21: OED examples for 14-15C, all Sc and Nthn; MED shows wider use. ENDLONGE, the whole length of (usually in an alliterative phrase with *overthwart*) 265.5, 718.36, 732.21, 784.13: OED from 14C, in Nthn and NMid dialect; MED, similar; EDD, primarily Sc and NCys, but also Leic. and Warw; Mustanoja in *ME Syntax* says influenced by ON *endilangr*, particularly Mid and Nthn. EVYSE, edge of wood, 1073.29: MED *ease*, in Nthn and NMid sources; EDD, eAngl.

FELLYS, hills, moors, 329.2: OED, Nthn; MED, similar; EDD, Sc. and NCys. FLATLYNGE, flat, at full length, 468.35, 1057.25: OED, Nthn quotations; MED, similar; EDD, Sc and Nhb. FLYNGE, hasten, 813.25, FLANGE (pret.) 656.1: OED, from ON *flinga, most citations Nthn and alliterative verse; MED, wider usage; EDD gives *flang* as the Sc, NCys and Yks preterite. FORFOUGHTYN, fought out, 77.4: OED, now obs. except in Nthn and Sc dialect, ME examples Nthn and Sc; MED, somewhat wider usage; EDD, Sc, NCys, Yks. FRYCKE, bold, lively, 1085.26 (in phrase "lusty and fricke"): OED, largely Nthn examples; MED, similar; EDD, *freck* Sc, Nhb, Yks. FRO, from, used very frequently (with "from"): OED, ON *fra*, mostly Nthn examples; MED, wider though Nthn predominance; EDD, Sc, NCys, NMid.

GAYNESTE, quickest, 329.5: OED, ON *et gegnsta*, Nthn citations; MED, same; EDD, NCys and Mid. GAP, opening, 547.3: OED, ON *gap*, 14-15C examples Nthn; MED shows use in Nthn and Mid placenames, but wider otherwise; EDD, wider use. GAR, cause to (*gart bren* 621.29, *gar make* 1199.32): OED, ON *ger(v)a*, chiefly Nthn and Sc dialect, quotations predominantly Nthn; MED, similar; EDD, Sc, Irel, NCys and NMid. GARNYSSHE, prepare for defense, 7.33, 24.25, 898.29: OED quotations, mainly Nthn; MED, wider use; EDD *garnish* meaning "to polish" is Yks slang. GATE, GATYS, way, road, direction, 173.1, 265.5: OED, now only Sc and Nthn, ME quotations Nthn; MED, same; EDD, wider use. GEFF, GYFF, if, 322.1, 1077.8, 1138.29: OED, Sc and Nthn dialect; mainly Sc citations. GERTE, great, 263.32: OED, dialectal; EDD records for Sc, NCys, Dev. GESTE, stranger, 262.33, 278.7: OED, now mainly Sc and Yks, early citations mostly Nthn; MED, somewhat wider usage; EDD, Sc, Lancs, Lincs, Yks. GNASTED, gnashed, 280.11 (in alliterative phrase *grenned and gnasted*): OED, prob. from ON **gneista*, citations mostly Nthn; MED, similar. GRYMME, formidable, 85.1, 266.6, GRYMLY, severely, 372.3: OED, Nthn and Mid citations; MED citations, largely from alliterative verse; EDD, *grim*, Yks, Hrf; in compounds Yks.

HANGERS, testicles, 643.24: OED does not record in this sense, but citations for things pendant are largely Sc. HALE AND HOW, a sailors' call, 320.29: OED *hale*, only other quotation Sc; EDD gives fairly wide use of *hale*, but *how* primarily Sc and Nthn. HALSE, embrace, greet, 87.26, 394.22: OED, ON *heilsa*, obs. except Sc, ME citations largely Nthn; EDD, Sc and NCys. HELED, HYLLED, covered, 280.21, 700.25 (cp. *unhylled*): OED, prob. from ON; EDD, NCys, Ches. Oxf, *hild* wYks. HETE, a reproach, 807.22, HETED, insulted, 1113.33: OED, from ON *haeþa*, rare and Nthn. HOPE, to think, 299.12: OED, obs., citations Nthn, NMid (and Chaucer).

YLLE, bad, evil, severely, 90.26, 258.15, 305.28, 325.23, 747.20, 911.22, etc. (also *evyll*): OED, ON *illr*, citations largely Sc, Nthn, NMid; EDD, Sc, Irel, NCys, Yks. INFELYSHYP, to join company, 418.7: OED does not list; EDD, does not list. INLIKE, INLYCHE, very, exceedingly 959.29, 1001.28, 1114.7: OED citations mainly Nthn and NMid. INWYTH, within, 1130.25: OED gives Sc and Nthn citations for 14-15C; Kaiser, Nthn. KEELE, to cool, 570.1: OED, mostly Sc and Nthn examples; EDD, Sc, Irel, NCys, NMid, eAngl, and Kent, Sur, Sus. KEMPYS, champions, 305.34: OED, citations show later ME narrowing from general use to Nthn; EDD, Sc, Irel, NCys, and Suff. KEST, thought, intended (pt. of "cast") 1067.33, etc: OED, Nthn in 13-18C; MED, somewhat wider use; EDD, Sc. NCys, nYks.

LADDYS, lads, 295.24: OED, citations Nthn and alliterative; EDD, Sc, NCys; Kaiser, Nthn. LANGERYNG, delaying, languishing? 500.2 (in phrase "wandrynge and langeryng"): OED has *lenger, linger* as rare and Nthn in ME. LANGUORE, lamentation, 579.18: OED cites in Nthn, Sc, and alliterative sources (and Chaucer). LAYNE, hide, 1075.38: OED, obs. except Sc, citations Sc, Nthn, alliterative; EDD, Sc, NCys; Kaiser, Nthn. LEARYS, cheeks, 501.34: OED *leer*, often in alliterative phrases and in Nthn sources; EDD, NCys and Mid. and Dor. LYTHE, joint, 117.15: OED, Sc and Nthn in 14-15C; EDD, Sc, Irel, NCys. LOPE, leaped, LOPYN, leaped, 102.29, 536.1: OED, ON *hloupa*, Sc, Nthn, and Langland; EDD, Lancs. LOVYNGE,

Appendix D 187

praise, 792.26: OED, Sc and Nthn sources; Kaiser, Nthn. LOWE, hill, 1150.18: OED citations from Sc, Nthn, and NMid sources; EDD, wider use though predominantly NCys. LOWSE, loose, free, set free, 268.26, 460.11, 496.30, 528.19, 777.31, etc: OED, ON *louss*, Nthn form *lous* against Mid and Sthn *lose*, citations Sc and Nthn.

MAKELES, peerless, 273.29, 427.11, 743.10: OED *make, makeles* predominantly Nthn; EDD *make*, Sc, Nthn (and Glocs). MAKER, poet, 493.4, 775.12: OED citations, Sc and Nthn; EDD, Sc. MARCH, boundary, 22.4, 272.22, 800.22: OED citations, predominantly Sc and Nthn (also Langland, Caxton); EDD, Sc, Irel, Nhb, Lincs. MARYS, MARES, marsh, 106.37, 278.25, 284.16 (in alliterative phrase *morys and mares*), 560.25, etc: OED, almost all citations from Nthn documents; EDD *marish*, Sc, Irel, Yks, Ches. MEANED, lamented, 821. 22: OED after 15C, only Sc and Nthn, and in 14-15C mostly so; EDD, Sc and NCys. MYKYLL, much, 9.5, 1015.3 and seven other uses: OED, infl. by ON *mikell*, this form chiefly Nthn and NMid; EDD has wider spread but chiefly Sc, Nthn, NMid, Irel. MON, must, 44.27, 1002.29 (MS has *mou* for former, but must be an error since Arthur is speaking of a prophecy "that I mou dye"; second has *mon* in MS, which editor amends to "ye mo(u) dye"): OED *mun*, 13-16C *mon*, Nthn and Mid examples; EDD, *mon*, Sc, nYks, nLancs. MORNE, lamentation, 79.35: OED, only other citation than this is Nthn; EDD as a noun, only Sc.

NEREHONDE, nearby, almost, 35.19, 1121.13, and thirteen other usages: OED, now only Sc and dial, ME examples all Nthn and Sc; Kaiser, Nthn; EDD, mostly Sc. Nthn, NMid. NYGHE, neigh, 256.25: OED, mostly Sc and Nthn citations (and Langland); Kaiser, Nthn; EDD, NCys, Yks, and Mid. OR, ere, 9.20 and frequently elsewhere (*ar* less frequent): OED, from late Nthmbn *ar*, ON *ar*, normal Mid form in ME: EDD, Sc to Lincs (and Gloc and Som). OS, as, 160.4 and several other examples: OED lists among 14-15C, Mid. spellings; MED (under *as*), all examples Nthn. OVERTHWARTE, OVERTWARTLY, 170.23, 305.29, 314.8, 324.5, 488.21, 718.35, 1198. 25, etc., often in phrase with *endelonge*: OED, ON *þvert*, now obs. or rare except in dialect, nearly all ME citations Sc, Nthn, NMid; EDD shows wider use, though mainly Sc, Nthn, NMid. PYKE, to go, 1202.2, PYCKED 557.35: OED, *pick*, possibly Celtic, *pyke, pike*-forms Sc and Nthn dialect. PLYTE, plight, 171.16: OED, ME citations all Nthn and NMid; Kaiser, Nthn. PLUMPE, clump, wood, 35.35: OED, now arch. and dialect, rare in ME, only Malory in exactly this sense but otherwise NMid examples; EDD, Aberdeen to Lincs. POYNT-LYNGE, point foremost, 799.31: OED, only other citation Sc. POUSTÉ, power, 920.5: OED, now Sc, obs. elsewhere, ME citations mainly Sc and Nthn (and Caxton); EDD, Sc obs.

RASS, RASYNG, charge violently, 145.14, 266.8, 309.24, 323.12, etc.: OED gives it as Sc and Nthn; EDD, Sc. (A)RAYSE, REYSE, to raise, 633.9, 1233.6, etc: OED, ON *reisa*, bulk of ME citations Sc and Nthn; EDD *rayse*, only eYks. RAKE, RAK (of bulls), string, 942.4, 946.5: OED *raik*, *rake*, ON *rak*, citations Sc and Nthn. RANSAKE, examine a wound, 885.28, 1152.27: OED, ON *rannsaka*, ME citations nearly all Nthn and alliterative verse (including *Piers Plowman*). REYSE, stimulate, 63.7: OED gives only Sc and Nthn examples for this meaning. RENNYNGE HOUND, hunting dog, 102.25: OED, obs., ME examples only Sc and Nthn; ROME(D), lament-(ed), ROMYNGE, 536.6, 912.21 (Vinaver amends to *ro(r)yng* unnecessarily), 1151.10: OED does not record this form, giving only *reme*; it is prob. the ON cognate, and appears twice in the alliterative *Morte Arthure* (Yks), for which OED has *rame*. ROSSHED, knocked, 394.14, 686.15: OED *rash*, chiefly Sc, now rare or obs., citations almost all Sc and Nthn: EDD, Sc. ROSTELED, fell violently, 736.3: OED, no entry, but cf. *rasteling*, tumult, uproar, which is obs. and cited only in alliterative *Alexander*; EDD has this form for "wrestled" for nYks, Lancs, Glocs, IW; the word appears in alliterative *Morte Arthure*. ROWYSSHE, knock, fall violently, 160.22, 400.27 etc: OED gives 15C spelling *rousch* as Sc, and the great majority of its 14-15C examples in all spellings are Sc, Nthn, and alliterative verse.

SAD, heavy, severe, 44.13, 44.14, 305.27: OED citations with this meaning nearly all Nthn and alliterative verse (also Chaucer). SCARYNG, loud of voice, 1163.16: OED, ON *skirra*, all ME examples are Sc, Nthn, and alliterative verse; EDD, wider use but especially Sc, Irel, NCys. SENSHYP, scandal, shame, 843.9 (in alliterative phrase *senshyp and shame*): OED *shenship*, almost all examples Nthn, NMid, and alliterative verse; Malory's spelling, mostly Sc: EDD, Sc.; the spelling SHONDESHYP, 320.13, is not recorded in OED, but may derive from ON form, *scand*, *scond*. SHAFFTEMONDE, handbreadth, 333.33: OED records this in wide use, but particularly in alliterative verse. SHIRLY, shrilly, 1090.8: OED gives general ME citations, but its modern examples are from Yks: EDD, Sc, Yks, Lancs, Der.

SYDELYNGE, sideways, 1217.30: OED citations are Sc and NMid. SYKER, certain, sure, 325.34, 816.12, 867.12, SYKERNESSE, agreement, 177.28: OED says that after 1500 the word is rarely used except by Scottish writers, but also remained current in North; 15C examples almost all Sc and Nthn; EDD records for Sc, Irel, Nhb, Cumb, Yks. SKATERD, scattered, 280.17: OED says this is commonly regarded as Nthn form against Sthn *shatter*; shown in Nthn and Mid texts; EDD, Sc, Nthn, and NMid counties. SKYFFTE, manage, 551.16: OED, ON *skifta*, citations from Nthn, NMid, and alliterative texts. SKYFFTE, lot, effort, 286.8, 682.15, SKYFTE, ridden of, 126.21: OED examples of first are Sc and Yks; does not record the adjective, but it may be pp. of verb. SLENTED, slipped, 981.27: OED, ON *slenta*, now dialect, ME citations of verb, largely Nthn and alliterative; EDD, Sc and NCys mainly, but also eAngl. and Nhp. SLO, to slay, 499.9: (Vinaver unnecessarily amends to *sle*): OED, from Nthn OE *slān* or ON *slá*, ME citations Nthn and NMid. SLY, SLYLY, skilful, clever, 175.31, 224.20, 464.28, etc: OED, this meaning obs. except in Nthn dialect: EDD, this meaning in NCys. SONDIS, messengers, 1228.25: OED *sand*, with fairly general spread, though most citations are Nthn and alliterative. SPARDE, shut, 432.9: OED, ON *sparri*, most of 14-15C citations are Nthn and eAngl. SPYRRE, SPURRE, SPARE, SPERE, ask, 351.8, 465.31, 495.14, 797.16, 808.29, 893.18, etc.: OED *speer*, examples chiefly Sc and Nthn; Kaiser, Nthn; EDD shows as far south as Derby, but mostly Sc and NCys. STAKIR, STAGERYNGE, stagger, 626.1, 323.8: OED, from ON *stakra*, obs. except dialect, citations except for Chaucer are Nthn and NMid; EDD records for Sc, NCys, NMid, and Hampshire. STE(A)VEN, STEVYN, voice, assignation, 84.7, 394.4, 1257.15: OED, apart from Chaucer citations, nearly all Sc, Nthn, and alliterative; EDD records for Sc, NCys, and Yks only. STUFF, to furnish men and goods for defence, 7.33, 677.12: OED, in this meaning the ME citations are almost all Sc and Nthn. SWALL, swelled, 1049.11: OED gives as Sc pret.; EDD, Sc. SWAP, to strike violently, 285.12: OED, now rare or obs., citations Sc, Nthn, and alliterative; Kaiser, Northern; EDD gives this sense as mainly Sc and Nthn.

TACCHIS, qualities, 63.27, 330.5: OED this meaning obs. except dialect; cites Malory and allit. *Alexander*. TAY, outer membrane of brain, 1237.21: OED, first example Bannatyne MS 1568. TENE, grief, 86.6 (in alliterative phrase *tray and tene*): OED, general use;

Appendix D

EDD, Sc, NCys, Yks, Ches. eAngl. THIRL, pierce, 106.6, 465.12: OED obs. except dialect and local; widespread in ME but citations since 1578 Nthn and Sc: EDD, Sc, NCys and NMid. THRALLE, thraldom, 892.13: OED, ON *praell*, in this meaning only citations are Sc, Nthn, and Cheshire; EDD; obs. Sc and Lancs. THRANGE, crowd, 262.30, 653.31, 1111.34: OED gives as Sc and Nthn form of *throng*, ME examples Sc, Nthn, and alliterative; EDD, Sc and NCys. THRANGE, pressed, 351.26, 654.24, 1177.32, 1183.23: OED *thring*, cites this preterite form in Malory and Nthn documents. THROOFF, prospered, 263.26: OED, ON *thrifa-sk*, all forms of the verb cited mostly from Nthn, NMid, and alliterative sources. TYLL, to, at, 27.19, 1216.6 and frequently elsewhere: OED says the word is characteristically northern in reference to place or purpose, although its citations show occasional use in Mid and Sth; Kaiser, Nthn; EDD, Sc, NCys, NMid. TRADE, trod, 1134.33: OED, possibly a Nthn form of the ON pret.pl. *traþum*, only this example. TRAY, pain, 86.6 (in alliterative phrase "tray and tene"): OED, ON *tregi*, obs., in general ME use, but in the alliterative phrase the citations are Sc, Nthn, and alliterative verse. TRAYNE, enticement, 511.6: OED, obs., examples after 1400 all Nthn; Kaiser, Nthn. TRESTE, lying in wait (hunting), 1104.8: OED *trist*, NMid sources.

UMBIR, shade, 372.28, 380.25: OED, now Nthn and Sc dialect, most ME citations similar; EDD, Lancs and Ches. UNBECASTE, UNBETHOUGHT, 1104.21, 421.18, 675.11 (cp. *umbelyclose* in Book V): OED *ymb-*, ON *umb-*, citations of words with this prefix almost all Sc, Nthn, and alliterative verse; Kaiser, Nthn; EDD records *umbethink* for Sc, NCys, NMid, and Dev. UNHAPPE, 271.1, 1161.7 (latter Caxton, in alliterating phrase *anger and unhap*), AT UNHAPPIS, unfortunately, 389.20, UNHAPPY, harmful, unlucky, 88.30, 90.23, 895.13, 1236.29, etc.: OED, ON *unhapp*, wide ME use but citations incline to Nthn. UNHYLLED, uncovered, 824.25, 908.2 (cp. *heled*): OED, fairly wide use, but majority of citations Nthn and alliterative. UNSYKER, unsure, 1036.28 (cp. *syker*): OED, obs. except Sc, ME citations show wider use but after Malory all are Sc. UNTYLL, to, 173.2 etc.: OED, ON *undtill*, originally Nthn; in application to place, all ME citations are Sc, Nthn, and NMid; EDD, Sc, Yks, Lincs, Som. VEARY, definite, 527.11: OED, obs. Sc spelling of "very."

WALTRED, tossed around, 805.9 (in alliterating phrase *wrythed and waltred)*: OED citations, Nthn, NMid, and alliterative; Kaiser, Nthn, EDD, Sc, NCys, Worc, eAngl. WEYKE (and similar comparative, superlative, and adverbial forms), weak, 164.26, 405.35, 719.9, 818.36, 919.28, 1069.20, 1237.25, etc. (the *weke, weak*-forms are lacking): OED, ON *veikr, ai*-forms occur almost entirely in Sc and Nthn citations (may be influenced by Nthn pronunciation of OE *wāc*). WANTIS, lacks, 116.8: OED, prob. ON *vanta*, citations almost entirely Sc and Nthn; EDD, Sc. Yks. WAP, beat (of water), 1239.25 (in alliterative line *watirs wap and wawys wanne*): OED, possibly related to "swap" and "whop," all citations from Sc, Nthn, NMid, and alliterative verse; Kaiser, Nthn. WARLY, warlike, strong, 320.26 (in alliterative phrase "warly wallys"): OED citations show wide use, but with Sc and Nthn predominance. WARKE, work, 1228.13: OED citations, Sc and Nthn; EDD, Sc. NCys. WARRE, worse, worst, 77.10, 596.16, 654.23, 686.10, 702.34 (including *mykyll the warre*): OED *war, waur*, ON *verre*, describes as Sc and Nthn, and all citations are from those areas; Kaiser, Nthn; EDD, wider use, but largely Nthn. WARS, worse, 931.23 and frequently elsewhere, WARSTE, 1076.35 and frequently elsewhere: OED gives this spelling as Nthn for 18-19C; EDD, Sc, NCys. WARWOLFF, werwolf, 1150.29: OED gives this as the Sc spelling in 15-17C. WAWIS, waves, 1025.27, 1239.14, 1239.25 (two last in alliterative phrases *wawys and wyndys* and *wawis wap and wawis wanne*): OED, in Nthn ME dialect would coincide in form with possible adoption of ON *vagr*; fairly wide use but particularly common in Nthn and alliterative verse; Malory borrows from stanzaic *Le Morte Arthur*. WESTIRLY, western, 1251.29; OED, chiefly Sc, ME examples Sc. WHATSOMEVER, WHANSOMEVER, WHERESOMEVER, WHOSOMEVER, WHOMSOMEVER, HOWSOMEVER, WHETHIRSOMEVER, WHAT(place, tyme, knight)SOMEVIR. These forms with the infix *-som-* are very frequent, e.g. 37.23, 407.29, 125.26, 624.29, 1119.21, 1162.1, 1202.19, etc.: OED *-sum-*, obs. Nthn; citations Nthn (though *howsomever* widespread): Kaiser says *-sum-* in such compositions is influenced by ON *sum* and is Nthn. WYGHT(Y), WYGHTLY, strong, 308.18, 418.13, 635.31, 1164.4, 1234.22: OED, ON *vigt*, citations predominantly Sc, Nthn, and alliterative verse; EDD, mainly Sc and NCys, but also SCys. WYLSOM, lonely, dreary, 332.33: OED, ON *villusamr*, obs. except Sc, ME citations mostly Sc, Nthn, and alliterative verse; EDD, obs. Sc. WYTE,

WYGHT, to blame, 56.8, 77.31, 146.30, 417.8, 897.13, etc.: OED, now Sc and Nthn dialect, although ME citations show wider spread; EDD, Sc, NCys and Glocs.

Summary. Allowing for repetitions, the total of these northern and northernish words is about 550. The items are spread throughout the book, but there are places where they occur more frequently than usual; e.g. I.16-17, II.6, III.8, 13; IV, 25; VI as a whole; VII.8, XIX.8-9, XXI.4, 5, 12. This variation of density is not related to the two copyists of the Winchester Manuscript, for the areas of density occur in both of their work. A partial explanation can be found in the nature of Malory's sources in different places: thus, the density of northernisms in Book V (described separately in Appendix E) is of course due to Malory's use of the Yorkshire poem, the alliterative *Morte Arthure*. The passages of density in Books XIX and XX may be because of Malory's use there of the stanzaic *Le Morte Arthur*, also composed in Yorkshire. Elsewhere, Malory's memory of these two poems might explain some of his northernisms; but it could only be a very limited explanation, for of the nearly two hundred different northern words that he used in sections that he translated from French, only seventy-five occur in the alliterative poem, and only twenty-two in the stanzaic one.

APPENDIX E
Linguistic Comparison of Winchester and Caxton Texts

In general the Caxton text is more standardized than the Winchester text. As the analysis in the first sections of Appendix B shows, the northern grammatical and spelling variants in Winchester are for the most part represented by standard forms in Caxton. A few northern forms however are confirmed as original by their appearance in both texts; and in a very few cases, Caxton has northernisms which are represented by standard forms in Winchester. These variations, which are reported on in detail in the analysis of the spelling and grammar of the Winchester text, suggest that the original from which both texts derive contained more such northernisms than either of the surviving texts.

In vocabulary the evidence is more extensive. A large proportion of the northern words in the Winchester text are also in the Caxton text, and so may be judged to have been in the original form of the work. There are however a good many variations between Caxton and Winchester. These, so far as they are reported in Vinaver's footnotes and so far as they seem relevant to the problem of dialect, are listed in the following two groupings.

a) In the following cases, the Winchester text (represented by the form in capital letters) is northern or old-fashioned while the corresponding Caxton form (in lower-case letters) is standard or more familiar:

ADREMED, dretched 1169
AFONNED, assoted 647
AR, ere 982, 1079, 1200

ARSTE, erst 969, 1013, 1079
AT UNHAPPIS, by unhap 389

Appendix E

AWGHE, owe 610
AWNE, owne 763
BANDES, landes 653
BEES, bedys 1238
BONE, yefte 109
BOTENETH, helpeth 1189
BRASTE, ranne oute 1057
BREKE, breche 817
BROSTE, broken 322
BYGHE, bye 1227
CHAFFLET, schaffold 518, skafhold 1069
CLEYGHT, caught 1240
CLYCHED, tooke 818
DARE "injure," they are 1212
DARF, nede 869
DAYSSHED DOWNE, fyl 1237
DONE "gift," bone 374, 571, 1148
DOUGHTYESTE, best 76
DURKED, darked 858, derke 974
DWERE, doubte 579, 685
EGGED, edgyd 580
woodys EVYSE, syde 1073
FELLYS, feldes 329
FRENDE HYM, get hym frendes 427
FRO, from 1183
FRYCKE, fresshe 1085
GART BREN, brente 621
GYFF, yf 1219
HERBEROW, lodgyng 172
HERBEROWDE, lodged 956
HETHYNDE, hethen 489
HOM, hem 72
ILLE, evyll 898
INWYTH, within 1130

JARFAUCON, gerfaukon 176
LEPE, lepte 432, 494, 818, 820
LOPYN, lepte 536
LOWSE, lose 813
LYGHE, lye 926
MASED, madde 825
MEANED, bemoned 821
MON, maye 1002
MOU "mon"?, mote 44
METE, dyner 1048
NEREHONDE, nyhe, 329, nyghehand 506
NYGHE, neye "neigh" 256
POUSTÉ, power 920
PUSYLL, chyld 794
ROMED "complained," ranne 1151
ROMYNGE, roryng 536, 911
SAMEFULLY, shamefully 1173
SAWE, shawe "wood" 548
SEETH, shethe "sheath" 995
SERE, drye 968
SHONDESHYP, shenship 320
SYGHE "saw," aspyed 961
SYKE, seche "seek" 687
SLY, wyly 175
SOLDE, sholde 1137
STAGERYNGE, scateryng 323
STERTE, lepte 433
stynte your STRYFF, noyse 1162
STURRES, sterres "stars" 991
SULDE, shold 982
TANE, taken 70
TAY, brayne panne 1237

Appendix E 195

THIRLED, ranne 106
THIRSTE, threst 390
TYLL(E), to 174, 328, 563, 821
THIRSTELEW, moche thursty 373
THRANGE "crowd," rayeng 653
THRYLED, thrulled 465
UNLY BLACK, inly "very" 911
UNTYLL, unto 464, 1082
VIGOURE, VYGOURE, fygur 880, 882
WAN ON HIS FEETE, rose 160
ME WANTIS, lacketh 116

WARE, were 945
WARRE, werste 596, werse 647, 686, 702
WARSE, wers 507
WARSTE, werst 1076
WAS WARE, knewe 975
WAYKELY, WEYKELY, wekely 405, 919
WHATSOMEVER, what 910
WHETHIRSOMEVER, whether 624
WHOTHIRWARD, whederward 462
WHOTHER, whyther 518
YODE, yede 971, etc.

b) The second group, however, reverses the situation: in these the Caxton text (represented by the forms in capital letters) has the northern or old-fashioned word or form and Winchester has the standard or more familiar one:

ALTHER, oure all 147
ANGER, hevynesse 564
AN-ANGRED, greved 1059
BANDES, bondys 813, 1169
BEE "ring," bye 360
BE SKYFTE HYM, be of of hym 126
BYGGE, grete 1187
BRASTE, falle 1196
BY HIS OWNE, by hymselff 78
CAN THANKE, I thanke 1203
CLAFE, claffe 270
CLEPED, called 469
CLEYGHTE, caught 255
CON, can 360, 1193
DOLE, sorow 1129

DRENCHED, drowned 916
ENDLONGE, longe 808
EURE "custom," hurte 34
FELAWES, knyghtes 1001, 1034, brother 925, felowis 540
FLANGE "flung," flowe 469
FLAY, flowe 981
FRO, downe 129, frome 253, 1077
GALHOUS, jybett 1154
GARTE HYM GO, stroke hym 111
GARTE UNARME, unarmed 254
GARTE TO UNARME, gan unarme 256

GART SETTE, made sette 396
GRAYTHED, (lacking) 171
GRETE, sadde 959
GRYMMYNGE, grennynge 688
HAPPE, fortune 82
HAPPE, so be 391
HELE, helth 1252
HETETH, is called 296
HYGHTE, his name was 495
HYLLED, coverde 1034
HYTTE, smote 647
HOVED, stondynge 92
HURTLED, smote 659, hurled 733
HURTELYNG, hurlynge 740
YLLE, evyll 282, 582, 777, 1162
INTYLL, untyll 1080
KENNE God thanke, yelde 897
KYNNE, kynnesmen 833
LADE, lode "loaded" 481
LAYTE, lyghtnynge 1004
LENE, lende 505, 508, 1111, leve 345
LYTH, joynte 263
LOOS "praise," love 963
MARYS, mores 282
MEDLE with, deale 728
MYKEL, muche 350, 502, 931
MYSHAPPED, mysfortuned 1177
NAY, I suppose nat 101
NEMLY, lyghtly 821
NENEME, name (inf.) "name" 753

ONY, any 398, 419
OR pryme, be 258
OVER HYP, overlepe 1154
RAFE, rove 821, smote 821
RASSHED, russhed 298, 469, 491, 1167, racith 748, raced of 734
RASYNGE, traversyng 298
RASSHYNGE, russhyng 523
REKE, recke 970
ROWNSPYKE, rowgh spyke 283
SCATHE, harme 80
SHEEF, threste 878
SYN, whan 967
SKUMME, skymme 26
SLAKE "valley," slad 260
can SPEDE, can do "did" 665
STEDYS, placis 314
by STYGH or by strete, fylde 353
STYNTED, staunched 326
SWARE, swore 25
TEETH, thyghe 678 (orig. *thee*? Fr. source has *cuisse*)
TEYED, fastenyd 893
TYL, (lacking) 821, to 843, 1078
UNGLADDE, sad 682
UN TYLL, unto 52, to 259
WAGGYNGE, sygnys 1139
thou WAS, that was 159
WERRE, worste 38, warse 507
WHATSOMEVER, what 1197, whatsoever 599
WHERESOMEUER, whoso woll 461
WHOSOMEVER, who 414
WISTE, knew 433
YERE, ere "ear" 1127

Appendix E

Comparison of these usages in the Caxton text with the glossaries in EETS editions of Caxton's works (A, *The Four Sons of Aymon*; C, *The Curial*; B, *Blanchardyn and Eglantine*; D, *Dialogues in French and English*; GB, *Godeffroy of Boloyne*; F, *Fayttes of Armes and of Chyvalrie*; P, *Paris and Vienne*) reveal Caxton himself using the following words in this second group: *an-angred*, A, B; *cleped*, P; *con(ne)*, A, C, D, G, P; *felau, felawship*, B, D, G, P; *fro*, D, P; *galhouse*, B; *gare*, A; *grymmeth*, C; *happed*, A, G, P; *heeled*, A; *in-tyl*, E; *lene*, A, D; *mareys*, F. G; *medle*, B, D, E, G; *mykyll*, A; *or*, F, P; *syn*, B, E, P; *scume*, E; *stynte*, P. Less than a quarter of these words and forms, therefore, were part of Caxton's own usage, and of those only four were normal with him. It is reasonable to conclude, therefore, that almost all these northernisms and old-fashioned usages existed in the manuscript from which Caxton printed.

Conclusion. The conclusion must be that both Winchester and Caxton are standardized texts, Caxton more so than Winchester. The fact that, despite this standardization, Caxton has some fifty words and a sprinkling of forms that are matched by standard usages in Winchester must mean that the text from which they both derive ultimately (and which must be akin to Malory's own) was considerably more northern in its language than even the Winchester text.*

---

* It is possible that complete comparison of the Caxton and Winchester texts might reveal still further northernisms in Caxton which are lacking in Winchester, for Vinaver's recording of the text variants, upon which we have mainly relied here, is somewhat fitful.

APPENDIX F
Linguistic Comparisons with Other Middle English Documents

I. *Comparisons with Yorkshire Middle English documents.* The central and most frequently mentioned area connected with the northernisms in Malory is Yorkshire. Comparison of Malory's words (and some forms) cited in Appendixes D, E, and G with the usage in several Yorkshire documents establishes that most of them were common in Yorkshire writing just before Malory's time.

a) The *Wakefield Plays* represent the language of the West Riding, about 30 miles south of Ripon, in the early fifteenth century. The following words and forms used by Malory appear in the glossary to A. C. Cawley's selection, *The Wakefield Pageants* (Manchester, 1958). *als, anger, are* "before," *at* "that," *awne, byr* "rush," *bowne, brast, breme* "fierce," *busk, bustus, can* "did," *can thank, carl, cast* and *kest, clater, crak, dede* "death," *dyke, doughty, dre, endlang, fellys, flyt, fond, gate, gar, gart, gnast, grete, grym, haill, how, hap, hope, hundreth, ill, keyle* "cool," *ken, kyrk, lad, layn, leyne* "give," *lig, loft* "high," *lowsyd, make* "compose, make," *masterman, mekill, mell* "speak," *mon* "must," *nerehand, nowder, or, overtwhart, rayse, rake, rase, renk, sekir, syn, skar, slo, spar, spyrd, steven, sty, tane, tene, thole, thrang, thrife, till, tray, trane, untill, wake, walteryng, war, wark, wars, wawghs, Yoyll* "Yule": also spellings and grammatical forms such as *betokyns, carpys, gyftys, gyf* "give," *lyffand, leyfe* "leave."

b) These parallels are taken from the glossary to Hope Emily Allen's selection, *English Writings of Richard Rolle of Hampole.* (Rolle was born about 1300 at Thornton Dale near Pickering.) *Als, anger, ar, at, awne, bowne, bren, bygge, dawyng, dike, dreghe, dwyne, eggen* "incite," *elde* "age," *felaws, flytte, gar, gate, gnaystynges, graithed, grete, gyf* "if," *grym, happe, haylce* "greet," *hethyng* "scoffing," *hilynge, hope, il, intil, kele, kene, kirk, kun* "be able," *layne, lene, lend, liggand* "lying," *lyth, make, makeles, mekil, mon* "must," *nerehande, nouther, or, os, sal, schendescip, scho, sen* "since," *siker, strande* "torrent," *sulde* "should," *tane, tene, thartil, thrille, thyrl, til, umbesette, umbethynk, war, wark, wayke*: also spellings and grammatical forms such as *thay, thair, thaym, es, lufes, begyles, lastand.*

c) *The Metrical Life of St. Robert of Knaresborough.* Joyce Bazire's EETS edition of this short poem of c. 1400 in Yorkshire dialect, lists these words in its glossary: *aghen, althir, awe, bryn, boune, brathe* "impetuous," *brest, busked, carle, kastes, carping, keyn, kempes, kenne, kyrke, crage, ded* "death," *dere, drye, felagh, flytte, fryth, gayn, gar, gate, gnaste, grathe, grim, yll, irke, layn, leynd, lyth, louse, outher, rayked, rayse, remed, sall, sulde, sen, shente, sekerly, slegh, spirred, sty and strette, tane, teyne, tharetyll, tyll, traye, tryst, umbeseged, umbythought, unhappis, wagged, waike, warlow, wyghtly, freke, carpyng, rayked, wrang.*

d) *The Poems of Laurence Minot,* ed. Joseph Hall, Oxford, 1897, glosses: *alder* "of all," *als, are* "ere," *bankes, big, boun, brim, busk, ded* "death," *dere, dik, droupe, frek, frith, fro, furth, gate, ger* "cause," *graythest, hundereth, ken, kene, kirk, lend, lig, mekill, mun* "must," *nowther, or, rese* "haste," *sal* "shall," *schende, sen* "since," *site* "sorrow," *sla* "slay," *suld* "should," *swire* "neck," *tane, tene, thai, thaire, tham, thrive, till, trey, umlap, umset, untill*: also spellings and grammatical forms such as *ligand, sayland; stremis, helmis; has, wakins, thai ligges, makes.*

e) *Ywain and Gawain,* ed. Albert B. Friedman and Norman T. Harrington, EETS 254 (London, 1964), is probably Yorkshire in language and about 1325 in date of composition; the manuscript is about a century later. These words in Malory's lists appear in the glossary: *als, anger, are, at, aw, awin, bir, boun, breke, bremly, brent, dede, dere, dyke, fell, flyt, frith, gaynest, gate, ger, graithly, gram, gret* "wept," *zone* "yon," *hailsed, hals* "neck," *herberd* "lodged," *hilles* "protects," *hope, intil, kan* "know," *karl, kene, kyrk, laine* "conceal," *lene* "give," *lende* "remain," *lig, lire* "flesh," *ment* "mourned," *mikel, mun, nerehand, or, outbrast, owper, rase* "plucked," *rese* "rush," *scath, seker, sekerly, sen* "since," *shende, sperd* "fastened," *spir* "ask," *sty, stoure, tane, tene, thole, umbithoght, untill, werr* "worse," *wharesum, wight*: also spellings and gram-

matical forms such as *awin, ware, kest, Yngland, shiferd, lufes,* under-
stands, *lyfand, syttand.*

f) Even larger numbers of Malory's northern words appear in the
Yorkshire and Lancashire alliterative poems of the late fourteenth century. Some seventy-five are used in *Morte Arthure,* about eighty in *Sir
Gawain and the Green Knight,* and even more in the *Geste Historiale of
the Destruction of Troy* (EETS, 1869, 1874), viz: *als, angarly,
angre, are* "ere," *at* "that," *awne, aurthewert, awkewardly, awe, banke,
bate* "contention," *beronnen* (in *blody beronnen*), *big, bygly, birr, boist-
ous, bonke, borly, boune, brast, brem, bren, brethe* "rage," *brig,
burbele, burd* "lady," *buske, bustious, can* "did," *carle, carpe, cast, caupe*
"a blow," *claterand, dere, dike, dregh, droup, dyke, eme* "uncle,"
endlange, flang, fleme, flit, fonnet "foolish," *forray, frek* and
frike, freke "man," *frith* "wood," *fryke* "hearty," *gaf* "gave," *gar* and
gart, gate "road," *gif* "if," *gyrd* "strike," *graithe, gretyng* "crying,"
grym, hailsen, hap, henge "hung," *hething, hundrethe, hurtelyng, kele,
ken, kene, kest, kyd, laite* "lightning," *langur* "linger," *lenge* "dwell,"
lere, lofte "sky," *lowse, lugg* "drag" (cp. Malory's *lugerand*), *maister-
men, make* "companion," *marche, mon* "must," *mykill, nemly, nowther,
or, overhild* "covered," *overthwert, owkewardly, owther, pike, plite,
pure* "thorough," *rake* "go," *reme* "cry," *renke* "knight," *ronk* "strong,"
sad, seker, sekurly, shake "set out," *shaw* "thicket," *shend, shenship, skant,
skathe, slade* "ravine," *slighly, soundismen, spere* "ask," *sprent, stake*
"stuck," *stale* "stole," *stevyn, stoure, stuff, stynt, suld* "should," *swang,
swap* "strike," *swire, sydelyng, syne* "since," *tane, tene, thai, thaim, thaire,
thirle, thole, thraldam, thrang, thrive, till, train* "trick," *umbcast,
umclose, umset, unhappe, unsiker, wag* "bob," *waghe* "wave," *walt*
"totter," *wap* "a blow, to beat," *wawe* "wave," *warloghe, waike* "weak,"
wite "blame," *wight* "brave": also grammatical forms such as *spekand,
prayand; suffers! hedys! me semes, me mervells, us likes, thou rises,
he loues, stake, rafe, scho.*

g) A less literary comparison is afforded by the *Plumpton Correspondence,* ed. Thomas Stapleton (London: Camden Society, 1839). These
letters were written to Sir William Plumpton of Knaresborough (an
associate and neighbor of the Yorkshire Malorys) by his family, tenants,
and business associates and so reflect the language of educated men in mid-
Yorkshire. The language is generally standard, but localisms appear here
and there mostly in spellings and grammar. The following details are
taken from letters written in the period 1460-85. Spellings: (*a*) *enpreson-*

ment 34, *Medilton* 37, *Trenete* 47, *ʒeftys* 49, *spetell* 106, *wedow* 123; (*b*) *raw* "row" 4, *awne* 30, *awing* 41, *snaw* 89; (*c*) *gud* "good" 17, *gude* 18, *livelihuds* 20, *gudly* 28; (*d*) *pauper* "paper" 46, *frrynds* 53; (*e*) *mistris* 15, *withoutyn* 21, *dellyd* 24, *wardin* 25, *resumyde* 49, *ʒeftys* 49, *citisins* 52, *plesyde* 49; (*f*) *lyg* "lie" 23; *mikle* 39, *beseketh* 39, *brygge* 139; (*g*) *gif* "give" 3, *haf* "have" 7, *lyfes* "lives" 46, *lyfing* 41, *ʒyffe* 49; (*h*) *oder* "other" 30, *fader* 43; (*i*) *sold* "should" 85, *hundreth* 11, *thof* "though" 7. GRAMMAR: (*a*) they, thaire, them (no *h*-forms); (*b*) *he sais* 10, *hase* 11, *knowes* 13, *semes* 17, *owes* 21, *stands* 32; (*c*) *they hase* 21, *threats* 25, *lyes* 54. VOCABULARY: *anenst* "opposite" 7; *angrie* 23; *at* "that" 31, 32, 41; *felaw* 2; *fro* 13, 22; *gar* 21, *gart* 36; *gif* "if" 13; *kan him thank* 32; *ky* "cows" 26; *kirke* 4; *latesum* "latish" 21; *or* "ere" 14, 32; *trussed in* 21; *siker* 28, *stub* "timber tree" 25; *whilk* "which" 36; *awort* "athwart" 85. These local usages are in substantial agreement with Malory's, the only striking difference being the *u*-spellings in words like *good*. Sprinkled as the northernisms are in the predominantly standard language of the Plumpton correspondence, they yield a linguistic texture quite similar to that of the Winchester manuscript of *Le Morte Darthur*.

h) It may be claimed therefore that the usages that have been characterized as northernisms in Malory on the basis of modern authorities, are supported as Yorkshire usages by the practice of Yorkshire and northern alliterative texts written during Malory's lifetime or not long before. Their continuance as Yorkshire dialect may also be checked in two substantial recent glossaries of the county's local vocabulary, C. Clough Robinson's *A Glossary of Words Pertaining to the Dialect of Mid-Yorkshire* (London, 1876), and Sir Alfred Edward Pease's *A Dictionary of the Dialect of the North Riding of Yorkshire* (Whitby, 1928). These are the relevant words and forms listed in these two works: *angery, angered, at, awe, awne, bait* "feed," *bank, boun, breeks, brigg, brast, bray* "beat," *busk, carl, clave, cleg* "stick to," *cleugh, click* "seize," *crack* "talk," *daftish, deead* "death," *dike, dwine, eam* "uncle," *egg* "incite," *endlang, fell, fill,* "fell," *flang, flit, fond* "foolish," *frack* "bold," *frind* "friend," *gain* "direct," *gait* "way," *gainest, gap, gar, gate* "way," *gert* "great," *gif* "if," *grutch* "begrudge," *hale* "call," *hap, hapment, harbour,* "lodging," *hawse* "neck," *hilling* "coverlet," *howsomever, ill, intil, keeal, kemp, ken, kest, kirk, lig, lith, lope, lowse, make* "friend," *marrish, mickle, moun, nearhand, nesh, nowther, ony, or, owther, raase, rome* or *raum* "shout," *rous* "rush," *sad* "heavy," *sal* "shall," *scar* "scare," *scattert, shaffment, shent ower, sidelang, sikker, sine, slack* "valley," *slee* "slay," *sly* "clever," *speir* "ask," *sprent* "sprinkled," *stakker, stale* "stole," *steven* "shout," *stour* "commotion," *strake* "struck," *sty* "path," *swang, swarth* "turf," *suld* "should," *taen,* "taken," *thrang* "crowd," *throof* "thrived," *thrumble* "tease," *til* "to," *trade* "trod," *umbethink, unheppen* "unpractical," *until, walt* "overturn," *wan* "won," *wantin* "deficient," *wap* "blow," *war, waur* "worse," *wark, warse, wayk, whatsomever, whensomever, wheresomever, whuther, wrang, yat* "gate," *yon.*

II. *Comparisons with Warwickshire dialect.* The foregoing comparisons establish that almost all Malory's apparent northernisms were used by Yorkshiremen and alliterative poets in the late Middle English period, but a further check is necessary to discover whether they may have also been used elsewhere. For Malory the two significant areas are Warwickshire and London.

(*a*) The *Coventry Leet Book,* ed. M. Dormer Harris, EETS 134, 135, 138, 146 (London, 1907-13) and *Two Coventry Corpus Christi Plays,* ed. H. Craig, EETSes 87 (London, 1902) represent the language of Coventry, the town nearest to Newbold Revel and one with which Sir Thomas Malory of Newbold Revel was associated in various ways. The *Leet-Book* provides nearly 300 pages of prose for the period 1440-1480 in a fair copy which may have standardized some local forms and introduced a few later linguistic developments. The two plays were rewritten by Robert Croo in 1534, and he certainly introduced some pompous language and some features of sixteenth-century standard English. Nevertheless, the two documents retain many features of east-Warwickshire dialect. These are the most striking localisms and a selection of examples:

Spelling. (*a*) The plays frequently reflect *y*-glides and *w*-glides before front and back vowels: *wold* "old," *whome* "home," *wonly* "only," *wonys* "once," *won* "one," *whomwarde* "homeward," *bwoy* "boy," *yeyre* "air," *yend* "end," *yorth* or *yarth* "earth"; and the *Leet-Book* uses similar spellings for "end" and "earl." (*b*) Frequently in the plays and occasionally in the *Leet-Book, w* and *v* are interchanged: *were* "very," *woise* "voice," *wengance, woide, trawelled, hawe* "have," *gawe* "gave," *hawyng* "having"; *veyis* "ways," *vast* "waste," etc. (*c*) Before *n, nd,* both texts occasionally spell *o* against standard *a*: *con, mon, ony, mony, womon, onsuerd, husbonde, stonde, honde, londe.* (*d*) OE *y* is occasionally represented by *i* in both texts in words where standard usage is *i*: *hull* "hill," *Colshull, bruge* "bridge," *dud, dudde* "did" in the *Leet-Book* and *cun* "kind," *furst* "first," *fure* "fire" in the plays ("much" and "church" have either *u* or *i*; "busy" and "rushes" have *e*). (*e*) Loss and addition of initial *h* is found in both texts: *hus* "us," which is used often; *horgans*, *hy* "I" in the plays; and *Erod*, *is* "his," *hete* "eat," *habundance* in the *Leet-Book*. (*f*) The *Leet-Book* always has *y* or *ȝ* in "gate," and these spellings are predominant in "give," "gave," "given," "again," "against," "gild." (*g*) The plays often show variant juncture between "mine" and a word beginning with an initial vowel: *my narmis, my nold age, my none darlyng*, etc. (*h*) In both texts the unstressed vowel is frequently *u*: *trybus* "tribes," *blossum, waxun, schorttun, mastur, weddur, systur, lyttull, tempull* in the plays; and *masturs, septur, bedull, myracull, bobbulez, fasus* "faces" in the *Leet-Book* are typical examples. (*i*) Miscellaneous spellings of nonstandard kind are: *nar* "nearer," *har* "higher," *lyggyd* "lay," *trauth* "truth," *quost* "quest" in the plays, and *dur, durr* "door," *lyggyng* "lying," *lone* "lane," which is frequently used, *thak* "thatch," in the *Leet-Book*.

Grammar. (*a*) In addition to the fifteenth-century standard pronouns, the following dialectal forms occur in the plays: *yche* "I," *ham* "them," *hit* "it." (*b*) Prior to 1480, the *Leet-Book* has no *-s* inflections for present-tense verbs, the third-person singular inflection being *-th* (*hurteth, useth*) and the plural *-on* (*aron, comon, han, notifion, mayn*, etc.); the plays, however, occasionally have *-s* in the third singular, even in the rhymes, and the plural inflection is normally zero. (*c*) In both texts, the past participle inflection in strong verbs is *-on, -un, or -en*: *sprongon, wuxun, cumon, hondon, ryden, bounden, holden*, etc.

Vocabulary. (*a*) The *Leet-Book*, which consists of brief reports on town business, has few words that might be called dialectal, these being the only possibilities: *bygge* "to build," *shaftmond* "handbreadth," *cast* "to intend." (*b*) The plays have rather more such words, though not many: *bayne* "ready," *enderes* "recent," *haft* "business," *tent* "to take heed," *glede* "fire," *kerne* "vagabond," *strangis* "news," *thee* "to prosper," *theal* "shaft," *wold* "hill," *looe* "hill," *a pyrie of wynd* "gust," *fryth* "wooded country," *lend* "remain," *till* "to," *untyll* "unto," *theretyll*.

In general, these features of the two documents agree with those of fourteenth-century literary texts from the Central West Midlands (cp. Mary S. Serjeantson's analysis). They are therefore features that might be expected to appear occasionally in any text that emanated from Warwickshire in the 1460's.

A few do appear in *Le Morte Darthur*: *con, stonde, honde, londe, dud, hit, yate, yiven, yaf*; and the words *shaftmond, cast, looe, fryth, tyll, untyll*. These, however, are the least significant items in the list, for they may sometimes be found in documents from London and other dialect areas: they are all found in northern documents, for instance. On the other hand, the most striking dialect features in the list do not appear in Malory at all.

From this, and also from the fact that almost none of the many northernisms in Malory's text appear in these Warwickshire documents, the conclusion must be that by far the greatest part of the forms and words which have been listed from *Le Morte Darthur* reflect an origin other than Warwickshire. A comparison with modern Warwickshire dialect emphasizes this conclusion. The only words in the Malory list that appear in G. F. Northall's *A Warwickshire Word-Book*, EDS (London, 1896), are: *egg* "to incite," *girt* "great," *howsumdever*, *mun* "must," *slade* "tract of land," *yon*.

III. *Comparison with London documents.* Checking of the words in the Malory list with the glossaries in EETS editions of some London and standard texts composed in the fifteenth century yield these results: (*a*) Stephen Scrope's lengthy translation of *The Dictes and Sayings of the Philosophers*, done in 1450, is a collection of anecdotes and tales; it contains only these items from the list: *carle, kele, plite, unbethinke(ynge)*. (*b*) Caxton's short prose romance, *Paris and Vienne*, which he published in the same year as *Le Morte Darthur*, contains only *happe*; his *Fayttes of Armes*, 1489, lists only *brenne, lovyng* "praise," *or, syn*; and the translation of the long romance, *The Four Sons of Aymon*, which he issued shortly after he printed Malory, contains: *an-angred, are* "ere," *brenne, conne* "know," *gare* "cause," *happed, heeled* "covered," *laddes, lene* "give," *mykyll, overhwarte, scathe, sin, spered* "asked," *stoure* "noise." (*c*) The anonymous translation of *The Book of the Knight of La Tour-Landry*, an earlier fifteenth-century work, lists only: *kiste* "cast," *lyge* "lie," *overthwartly, steven, taches* "blemishes."

(*d*) Nearly a century before, Chaucer had used rather more of the words in the list, and that may possibly be because he had Yorkshire friends and an unusual interest in northern dialect. Skeat's glossary in his six-volume edition of *The Works of Geoffrey Chaucer* lists less than forty of the words, including *boun, crag, droupe, gnaistinge, louse, makeles, note, poustee, yon, werre* "worse," which are used only once, and *mareys, mikel, tache, thirl*, which are used only two or three times. Only a very few of the words, *brenne* and *hap* most notably, appear often enough to suggest that they may have been part of the ordinary London vocabulary.

What is most interesting and significant in Chaucer's usage in these matters, however, is that in the imitation of northern (probably north-Yorkshire) dialect used by the clerks in the *Reeve's Tale* there are more northernisms than in all the rest of Chaucer's writing, and that several of them are items similar to those listed from *Le Morte Darthur*. Thus, the clerks use: -*s* inflections for third-person verbs, *fares, has, falles, bringes, says, tydes*; spellings such as, *awen, na, swa, banes, waat, sal, taa* "take," *wrang*; and words like, *als* "as," *ay* "always," *dawe* "dawn," *daf* "foolish," *fonne* "fool," *gif* "if," *hethen* "hence," *ille* "evil," *il-hayl, los* "praise," *y-mel* "mixed," *sin* "since," *til* "to," *wagges, wanges* "cheeks," *whilk* "which," *wight*.

The conclusion to be drawn from these London comparisons is that few of the words and forms in the Malory lists were ordinary London usage, and that most of them (and probably far more than Chaucer parodies) would have been readily recognized as northern (and Yorkshire) by any attentive contemporary reader.

APPENDIX G
Linguistic Analysis of the Roman War Episode

Malory's version of the Roman war (Book V in C, pp. 181-247 in Vinaver's edition of W) presents a special linguistic problem, for it is a prosing of the Yorkshire alliterative poem called *Morte Arthure*. C is a radically revised version, which is also linguistically adjusted to standard usage; W contains a great many northernisms, a large part of them taken from the poem. The poem survives in a single medieval text, that of the Thornton MS, which is a somewhat corrupt text.

The poem is not only written in Yorkshire dialect, it is also heavily charged with the traditional language of alliterative verse. As a result, it is formidably difficult. The consequent problems relating to Malory's prosing, therefore, are the degree of his understanding of the poem, particularly in the details of its language, and the extent to which his northernisms are taken from the poem. These problems are not simplified by the theory, which is sometimes advanced to explain his differences from the poem, that he used a different text than that in the Thornton MS. The conjecture, convenient as it may be for some arguments, renders rational analysis impossible. The present analysis proceeds from the belief that much can be learned—even as to whether it is necessary to postulate a lost variant text of the poem—by making a close and full comparison of Malory's prosing, as it is represented in W, with the poem as it is represented in the Thornton MS. (Brock's EETS edition is the text cited here.)

I. *GRAMMAR*. For the most part, W of this episode is written with the grammar of fifteenth-century standard English, the same forms that

Malory usually used elsewhere in his book. Varying these, however, is a much larger proportion of northernisms than he used elsewhere. Some of these are simply transferred from the poem; others are independent of it in the sense that they do not occur in the poem, that they occur in words that Malory replaced by synonyms, or that they appear elsewhere in the poem than at the points where Malory used them.

The largest group consists of verbs which have northern inflections in the present indicative. For the second person singular, W uses the standard *-yst* inflection ten times; but it has six examples of northern *-ys*, and of these five are not matched in the poem: *berys thou* 201.2 (the poem has *buskys*), *thou sittes* 202.17 (*lygges*), *thou lovys* 212.12 (lacking), *thou wynnys* 218.10 (lacking), *thou bebledis* 230.16 (lacking). For the third person singular, the episode has thirty-nine examples of the standard *-th* inflection: *greyth* 188, *longyth* 191, *metyth* 239, etc. But it has far more examples of northern *-ys*; there are 117 all told, and of these, sixty-eight are not matched in the poem, but appear in Malory's substitute synonyms or in passages that he apparently added or paraphrased radically. As examples we may cite these which occur on two pages: he *buskes* 200.5 (poem, *bounede*), he *stertes* 200.6 (*sterte*), *hentys* 200.6 (lacking), *fyndis* 200.6 (lacking), *kepys* 200.14 (*gemez*), *nedys* 201.3 (lacking), *lodgys* 201.23 (lacking).

The plural inflection is sometimes the standard one, *e/en/*zero, as in *they make* 245. More numerous, however, are the twenty examples of northern *-ys*, of which four-fifths are not matched in the poem; e.g. *knyghtes and lordis longis* 246.3, which occurs in the added conclusion, *three fayre maydens that turnys* 202.1 (where the poem has *turne*), *they fyghtes* 230.1 (*feyghtten*), *they castys* 237.6 (*caste*), and *they longis* 243.14 (*longede*). W also has three imperatives with *-ys* inflections; of these, two are not matched in the poem: *now fastynys* 200.12 (the poem has the indicative form), *herkyns me* 212.30 (lacking).

Against the poem's normal northern *-ande* inflection in present participles, Malory commonly has standard *-ynge*, as in *commaundynge* 185. But he has also six examples of the northern inflection: *lugerande* 196.24, *flamand* 200.18, *wryngande* 200.20, *syttande* 200.20, *glystrand* 229.3, *baytand* 233.20. (And *recrayedand* 185.19, which Vinaver amends silently to *recrayedest*, may be a seventh.) Of these, *lugerande, syttande, glystrand* are not matched exactly in the poem, which has synonyms.

W also uses the northern preterites *leepe* 189.31, *keste* 215.2, *swange* 215.21, which also appear in the poem. The substantival adjectives *that mylde* 201.5, *the kene* 216.14, *a doughty* 227.15 are not matched in the poem, although similar usages appear elsewhere in the poem and in other northern alliterative verse.

II. *SPELLING*. The most prevalent northernism in Malory's spelling in this episode is the representation of the unstressed vowel as *i/y*. This is also the predominant habit of the poem; but Malory often has *i/y* where the poem uses the more standard *e*. Examples taken from the first two pages are: *knyghtis* 185.3, *takyn* 186.21, *aftir* 185.3, *messyngers* 185.9, *knelyd* 185.14, *feryst* 186.1, *londis* 186.3, *gretis* 186.7, *fadir* 186.10, *ellys* 186.10, *weldyst* 186.11, *erlys* 186.20.

Other northern spellings may be listed and exemplified briefly: (*a*) Malory uses *mykyll* 204.12, 205.3, 234.14, where the poem either has *myche* or lacks the word. The northern *beseke* "beseech" 244.12 occurs in an added passage; *lygge* "lie" 244.9 occurs in an added passage; *kyrke* 205.17 repeats the poem. (*b*) Like the poem, Malory often spells *e* where standard usually has *i*, in such words as *rever* 190.18, *geff* 202.16, *geffyn* 201.14, *gresly* 208.13, *presoners* 211.18, *strekyn* 196.8, *setthen* 225.8, *overredyn* 231.10, *prevely* 218.20. (*c*) In a few words, W employs *ey*, probably a northern spelling for long *e*, where the poem uses *e*: *feyble* 201.1, *kneis* 221.9, *freyke* 199.9, *beystys* 235.22, *creyme* 227.22, and also *raynke* 236.25. (*d*) Between a vowel and *sh* M often inserts *y*, which is a practice found in northern documents and occasionally in western ones: *freysshly* 229.24, *fleysshe* 236.22, *abayssed* 238.2 (also, cp. *cleyghte* 198.15); *cruysshed* 203.6, *buysshemente* 243.2, *fruysshed* 208.16. In these cases, the poem has the simple vowel spelling. (*e*) Like the poem, Malory has usually *g* in such words as *gyff* 189.5, *gotyn* 193.26, *geffyn* 201.14, *gaff* 232.4, *gyff* 189.5, *geff* 202.16, *gatis* 243.6, but also sometimes uses (as does the poem) the native *y* which was common in standard English: *yatys* 227.28, *yeff* 188.24, etc. (*f*) Against standard final *v*, W often spells *ff*: *sauff* 205.4, *gyff* 190.25, *gaff* 232.4, *greffe* 235.7, *preff* 235.4, *droff* 239.24. This is a northern spelling and it also occurs in the poem, although not always in the places where W uses it. (*g*) Isolated spellings of northern type are these: *or* "ere," which is used several times; *hundretthis* 243.1 and *hunderthes* 196.9, *furth* 193.5, *fourmed* 202.18, *infourmede* 203.8, *whother* 229.11, *Yole* 232.4, *bowske* 206.11, *ony* 192.1, *thonke* 192.4. Except for *bowske, thonke, whother*, the same spellings occur in the poem.

III: *VOCABULARY*. The following groupings are concerned with northern words which Malory transferred directly from the poem or used

Appendix G

with different measures of independence from the poem. Characterization of the words as northernisms is based upon specific statements or the nature of the citations in the OED, MED, EDD, Kaiser's study, and the glossaries of Yorkshire dialect compiled by Robinson and Pease.

a) Simple Transferals. Thirty words, representing forty-one uses, are simply transferred from the poem, occurring at exactly the same points in the narrative and in the same contexts. AWKEWARD 230.10. BAYTE "to feed" 234.7, BAYTED 228.18. BEEKYS "warms" 202.10. BOWSKE "hasten, prepare" 206.11, BUSKED 243.6. CARLE "man" 202.19 (in 199.12 it replaces *kene*). CARPE "speak" 200.23, 215.12. CRAGGE "rock" 200.16, 205.17. DERE "brave" 242.10. EASE "edge of a wood" 228.21. FORREY "to pillage" 228.7. FREYKE "warrior" 199.9, 202.17, 236.23. GARTE "caused to" 216.32. GLOORED "stared" 202.26. HAPPE "fortune" 232.6. HAYLESED "greeted" 202.15. HOWGE "great" 205.11. KEN "to instruct" 199.11. LENDYS "loins" 202.10. UPPON LOFFTE "aloft" 200.6, ON LOFFTE 206.24. MAYSTIRMAN "hero" 200.14. RAYKED "went" 226.9. RANKE "strong" 223.5. RENCK "warrior" 216.30, 236.25 (latter spelled *raynke*). ROMED "lamented" 196.25. SWAPPYNG "striking" 210.19. SWARFFE "meadow" 203.15. THIRLED "pierced" 234.1. TYLL "to" 200.5. WARLOW, WERLOW "warlock" 200.24, 203.23 YON "yonder" 215.11.

Some explanation for Malory's confidence in transferring these words and integrating them into his own narrative may be found in the fact that nearly half of them are part of his own active vocabulary in the rest of his work (cp. App. B).

b) Possible Transferals. The following forty-five northern words, representing some sixty-nine uses, also occur in the poem. But they do not occur at the same points as Malory has them. Sometimes the placing differs by only a few lines, but often the placings in the poem and Malory are remote from one another. In an attempt to differentiate uses that may be independent of the poem, an asterisk has been placed before words which, judging by the glossary in the EETS edition of the poem, are separated by one hundred lines or more in the two versions. ANGIRFULL 202.15, replacing *hawtayne* (poem has *anger* and derivatives several times elsewhere). *BANKE 198.4, replacing *coste* (poem has *banke* at 728, 3715, 2732). *BESEKE 244.12, replacing *beseech* (*besekes* 127, 305). *BOWERLY "noble" 208.1, replacing *stelyn*; *BOURELYEST

Appendix G 211

214.33, BOURELY 240.29 (*burliche, burelyche* 304, 586, 730, 1002, 1111, 2010, 2190, 4200). BRAGGE "boast" 207.20 (*braggers* 1348). BRENTE "became hot" 239.20, BRENNYS 197.9 replacing *bryttened* (poem has *brynne, brynte* frequently elsewhere). *BRYM "fierce" 215.30, BRYMMYST 209.18 (*brymly* 117, 4215, *bremly* 4108, *breme* 1380). BUSKYS "hastens" 200.5, replacing *bounede* "prepared" (*buske*, etc. often used elsewhere in poem). *CARPYS "speaks" 190.7, replacing *meles* (poem has *carpe* and derived forms at 143, 220, 1929, 2126, 2750). CASTE "think, intend" 192.22, replacing *ettylle* "intend" (poem has *cast* in the same sense frequently elsewhere). CLEGGED "seized" 204.9, replacing *clekys*; CLEYGHTE 198.15, replacing *taken*; ICLEYGHT 204.6, 217.7 (poem has *clekes* also at 1164, 1865, 2123). *CLOWYS "steep valleys" 224.12, 204.10, latter replacing *clyffez* (poem has *cloughes* 941, *clewes* 1639, 2019). EASE "edge of wood" 228.21, poem *eynis* (also at 1283 in slightly different sense). *FELLE "hill, moor" 191.2, replacing *felde* (*felle* occurs in 2489, 2502). FLYNGIS "charges" 236.21, poem has *flyngande* 2758. *FREKE, FRAYKE "warrior" 235.22, 236.18 (*freke* 557, 742, 873, 973, 1364, 2898). *FRUYSSHED "dashed" 208.16, 214.33 (*ffruschene* 2805). *GAYNESTE "quickest" 239.9, 242.27 (poem has this word at 487, 1041, 3007). *GARTE "caused to" 225.2 (poem uses this word in *ger-* or *gar-*forms at 1780, 1886, 1946, 1975, 3641). *GRAME "grief, harm" 229.16 (poem uses the word in meaning "anger" at 1077, 3009). GREKYNGE "dawn" 228.19, replacing *grygynge*. *HALSE "neck" 239.18, replacing *swyre-bone* (*halse* 764, 1798, 4121). *HAPPYNS "befalls" 226.8 (poem *happene* 1269, *hapnede* 1154, 3305). *KYD(DE) "famous" 218.22, 223.11, 203.5 replacing *kene*, 214.30 (used in poem at 65, 96, 232, 1272, 1390, 1651, 3674). *LENDIS "remains" 243.15 (*lende* 1970). *LYGGE "to lie" 244.9 (poem has this form at 459, 805, 1060, 1184, 1773). *MARCHE "to border" 190.2 (poem has the verb at 77, 318, 631, 1232, 1588). MYKYLL "much" 205.3, 234.14, replacing *myche* (poem has *mekille* 711, 1236, 1314, 1382, although it uses *myche* more frequently). *RENCK, RAYNKE "warrior" 207.15 replacing *rebawde*, 219.1, 238.9 (poem has the word at 17, 147, 391, 1057, 1410, 1994, 2135). *RENSAKED "examined a wound" 224.25, 211.25 (poem has the word at 1884, 3939, 4304). *RYCHE "powerful" 213.27 (used in poem at 147, 108, 173, 833). *SHUNTE "move aside" 203.10 replacing *eschewes*, 213.31 replacing *shone* (poem has *schounte*

736). SYKERLY "surely, carefully" 199.17 replacing *in faythe*, 222.18 (*sekyrly* 439, 441, 969, 1420, 3499, etc.). SKYFFTED "divided" 205.15 replacing *delte* (poem has *schifte, skyfte* in various forms at 32, 725, 1213, 1325, 1561, 1651, 1717, 2456, 3848). *SONDISMEN "messengers" 212.27 (poem has word at 266, 1419). STALE "troop of armed men" 209.31, 237.21, 235.9 replacing *stede* (poem has the word in this sense and also as "place" 377, 1355, 1435, 1932, 1980). *STERNE "strong" 213.8, 215.31 (word occurs in poem at 157, 377, 3623, 3872). *STOURE "battle" 210.34 (poem has word at 1488, 1747, 2086). STRENDYS "streams" 199.16 (poem has *strandez, strondes* here and at 598, 883, 947, 1227, 1337, 3628, 4068); at 226.21, Malory gives *stremys* as a synonym substitute. *SWANGE 215.21 replacing *swapped* (poem has *swangene* 2146). SWAPPIS "strikes" 203.5, 203.12 replacing *jaggede* (poem has *swappez*, etc. 314, 1126, 1464, 1465, 1795, 4245). SOWGHE "rushing noise" 197.7 (*swoughe* 1127). *TENE "pain" 230.22, replacing *tourfere* (*tene* 1396, 1956). WELTRYNG "rolling about" 203.27 but only in C (poem has *welters* at 890, 1140, 1142, 2147).

(*c*) *Non-transferals*. The fact that Malory's uses of over half the words in the foregoing subsection are so far removed from the places where they occur in the poem makes it probable that they were part of his own vocabulary. This possibility is strengthened by the fact a considerable number of northern words in Malory's version do not appear in the poem at all. ANGURLY 203.13 replacing *ruydly*. BRAY "conflict" 227.26. CRAKED "spoke" 215.10 replacing *meles*. DYNDLED "resounded" 219.17 replacing *dynned fore dyn*. GLYSTRAND 229.3 replacing *gessenande*. YLLE "severely" 207.19. JOWKED "struck" 238.5. LUGERANDE "hanging loosely" 196.24 replacing *lutterde*. NEREHANDE "almost" 217.26. NOTE "business" 234.4 (nearest use in the poem is the verb *notez* 1815). OVERTHWARTE 223.17 replacing *awkwarde*. PURE, *the pure provoste* 217.2 in intensive sense common in northern verse. PYKYS "goes" 220.3. SYTTANDE 200.20 replacing *gretande* "lamenting": M's word could mean either "lamenting" or "sitting"; if it means the former, it is a rare northern word of ON origin. SQWATTE "crushed" 221.2 replacing *craschede*. THERETYLL "thereto" 243.18. THRUMBELYNG "in a heap" 224.14. TORONGELED "ragged?" 196.24. UMBELYCLOSED "surrounded" 215.31 replacing *umbelappez*. UNTYLL "unto" 220.27.

IV. *MALORY'S HANDLING OF THE VOCABULARY OF MORTE ARTHURE*. It is sometimes suggested that northern words in this section of Malory which do not appear in the poem are to be explained by Malory's using a text of the poem different from that which has survived in the Thornton MS. This explanation, usually applied to a few isolated words, does not face the large number of such words that is listed in this Appendix; and it therefore takes no account of the extensive textual differences that such a theory would entail if it were to account for the eighteen words (and more usages) listed above in subsection (c) and the still more numerous words in subsection (b) which occur in the poem only at points remote from those where Malory used them. To assume that these fifty or so forms were in the text of the poem that Malory used would usually entail altering the alliterative patterns of the lines in which the words occurred, and therefore changing the phrasing not only of those lines but of contiguous lines too. Since the poem as we have it usually reads satisfactorily in these places, a consistent application of this explanation would necessitate postulating a text which differed frequently and extensively from the Thornton text, but apparently without any recognizable reason in meaning or poetics.

A simpler explanation is that the differences are Malory's doing. This explanation may be supported by the fact that elsewhere in his work—when he is working from French sources—Malory used a good many of these words, e.g., *banke, beseke, brente, brym, felle, flyngis, garte, gayneste, happyns, ylle, lygge, march, nerehande, overthwarte, pyke, rensaked, skyfte, tene, theretyll, unbecaste*. It is also supported by the numerous northern grammatical forms and spellings that Malory added in the prosing of this poem, even though it is generally written in standardized language. These forms and spellings certainly necessitate no theory that Malory used a different text of the poem. Taken together with the northernisms in grammar, spelling, and vocabulary that are scattered throughout the rest of Malory's work, they indicate almost certainly that Malory's northernisms in the whole of his work—those which he transferred from the poem and those that he used additionally in the Roman war section and elsewhere—are best explained by his being very well versed in the language of northern dialect and northern alliterative verse. That they are more numerous in this section is readily explained by the stimulus of his northern source.

A more precise estimate of Malory's grasp of the difficult northern

Appendix G

dialect and alliterative diction of *Morte Arthure* may be based upon his dealing with individual words and usages in the poem. Unfortunately, it is impossible to make a complete and exact analysis. Malory's version is not a literal translation: he paraphrased as well as abbreviated, and many of his verbal changes may have been determined by his own literary objectives rather than by any intent to restate the poem exactly. Verbal equivalences between his prose version and the poem are therefore limited. The following list provides an accounting of those usages which may be regarded as translation. The capitalized words are those in the poem; the lower-case equivalents are Malory's. The asterisks distinguish words which seem to have been poetical, obsolescent, or dialectal in Malory's time.

*ABOWNE "above" 3072, *abovyn* 243.6. ALFYNE "bishop in chess" 1343, *elffe* 207.20. *ANLACE 1148, *a shorte dagger* 2041. ASKRYEDE "shouted" 2773, *had grete care* 236.16. *AWKWARDE 2247, *overthwarte* 223.17. *AYERE "go" 455, *ryde* 191.3.
*BALE "sorrow" 1054, *sorow* 202.15. BALEFULLE 1029, *fayre* 202.1. BALE FYRE "signal" 1048, *bryght fyre* 202.11. *BEDGATT "going to bed" 1030, *go to his bed* 202.16. BELYFE "quickly" 1263, *blythe* 206.12. *BYERNS "warriors" 1391, 2785, 2656, *felowys* 209.4, *barowne* 236.25, *kyngez* 233.5. *BIRDEZ "girls" 1029, 1136, *maydens* 202.1, 203.21. *BLONKES "horses" 615, 895, 2518, 2672, *horsys* 194.4, 196.2, 199.24, 228.22, 233.20. *BLYSCHIT "glanced" 116, *loked up* 185.12. *BOWES "goes" 2310, *were brought* 225.15. *BOWNEZ "goes to ground" 1136, *kneled* 203.22. BOURDEZ "jests" 1170, *lough* 204.16. *BRAYEDEZ "drives" 3126, *rode unto* 243.3. *BREDE "roast meat" 1052, 2716, *birdis* 202.13, *byrdys* 234.23. *BRENES "cuirasses" 1413, *helmys* 209.14 (cp. *buskede in brenyes* 2517), *armed* 228.20. BRYNNEZ "burns" 1241, *destroyed* 206.2. *BRYTTENYD, BRITTENES "destroy(s)" 802, 823, 1067, 1242, *rentyth* 197.9, *slowe* 197.21, *mourtheryng* 202.21, *made grete slaughtir* 206.2. *BROTHELY "fiercely" 1408, *on bothe sydys* 209.11. BRUSTENE "break" 2772, BRISTE 2808, *brake* 236.15, 237.8. *BUS "behoves" 2576, *bade hym* 230.14. *BUSKES "goes, hurries" 1223, 1378, 2068, *remevyth* 205.19, *turned to* 208.18, *gyrde thorowoute* 220.9. BUSTOUS "rough" 775, *grymly* 196.22.
*CAYRE, CAYERS, KAYRES, KAIRE 1272, 480, 1707, 1319, *remeve oute* 206.15, *rode* 213.27, *passed* 191.10, *ryde* 207.11. *CAREMANE "carl" 957, *knyght* 200.23. *CHARE "carry" 1886, *sende* 216.32. CHERE 2965, *mode* 239.22. *"CHESES a way to" 2954,

chasis to 239.14. *CLEKYS OWTTE 2123, *toke oute* 221.7. *CLOUGHES "cliffs" 941, *creste* 200.16. COWNTERE "accountant" 1672, *cowarde* 213.17. *COWPEZ "strikes" 2059, *smote* 220.6. DALE 2031, *vale* 219.16. *DERFE "strong man" 2971, *deuke* 239.24. DYGHTE, DYGHTTES 2626, 3045, 3066, *dresse(d)* 232.3, 241.14, 242.9. *DRAGONE ON DREGHE "aside" 786, *dredfull dragon* 197.1.
*ELDES 301, *ayges* 189.2. EME "uncle" 1347, *cosyn* 207.23. *ENGLAYMEZ "makes slimy" 1131, *foule begone* 203.18. *ENKERLYE "eagerly" 2066, *boldely* 220.9. ENNELLED "enamelled" 1294, *displayed* 206.24. ESCHEWE(S), ESCHEWEDE 1116, 1750, 1881, *shuntys* "avoids" 203.10, "recover" 214.30, *recovirde* 216.29. *ETTELLES, ETTYLLE "intends" 520, 554, *thynkys* 192.9, *caste* "intend" 192.22.
*FANGEZ "takes" 1005, *had he none* 201.20. FARES 788, *come* 197.2. FARLANDE "foreland" 1188, *montayn* 204.24. *FEEMENE "vassals?" 2488, *foomen* 228.6. FELE 2783, *many* 236.23. FERE "terror" 2735, *faare* "behavior" 235.13. FERES "companions" 1884, *noble knyghtes* 215.32. *FERKE "go" 1037, 1188, 2501, *fare* 202.6, *go up to* 204.24, *forth yode* 228.14. *O FERROME "afar" 934, *none nyghe* 200.13. *FEY LEVYDE "dead" 1070, *slayne* 202.23. *FILSNEZ "lurks" 881, *shalte thou fynde* 199.15. FIRTHE "wood" 1708, *woodis* 213.29. *FLAYRE "scent" 772, *flame of fyre* 196.19. *FLENGES "goes" 2763, *flyttys* 236.11. *FFLERYANDE "scoffing" 2779, *eregned* "heretical" 236.20. FOLE "foal" 449, *horsis* 190.27. *FOR-SETT 2012, *besette* 219.10. *FOWNDES "goes" 3113, *passed* 242.25. (also FOONDE 2489, *go* 228.7). *FORCYERE "stronger" 1176, *ferser* "fiercer" 205.5. *FRAYNEZ "asks" 954, *asked* 200.22. *FRAYSTEZ A FURTH "seeks a way" 1227, *shooke over* 205.20. *FREKE "warrior" 1364, *knyght* 208.9. FREKE "bold" 1174, *freysh* 205.2. *FREKLY "boldly" 1360, *faste* 208.6. FRETTE "rubbed" 2708, *putt* 234.15. *FULSOMESTE "foulest" 1061, *fowlyste* 202.17.
*GADLYNGES 2855, *boyes* 238.2. GARRETT "tower" 3104, *Gareth* 242.22. *GERTE "caused to" 1780, *commaunded* 215.8. *GESSENANDE (meaning uncertain, possibly "jessant" or "glistening") 2521, *glystrand* 229.3. GYRDES "goes" 2527, *rode* 229.5. *GLADE "glided" 2973, *droff* (of a spear) 239.24. *GLAVERANDE "foolish" 2538, *proudly* 229.14. *GLYFTES ON "looks at"

2525, *was ware of* 229.4. *GLOPNEDE, GLOPYNE, GLOPPYNS "lament" 1074, 2580, 2854, *grevid* 202.26, *feare* 230.20, *greve* 238.1. *GOME "man" 1209, 2525, 2562, *man* 205.14, *knyght* 229.5, 230.8. *GRAYTHE "prepare, go" 1279, 1384, 2124, *dressed* 206.19, *gyrdis* 208.12, *gurdys towarde* 221.8. *GREFES "groves" 2882, *grevys* 238.10. *GRETES "weeps," GRETANDE 2963, 951, *wepte* 239.19, *syttande* (meaning either "grieving" or "sitting") 200.20. GREYHONDES 2521, *gryffons* 229.3. *GUYTE "young man" 2964, *Gotelake* 239.21.

*HALLE "whole" 2709, *hole* 234.16. HAPPENEDE 2365, *happed* 226.17. *HARAGEOUS "cruel" 2448, *noble* 227.23. *HENDE "gracious one" 2631, *lyege lorde* 232.6. HENTEZ "catches" 1132, *caughte* 203.19. HERTELYCHE 2551, *hatefull* 229.23. HOSTES 2889, *boste* 238.15. HOWGE 2890, *myghty* 238.16. *HULKE "crude fellow" 1058, *hym* 202.15.

*ILKE A ȜERE 3145, *yerly* 243.26 (C only). *JAGGEDE "chopped" 1123, *swappis* 203.12. JOURNEE "battle" 825, *to fyght* 197.22. KALENDEZ 2371, *moneth* 226.20. *KENE "inform" 2620, *telle* 231.22. *KENE "bold man" 876, *carle* 199.12. *KNAWE 2637, *telle* 232.11. KYNGRYKEZ 820, 1272, *kyngdomes* 197.18, *londys* 206.16. KYRNELLES "crenelations" 3047, *kyrtyls* 241.16.

*LACHENE "catch" 2541, *handylde* 229.17, LAUGHE 2999, *lyffte* 225.2, *takyn* 240.10. *LATES "features" 2536, *lokys* 229.13. LAUNDE (for *launge?*) 2531, *langage* 229.9. LAYE "law" 2594, *lorde or legeaunte* 231.8. *LECHENE "heal" 2388, *laughte* "caught" 227.5. *LEDE "man" 854, 1820, *lyff* 198.18, *good man* 215.33. *LELE "loyal" 2999, *noble* 240.10. *LENGE, LENGES "remains, dwells" 152, 469, 3058, *abyde* 186.18, 191.1, *lay* 242.20, *lygge* 244.9. *LYGGES "lies" 1060, *syttes* 202.17. *LYKANDE "pleasing" 2406, *ryche* 227.7. *LUTTERDE LEGGES 779, *lugerande lokys* 196.24.

*MAKKE "fellow" 1166, *makyng* "fashion" 204.13. MEES "Metz" 2951, *Moyses-londe* 239.11. *MELLE, MELE(S) "speaks" 382, 938, 1781, 3109, *carpys* 190.7, *speke* 200.14, *craked* "spoke" 215.10, *spekyth* 242.23. MELLES "smites" 2951, *smytyth* 239.11. MYCHE 2708, *mykyll* 234.14.

ONE "alone" 937, 1044, *alone* 200.14, 202.9. OUNDYDE "wavy" 765, *enamyled* 196.15. PAYES "pleases" 2647, *pleased* 232.19. PLATTES 2478, *plantys* 228.1. POYNE HIS PAVELYOUNS

2625, *poynte all the paltokkys* 232.2. *PREKER "horseman" 1374, *bolde barowne* 208.14. PRYSE "fame" 2650, *loose "praise"* 232.22.
*RAREDE "roared" 1124, *brayed* 203.13. *RAYKEZ "goes" 889, 2920, *turnys towarde* 199.21, *folowed* 238.25. REONE "Rouen" 424, *Rome* 190.18. RYDE UTTERE 2438, *fle* 227.19. RYALLE STEDE 2792, *rede stede* 236.28. *RYCHE 2518, 2527, *stronge* 228.22, 229.6. *ROMYEZ "laments" 888, *seyde* 199.19. ROWME "roomy" 432, *Roome "Rome"* 190.22.
SADE "full" 847, *cesid "done"* 198.13. *SALLE IDENE 3062 (meaning uncertain), *shall have lyvelode* 242.2 (M. may have read as "dine"). SALL SOFTENE 2692, *woll hele* 234.3. SALE "hall" 134, *halle* 186.2. SAUGHTE "security" 1007, *savyng* 201.22. *SCHAFTMONDE 2546, *the brede of an honde* 229.20. SCHANKEZ 1104, *leggis* 203.3. SCHREDE 2689, *shorne* 234.2. *SEKE "go" 1336, *ryde* 207.16 (also SOUGHTE 1977, *dressid* 218.21). *SKYFTES "shifts" 3118, *skyrmysshed wyth* 243.1. *SKOVEROURS "scouts" 3118, *foreryders* 243.1. SOPPE "troop" 2819, *small parte* of thy men 237.15. SOTTE "fool" 1060, *theeff* 202.16. *SOWRE OF THE REKE "source of the smoke?" 1041, *creste of the hylle* 202.8. SPRENTE "sprang" 2062, *braste* 220.7. STAKE 1178, *sette hit on a trouncheoune* 204.18. STEDE 1748, *stale "place"* 214.28. *STYGHTYLLE "arrange" 157, *seteled and served* 187.7. STOKES 2554, *stabbis* 229.23. *STOTAIS "falters" 1435, *stoode* 209.31. *STRANDEZ "rivers" 883, 947, 1227, 2373, *strendys* 199.16, *stremys* 200.18, 205.21, 226.21. *STREKEZ "pitches tent" 1229, *pyght* 205.22. SUPPOWELLE "support" 2819, *succoure* 237.15. *SWANGE "loins" 1129, *baly* 203.17. SWAPPES, SWAPPEDE OWTTE, 2982, 2959, 1795, *smyttyth* 239.32, *smote* 239.18, *swange oute* 215.21. SWEFNYNGE "dreaming" 759, *slumberyng* 196.12. *SWYRE-BANE "neck bone" 2960, *halse "neck"* 239.18. SYNE "after" 1182, *aftir* 204.21. *SYTE "sorrow" 1305, *sorow* 207.7. SYTHIS "times" 2216, *tymes* 222.26.
TACHESESEDE "spotted" 821, *to-tatered* 197.19. TAKLE 2444, *toolys* 227.20. *TALMES "falters" 2581, *tame* 230.21. *TASE A SOPE "takes a sup" 1890, *dranke* 217.4. *TENES "sorrows" 264, *grevyth* 188.3. *THIRLLEZ "pierces" 2167, *bare hym thorow* 221.30. THOFE "though" 2645, *if* 232.16. *THREPIDE "fought" 2216, *russhed* 222.25. *TILTINE "topple" 1144, *rolled doune* 203.28.

*TYTTE "quickly" 1891, 2583, *in a brayde* "rush" 217.5, *in haste* 230.22. *TORFERE "harm" 2582, *tene* "harm" 230.22. *TRAISE "goes" 1629, *turned* 212.25.

*UMBECLAPPES 1779, *toke hym in his armys* 215.8. *UNBELAPPEZ 1819, *umbelyclosed* 215.31. *UNSAUGHTLY "violently" 1847, *sore* 216.10. UNSENE "unseen" 3114, *cite of Virvyn* 242.26. UNWYNLY "unpleasantly" 1303, *with hawte wordys* 207.6. VERTONNONE VALE 3170, *vertuouse vale* 244.9. VOUTE "face" 137, *face* 186.5.

*WAFULLE 955, *carefulle* 200.23. WANDYRS 798, *wyndis* 197.6. WARPE OF 901, *caste on* 200.3. *OR THE WATHE "harm" 2669, *over a water* 233.17. WEPEDE 1920, *with a keuercheff wyped his iyen* 217.24. *WEYNDE(Z) "goes" 450, 2493, *go* 190.27, 228.8. *WYDERWYNE "adversary" 2045, *Lucyus* 220.1. WILLNEZ "desires" 2224, *sekyst* 222.31. *WITH BIRENNE (apparently copyist's error) 2519, *withoute* 229.1. *WONE "dwelling" 1300, 2472, *tente* 207.1, *cite* 227.28. *WOROWS "kills" 958, *destroy* 200.24. *WYE "man" 2515, 2670, 2657, *man* 228.20, 233.5, *knyght* 233.18.

*ƷEMES "protects" 938, 1069, *kepys* 200.14, *owyth* 202.22. ƷERNES 1032, *askys* 202.3.

In the texture of his own narrative, the greatest part of Malory's substitutes in these pairs are thoroughly appropriate in representing the meanings in the poem. A fair proportion, however, are different enough as to raise questions about the way he read the poem or the measure of his understanding of particular words. The following paragraphs deal with representative items in these classes.

Some words which Malory represents by words different in meaning were so familiar in the general usage of his time that his substitutions must have been quite deliberate, prompted by his own narrative intentions. Among these are his substitutions for *balefulle* (fayre), *cowntere* (cowarde), *dale* (vale), *enelled* (displayed), *frette* (putt), *grayhondes* (gryffons), *pavelyouns* (paltokkys), *oundyde* (enamyled), *ryalle* (rede), and *sotte* (theeff). The same explanation must also apply to those words which, although they were not so widely used in his time, were part of his own active vocabulary elsewhere in *Le Morte Darthur*; among these may be cited: *bustous* (grymly), *cloughes* (creste), *eme* (cosyn), *lygges* (syttes), *skyftes* (skyrmysshed). In a few cases, it is possible to guess at his motive for such a change. Since *garrett*, "tower," was a commonplace word, the substitution of *Gareth* may have been prompted by the fact that Gareth was to be a major hero in later sections of Malory's book. That he replaces *flayre*, "scent," by *flame* may be a detail in his emphasis of the firedrake characteristics of the dragon of Arthur's dream. Some substitutions —such as Malory's *birdis* (poem, *brede*), *poynte* (poem, *poyne* "place"), *faare* "behavior" (poem, *fere*), *stoode* (poem, *stotais* "falters")—may result from his fondness for a simple word of similar sound, even if its meaning were only approximately the same.

Examples such as these show how hazardous it is to label any of Malory's variants as simple errors. Some, however, might be thought to be misreadings—e.g., *forcyere* (M, *ferser*), *feemene* (M, *foomen*), *hostes* (M, *boste*), *Mees* (M, *Moyseslande*), *Reone* (M, *Rome*), *sere* (M, *sore*)—where mistaking of two similarly written letters might have led to confusion. A different punctuation from that of the modern editor could explain his substituting *makyng* for *makke*. Three changes: *glystrand* for *gessenande*, *langage* for *launde*, *withoute* for *with birenne*—may show him correcting or rationalizing imperfect readings in his copy of the poem, if that copy were the Thornton MS or one that had the same errors.

Several variants: *blythe* (poem, *belyfe* "quickly"), *chasis* (poem, *cheses* "goes"), *faare* "to-do" (poem, *fere*), *kyrtyls* (poem, *kyrnelles*), *laughte* (poem, *lechene*), *plantys* (poem, *plattes*), *tame* (poem, *talmes*), *Virvyn* (poem, *unsene*), *vertuouse* (poem, *Vertonnone*)—may have resulted from rapid and careless reading. But they may also be deliberate changes; for, except for *gessenande* and *talmes*, there seems no reason at all why Malory should not have understood these words. That he worked rapidly and sometimes carelessly, is shown by many obvious and simple errors in French words which normally he translated with assurance. The same explanation might also hold for his substituting *water* for *wathe*, *hatefull* for *hertelyche*, and *freysh* for *freke* "bold": he may simply have misread these words as "wather," "hetelich," "frick"—all of which he uses elsewhere in his work.

A few of Malory's substitutions might be thought to show only approximate understanding, e.g., *bryght fyre* (poem, *bale-fyre*), *bade hym* (poem, *bus* "behoves"), *helmys* (poem, *brenes* "corslets"), *foule begone* (poem, *englaymez* "makes slimy"), *eregned* "heretical?" (poem, *fflery-ande* "scoffing"), *proudly* (poem, *glaverande* "foolish"), *lyege lorde* (poem, *hende* "gracious person"). But the misunderstanding is far from certain; the substitutes are within the same areas of meaning, and they may simply represent Malory's stylistic preference and the range of substitutes that occurred to him at these times.

In notes and articles devoted to this aspect of Malory's work, various scholars have combined to declare a dozen or so of Malory's substitutions to be outright errors: his *elffe* for *alfyne* "the bishop in chess," *birdis* "maidens" for *brede* "roast meat," *on bothe sydys* for *brothely* "fiercely," *brennys* "burns" for *bryttenyd* "destroyed," *dredfull* for *on dreghe* "aside," *had he none* for *fangez* "seizes," *syttande* for *gretande* "lamenting," *stoode* for *stotatis*, *creste of the hill* for *sowre of the reke*, *seteled* for *styghtylle* "arrange," *noble* for *haragous* "violent," *Gotelake* for *guyte* "young person," *lugerande lokys* "straggling hair?" for *lutterde legges* "bent legs?"

In most of these cases, Malory's substitutes are certainly remote in meaning, and this might be explained by his understandable ignorance of some very rare words. On the other hand, it is not at all certain that all these substitutions are errors resulting from incomprehension. His *elffe* achieved the same mockery as *alfyne*, and does so with a word of similar sound and much greater familiarity; moreover, the poem's chess term is not a word that a gentleman of his standing would have found strange. His *dredfull*, when read in the full context of his statement and the poem's, appears not to be a substitution for *on dreghe*, but an addition to it. That his *brennys* for *bryttenyd* is not the result of ignorance is proved quite certainly by the fact that on three occasions elsewhere in this section he made thoroughly competent substitutions for this same word. And in any case, it seems most probable in this instance that his substitution is actually *renteth* "rends," a very competent translation. The meaning of *styghtylle* is actually represented in Malory's complete and alliterative phrase, *seteled and served*, which he devised to represent two lines in the poem. And the substitution of *syttande* for *gretande* may be no error at all: elsewhere in this section, Malory correctly translates the very rare northern word *syte* as *sorow*, so it is reasonable to believe that in using *syttande* for *gretande*, "grieving," he meant exactly the same thing as the word he replaced.

This apologia for Malory's variants does not cover all examples, but it applies to almost all. Malory worked so freely and confidently in making his own version from the poem, that it is risky to indict him with ignorance in particular instances. In view of the difficulty of the language of the alliterative poem—some of its words are seldom encountered even in other northern alliterative verse—it is possible that Malory did not grasp the

Appendix G

meaning of quite a number of its words. Some he may therefore have avoided altogether, some he may have represented only approximately, or even incorrectly.

Against this, however, is the positive evidence in these pairings of the degree of Malory's grasp of the northern and alliterative vocabulary of his source. It is dubious indeed that anyone who was tackling alliterative and northern verse for the first time, anyone who was unfamiliar with northern dialect, would have dealt so competently—and often in northern fashion—with such unusual words as these, for example: poem's *bedgatt* (Malory's *go to his bed*), *birdez* (*maydens*), *blonkes* (*horsys*), *cowpez* (*strikes*), *caremane* (*knyght*), *eldes* (*ayges*), *enkerlye* (*boldely*), *ettelles* (*thynks, caste*), *fey levyde* (*slayne*), *fraynez* (*asked*), *freke* (*knyght*), *gretes* (*wepte*), *jaggede* (*swappis*), *glopyne* (*grevid*), *gerte* (*commaunded*), *glyftes on* (*was ware of*), *gome* (*knyght*), *lates* (*lokys*), *lede* (*good man*), *lenge* (*abyde*), *mele* (*carpys, craked*), *ryche* (*stronge*), *romyez* (*seyde*), *saughte* (*savyng*), *sprente* (*braste*), *strandez* (*stremys*), *strekez* (*pyght*), *swange* (*baly*), *swappes* (*smote*), *syte* (*sorow*), *tiltine* (*rolled doune*), *thirllez* (*bare thorow*), *tytte* (*in haste*), *torfere* (*tene*), *unbelappez* (*umbelyclosed*), *wye* (*man*), *worows* (*destroy*), *zemes* (*kepys*). Nor does it seem likely that a tyro would show such command as Malory had of the rich alliterative vocabulary relating to movement: *ayere, bow, brayde, buske, ferke, flenge, founde, graithe, gurde, rayke, seek, traise, weynd,* and so on. Usually he replaced these words by *go, ride, pass, turn*; but sometimes—and this is also true of his substitutions for other words—he replaced a poetical or a dialect word with another word that was part of the vocabulary of northern and alliterative verse.

Detailed analysis indicates, therefore, that despite the approximateness of some of Malory's substitutions, despite the possibility of misunderstanding in some instances, Malory's command of the difficult vocabulary of the alliterative *Morte Arthure* was remarkably competent. This conclusion is sustained by, and also probably explained by, the evidence elsewhere in his book that he was familiar with northern dialect and with alliterative poems other than this one.

APPENDIX H
Alliteration in Le Morte Darthur

The following alliterative phrases occur elsewhere than in Book V, in sections where Malory was translating from French. Some of the phrases occur frequently, but it has been felt that one citation will be enough here. Phrases like *wit ye well, swange oute a swerde, wax woode, sounde and sauff*, or *smote sore*, which may be merely colloquial, proverbial, or happenstance, have been omitted. Phrases which are cited by Oakden as characteristic of alliterative verse are marked with asterisks. The alliterations are spread throughout Malory's work, but they are especially frequent in *Gareth, Lancelot, Urry*, and the *Death of Arthur*.

Anger and unhapp(e) 1161.7; *bare in a beere* 909.9; *I may beare well the blame for my bak is brode inowghe* 757.28; *as beste tylle a bay* 1216.6; *blacker than ony bere* 910.5; *blacker than a byry* 962.28; *that blast, said Balyn, is blowen for me* 88.20; *blossom and burgyne* 1119.5; **blowe such a boste* 312.4; *brym as ony boore* 1193.6; **brochys and bees* 1238.2; *the brachet ever boote hym by the buttocke* 102.27.

Cowrith within a castell 839.34; *crakynge and cryinge* 865.17; **daysshed down starke dede* 1237.22; *delyverly devoyded* 1219.32; *depe draughtys of deth* 372.7; *dryed and dwyned awaye* 1257.3; **droupe and dare* 1212.5; **endelonge and overtwarte* 784.13 (and 808 only in Caxton); *as faste as ever he myght flynge* 813.25; **fayre faryn wythall* 819.30; *flow into the felde* 29.35; **flowryth and floryshyth* 1119.22.

*Gyff me my gyffte 112.23; **grene os ony grasse* 990.35; *grenned and gnasted* 280.11; **greselyest grone* 807.29; **hale and how* 320.29;

223

hyghe in haste 127.9; *hylde downe her hede* 756.18; *holtis hore 1241.5; **huntyth and hawkyth* 839.33; *hurteled there horsys* 746.10; *layne hit no lenger* 1162.20; *his learys and hys earys* 501.34; **ley the as low as thou laydest me* 1219.13; *lycoures lustis 1120.4; *lykynge and luste* 810.9; *lope a grete lepe* 102.29; *lyghtly lepe up and leffte* 753.17.

Morys and mares and many wylde wayes 284.16; **naked as a nedyll* 792.14; *ovirtwarte and endelonge* 718.36; *pycked her away pryvayly* 557.35; *renne over and rosshed* 686.15; *me repentis of youre recoverynge* 502.32; *many sad strokis* 1217.18; *sanke downe and sowned* 1220.29; *salved them with soffte salvys* 1232.29; *sealed with their synattes* 1134.4; **senshyp and shame* 843.9; *serched and salved hym wyth souftte oynementis* 1218.10; *sette at a sydebourde* 301.24; *she shryked shirly* 1090.8; *shrede hem downe as shepe* 1211.27; *syke for sorow 1218.22; *syke and unsounde* 1218.28; *synne and shame 1239.20; **smote with spearis* 659.18; **their spearys all to-shevirde* 656.21; **by styghe and by strete* (Caxton) 353.20; **stynte youre stryff* 1162.22; *strayned hymselff so straytly* 1086.1; *styke as a swyne* 301.21; *thorow the thyckyst pres he thryled thorow* 465.12; *led him tylle hys tente* 1058.7; *tyed hys horse tyll a tre* 776.28; **from toppe to too* 1256.19; *traced and traverced* 1217.15; *trasynge and traversynge* 843.28; *trade on a trappe* 1134.33; *dole tray and tene* 86.6; *traytour and untrew* 1239.27.

The waytis uppon the wallys 352.29; *ware and wyse 1211.23; *warly wallys* 320.25; *warre and wrake 1162.4; *watirs wap and wawys wanne* 1239.25; *wawis and wyndys 1239.14; *much weale and much worshyp* 1169.25; *wente his way 1221.8 (Caxton); *wepte and wayled 1241.3; **wepte as she had been wood* 1086.13; **weale and worshyp* 1169.25; *as wyȝte as ever was Wade* 308.18 (Caxton); *I will wynne worshyp worshypfully* 321.6; **whyle that I wynne worshyp* 311.5; **wynne no worship at thes wallis* 1218.13; *wynde and wedir 810.9; **the woo with the weale* 1171.22; **the worshyp I wanne* 770.32; **worshyp of the worlde* 311.8; *my wretthe I wrekid* 312:37; *wrythed and waltred as a madde woman* 805.9.

These alliterating phrases and lines indicate that Malory was fond of alliterative rhythms and familiar with some of the patterns used in northern alliterative verse. Sometimes he used them almost as a refrain: *tied his horse till a tree*, and *win worship in the world* are his favorites.

This mannerism is important in relation to understanding his procedures in Book V, where he was prosing the alliterative *Morte Arthure*. It is also important in judging what text of that poem he may have used.

The Thornton text of the poem, the only medieval copy that has survived, is far from perfect; names often appear in strange form and there are places where the meaning is obscure. These details are not likely to be due to carelessness on Thornton's part; no such objections are raised to the many other texts that he copied.

Although the poem of itself is sometimes obscure, it is doubtful that its obscurities would have led to the latter theories had it not been for Malory's prosing. They were mostly evoked by the discovery of the Winchester manuscript of Malory's book. The Caxton text of Book V is so far rewritten as not to prompt any theory beyond that it is probable that Malory worked from the poem. The Winchester text, twice as long as Caxton and very much closer to the poem in its language, converted this probability into certainty. But the many details in which it differs from the poem—in vocabulary, grammar, alliteration, even in subject matter—led some scholars to conjecture that Malory's variants were derived from a correcter text of the poem, or even that he used a variant text in which there existed the differences of subject matter and structure which appear in his prosing. The corrollary to that belief is that the Thornton text is so corrupt that it may confidently be emended in accordance with Malory's version.

What has not been adequately considered, however, is the possibility that Malory could have used the Thornton text or one very similar to it and that his divergencies are of his own doing. Nor has any complete comparison been published between the Thornton text and his prose version. Before any theory is adopted about any other form of the poem, before any emendation is proposed for either Thornton or Malory, it is essential to examine as a whole the correspondences and differences between them. In Appendix E, the grammar, spelling, and vocabulary of these two texts were compared. The conclusion that resulted was that while the Winchester text standardizes the language, it retains many of the northernisms of Thornton and adds a good many northern usages besides. In the present Appendix, a similar analysis is made of the alliteration in the two texts.

Malory's version has nothing corresponding to the last and tragic quarter of the poem; instead, it has a brief triumphant ending, which is nowhere suggested in the Thornton poem, and is indeed aesthetically alien to the poem's tragic design. The rest is reduced to about half the length, partly summarized in Malory's own words, partly abbreviated by linking and adapting ruling phrases from the poem. In the latter process, Malory took over many alliterating phrases, and sometimes he transferred complete alliterative lines, some of them scarcely changed, others altered in varying degrees. Not infrequently, Malory also used alliterative phrases or lines which do not appear in the poem. The following lists show the various degrees of relationship and provide a pretty complete coverage.

Instances of Malory's taking over a line without any change except those demanded by prose syntax are so numerous that a few examples will suffice. Here and in the following lists, Malory's reading is given in the left column and the poem's in the right:

into the vale of Vyterbe, and there to vytayle my knyghtes 189.28	In the Vale of Viterbe vetaile my knyghttes 353
by the rever of Rome hold my Rounde Table 190.18	By the reyuere of Reone halde my Rounde Table 424
than ever had Arthure or ony of his elders 201.23	Thane euere aughte Arthure or any of hys elders 1016
where lay many lordys lenyng on there shyldys 233.20	Lordes lenande lowe on lemand scheldys 2672

Almost as numerous are the instances of Malory's taking over a line from the poem but replacing one or more of its dialectal or unusual words with familiar words that retain the alliteration:

1. and syth ryde unto Roome with my royallyst knyghtes 190.22	Ryde all thas rowme landes with ryotous knyghttes 432
2. an hydeouse flame of fyre there flowe oute of his mowth 196.16	And sych a vennymous flayre flowe fro his lyppez 772
3. Than the dredfull dragon dressyd hym ayenste hym 197.1	Thane the dragone on dreghe dressede hym aȝaynez 786
4. as she rode by a ryver with her ryche knyghtes 198.16	Beside Reynes as scho rade with hire ryche knyghttes 853

Appendix H

5. Many folkys folowed hym, mo than fyve hondird 198.19

   We folowede o ferrome moo thene fyfe hundrethe 856

6. woldist thow ken me where that carle dwellys 199.11

   Bot walde thow kene to the crage thare that kene lengez 876

7. to Seynte Mychaels Mounte where mervayles ar shewed 200.2

   In seynt Mighelle mount, there myraclez are schewede 899

8. they sente hym in faythe for savynge of their peple 201.21

   They send it hym sothely for saughte of the pople 1007

9. Than fare thou to yondir fyre that flamys so hyghe 202.6

   Ferke fast to the fyre, quod cho, that flawmez so hye 1037

10. For thou art the fowlyste freyke that ever was fourmed 202.17

    For the fulsomeste freke that fourmede was euere 1061

11. Than the gloton gloored and grevid full foule 202.26

    Thane glopnede the glotone and glorede vnfaire 1074

12. Than he swappis at the kynge with that kyd wepyn 203.18

    He walde hafe kyllede the kynge with his kene wapene 1106

13. the grasse and the grounde all foule was begone 203.18

    That alle englaymez the gresse one grounde ther he standez 1131

14. othir ellys shunte for shame, chose whether ye lykys 213.31

    Whedyre we schone or schewe, schyft as the lykes 1717

15. stondys in your stale and sterte ye no ferther 214.28

    Standez here in this stede and stirrez no forthire 1748

16. and gurdys towarde Galapas that grevid hym moste 221.8

    Graythes hyme to Golapas that greuyde moste 2124

17. in the contrey of Constantyne by the clere stremys 226.21

    One the coste of Costantyne by the clere strandez 2373

18. of golde glystrand three gryffons in sabyll 229.3 — He bare gessenande in golde thre grayhondes of sable 2521
19. thou gryppe to the thy gere or more grame falle 229.15 — Bot if thowe graythe thy gere, the wille grefe happene 2539
20. Than groned the knyght for his grymme woundis 230.8 — Thane granes the gome fore greefe of his wondys 2562
21. Bade hym bynde up his wounde or thy ble chonge 230.14 — Us bus haue a blode-bande, or thi ble change 2576
22. Thow trowyste with thy talkynge to tame my herte 230.21 — Thow trowes with thy talkynge that my harte talmes 2581
23. swyfftly with his swerde he smyttyth hym thorow 239.32 — And with a swerde swiftly he swappes hym thorowe 2981
24. and so goth in by Godarte that Gareth sonne wynnys 242.22 — Gosse in by Goddarde, the garett he wynnys 3104

None of Malory's variations casts serious doubt on any of the readings in the Thornton text: even *gessenande* (18) may be simply a careless error for the heraldic term "jessant," which Malory rationalized as *glessenande*. Some variants might be characterized either as Malory's misunderstandings of a rare or dialectal word or as deliberate substitutions prompted by his wish to use a more familiar word with approximately the same sound (3, 4, 5, 8, 13, 18, 23). The change of *garett* to *Gareth*, which Vinaver took to be an error, is likely to be deliberate: there was nothing strange about *garett* "keep, tower," and in Book V one of Malory's devices is obviously to introduce or to emphasize knights who are to be important in his later books.

The feeling for the rhythmic and letter-rhyming demands of an alliterative line, the general understanding of the difficult vocabulary, and the ease in making a simple prose adaptation which are displayed in these passages are even more striking when Malory took elements from two lines of the poem and combined them into one shorter alliterating phrase, as in:

Appendix H

1. bare hym thorow the brode shylde and the brode of his breste 208.18

   With a bustous launce he berez hyme thurghe
   That the breme and the brade schelde appone the bente lyggez 1379-80

2. there commaunded knyghtes to kepe well the corse 215.8

   Vmbeclappes the cors, and kyssez hym ofte
   Gerte kepe hym couerte with his clere knyghttez 1779-80

3. Than they lette brayde of hir basnettys and hir brode shyldys 234.7

   Braydes of his bacenette and his ryche wedis
   Bownnes to his brode schelde 2695-6

4. and the deuke of Douchemen dressys him aftir 237.26

   Than the duke of Lorrayne dresesse thare-aftyre
   With dowbille of the Duche-men 2833-4

In these cases, certainly, the fact that Malory produced a satisfactory single alliterative long line does not necessitate doubt that the two lines of the Thornton text are authentic and original. All that it suggests is that Malory was familiar enough with alliterative verse to be able to produce good lines even when abbreviating and simplifying his source.

Not infrequently, Malory employs more complete or more conventional alliteration than the corresponding lines of the poem:

1. I make myne avow unto mylde Mary 188.2

   And I salle make myne avowe devotly to Criste 296

2. there to vynquysshe with victory the vyscounte of Roome 189.12

   Tylle that I haue venquiste the Vicounte of Rome 325

3. Thou haste made many martyrs by mourtheryng of this londis 202.20

   Thow has marters made and broghte oute of lyfe 1066

4. Be God, sayde Sir Gawayne, hit grevys me but lytyll 230.19

   ȝa, quod sir Gawayne, thou greues me bot lyttille 2570

5. I graunte, seyde sir Gawayne, so God me helpe 231.5

   ȝis, quod Sir Gawayne, so God me helpe 2589

6. and his knavys be so kene, his knyghtes ar passynge good 232.8
   Giffe his knafes be syche, his knyghttez are noble 2632
7. for they woll hyde them in haste for all their hyghe wordys 235.25
   They wolle hye theyme hyene for all theire gret wordes 2744
8. and prestly prove yourself and yonder pray wynne 236.3
   We salle proue todaye who salle the prys wyne 2751
9. Be God, sayde sir Gawayne, this gladys my herte 238.11
   Peter, sais sir Gawayne, this gladdez myne herte 2883
10. for to cese of their sawte for the cite was yolden 242.5
    For to leue the assawte, the cete was zoldene 3063

Vinaver suggested that in No. 9, Malory has an original reading that has been corrupted in the Thornton text; for the knight who normally swears "By Peter" in this poem is Priamus. Be this as it may, there is nothing either here or in the rest of the examples to prove that the additional alliteration is not Malory's doing. Fourteenth-century alliterative poems frequently employ different alliterations in the two halves of a line; sometimes they have half-lines, even whole lines, with no alliteration at all. Björkman and other early editors of *Morte Arthure* were prone to emend such lines on text-book principles. Vinaver rejected several of these regularizations of the poem (186.4, 189.2, 202.21, 236.21, 243.27) because the Thornton reading is the same as Malory's. The fact that Malory's alliteration is sometimes more regular is, therefore, no logical basis for emending the poem, especially when it gives good sense and good rhythm. Alliteration is never mechanical in poems like *Morte Arthure*, and Malory had his own inclination toward alliteration.

At times Malory was independent in his alliteration, expressing the same meaning as a line in Thornton, but expressing it with different words and different letter-rhymes:

1. And of all the soveraynes that we sawe 192.13
   Of all the wyes thate I watte in this werlde ryche 533
2. Than he turnys towarde his tentys and carpys but lytyll 199.21
   Raykez ryghte to a tente, and restez no lengere 889

3. For in the moneth of May this myscheff befelle 226.20	In the Kalendez of Maye this caas is befallene 2371
4. so worched his wounde that his wytte chonged 230.12	That voydes so violently that all his witte changede 2571
5. for garneson nother golde have we none resceyued 239.4	Our wages are werede owte and thi werre endide 2930
6. That the wete watir wente doune his chykys 239.22	That the chillande watire one his chekes rynnyde 2965
7. alle the tale truly, that day how they travayled 240.22	Alle the tale sothely, and how they hade spede 3016

In these examples, Thornton reads satisfactorily both in sense and form. Malory's variations, radical as they are, demand no further explanation than his own narrative intent and his disposition—under the influence of this poem, and probably others like it—to employ alliterative rhymes and rhythms.

Malory often changed the meaning slightly or added small details, and these he sometimes expressed in alliterative style:

1. dame Elyneys son of Ingelonde was Emperour of Roome 188.10	That ayere was of Ynglande and emperour of Rome 283
2. Than leepe in yong sir Launcelot de Laake with a lyght herte 189.31	By our Lorde, quod Sir Launcelott, now lyghttys myne herte 368
3. Than lowghe sir Bawdwyn of Bretayne and carpys to the kynge 190.7	Than laughes sir Lottez, and alle on lowde meles 382
4. by the sonne was sette at the seven dayes ende 191.14	By the seuende day was gone the cetee thai rechide 488
5. that the mountaynes of Almayne be myghtyly kepte 192.20	Be sekyre of the sowdeours and sende to the mowntes 551

6. the Grekes were gadirde and goodly arayed 193.17 — Be that the Grekes were graythede, a fulle gret nombyre 602
7. and caughte the corseynte oute of the kynges armys 204.11 — That thus clekys this corsaunt owte of thir heghe clyffez 1164
8. Now geff the sorow, sir Emperour, and all thy sowdyars the aboute 207.6 — Gyffe ȝow sytte in your sette, Sowdane and other 1305
9. the kynge thanked Cryste clappyng his hondys 211.11 — Christ be thankyde, quod the kynge, and his clere modyre 1359
10. Be he kyng other knight, here is his rencounter redy 213.11 — Es there any kyde knyghte, kaysere or other? 1651
11. with mo than fyve hondred at the formyst frunte 214.34 — Fif hundreth one a frounte fewtrede at onez 1756
12. Than the kynge mette with sir Cadore his kene cousyn 223.22 — Cosyne of Cornewaile, take kep to thi selfene 2262
13. Stabbis at hir stomakys with swerdys well steled 229.23 — Stokes at the stomake with stelyne poyntes 2554
14. So freysshly tho fre men fyghtes on the grounde 230.1 — Feghttene and floresche withe flawmande swerdez 2555
15. I am knowyn in his courte and kyd in his chambir 232.13 — Kidd in his kalander a knyghte of his chambyre 2640
16. with lawghyng and japyng and many lowde wordys 233.21 — With lowde laghttirs on lofte for lykynge of byrdez 2673
17. chyfften of this chekke and cheyff of us all 235.10 — Chiftayne of this journee with cheualrye noble 2732
18. ye are fraykis in this fryth nat paste seven hondred 235.22 — ȝe are at the ferreste noghte passande fyve hundrethe 2741

Appendix H

19. on a rede stede rode hym agaynste 236.28	One a ryalle stede rydes hym aȝaynes 2791
20. but yf they be stadde wyth more stuff than I se hem agaynste 237.21	Bot they be stedde with more stuffe than one ȝone stede houys 2824
21. Greve you nat, good men, for yondir grete syght 238.1	Gloppyns noghte, gud mene, for gleterand scheldes 2863
22. But Chasteylayne, thy chylde, is choppede of the hede 240.25	Bot a childe Chasteleyne myschance es befallene 3028
23. grete sommys of sylver, syxty horsys well charged 243.20	Grete sommes of golde, sexti horse charegid 3136
24. With septure, for sothe, as an Emperoure sholde 244.21	With his ceptre, as soueraynge and lorde 3186

Some of these variants are obviously results of Malory's adapting the poem to his own larger work, particularly of his antedating the Roman war to an earlier stage in Arthur's reign (Nos. 2 and 3). No. 1 is an addition taken from some other version of the story, Geoffrey of Monmouth's or Wace's or the French *Merlin*'s. The rest seem to be changes made by Malory himself in the interests of firmer alliteration (4, 6, 17, 18, 23), a livelier picture (6, 9, 11, 12, 19, 24), or clarification (7, 8, 13, 15, 16, 20, 21, 24). Sometimes Malory's reading is superior to the poem's; but since the poem's reading is satisfactory in both meaning and form, there is no compelling reason to rob him of the credit by assuming that he took them from a better text of the poem than the Thornton one.

There remain some forty alliterative passages, half-lines, full-lines, and two extended sequences, which have no parallels at all in the Thornton text:

1. I complayned me to the Potestate the Pope hymself 189.16
2. they helde Irelonde and Argayle and all the Oute Iles 189.24
3. Sir, sayde the senatours, lette be suche wordis 192.3
4. and of Calabe and of Catelonde, bothe kynges and deukes 193.19
5. Thy soth sawys have greved sore my herte 199.20
6. they boste and bragge as they durst bete all the worlde 207.26
7. Than the Romaynes folowed faste on horseback and on foote over a fayre champeyne unto a fayre wood 208.6

Appendix H

8. were formeste in the frunte and freyshly faught 209.23
9. Sir Borce and sir Berell, good barounnes, fought as two boorys 209.27
10. Loo, where they lede our lordys over yondir brode launde 210.13
11. Strode uppon a steede 210.13
12. the brayne and the blode 210.25
13. and the kynge thanked Cryste clappyng his hondys 211.11
14. that the messyngers ded that day thorow dedys of armys 212.6
15. the dalys and the downys 213.6
16. worship to wynne 214.16
17. Kylle doune clene for love of sir Kay 223.23
18. Than sir Cadore, sir Clegis, caughte to her swerdys 224.5
19. and ever he slow slyly and slypped to another 224.20
20. forth yode sir Florens and his felyshyp was sone redy 228.14
21. the rubyes that were ryche 230.6
22. for thou all bebledis this horse and thy bryght wedys 230.15
23. That may I do, and I woll, so thou wolt succour me that I might be fayre crystynde and becom meke for my mysdedis. Now mercy I Jesu beseche, and I shall becom Crysten and in God stedfastly beleve, and thou mayste for thy manhode have mede to thy soule. 230-231
24. Yet woll I beleve on thy Lorde that thou belevyst on 231.16
25. for here hovys at thy honde a hondred of good knyghtes 233.12
26. how he had macched with that myghty man of strengthe 233.25
27. they myght sitte in theire sadyls or stonde uppon erthe 234.9
28. New tell us, sir Pryamus, al the hole purpose of yondir pryce knyghtes. Sirs, seyde sir Pryamus, for to rescow me they have made a vowe, other ellys manfully on this molde to be marred all at onys. This was the pure purpose, whan I passed thens at hir perellys, to preff me uppon payne of their lyvys. 234-5
29. they jowked downe with her hedys many jantyll knyghtes 238.6
30. no knavys but knyghtes kene of herte 238.10
31. for the love of our lyege lorde Arthure 239.2
32. Now and thou haddyst ascaped withoutyn scathe, the scorne had been oures 240.1
33. But ye shall have lyvelode to leve by as to thyne astate fallys 242.2
34. Than the kynge with his crowne on his hede 242.11
35. moste governoure undir God for to gyff them lycence 244.17
36. There they suggeourned that seson tyll after the tyme 245.8

37. none that playned on his parte, ryche nother poore 245.11
38. suffir nevir your soveraynte to be alledged with your subjetes 245.17
39. As long as I live my servys is your own 245.31
40. myghte playne of his parte 246.1
41. for of rychesse and welth they had all at her wylle 246.2
42. the knyghtes and lordes that to the kynge longis 246.3
43. we have wyffis weddid 246.7

Some of these alliterative passages have provided the chief basis for the theory that the copy of *Morte Arthure* that Malory used was different from the Thornton text of the poem: Vinaver, for example, suggests that Nos. 1, 5, 9, 10, 14, 18, 20, 21, 23, 26, 29, 30, 31 must have been drawn from another version of *Morte Arthure*.

While this theory may seem plausible when Malory's variations are considered one at a time, it is not so persuasive when all the variations are considered together. Occasionally the inclusion of Malory's line in the poem might make for better narrative, though the poem usually reads intelligibly without the addition. But sometimes such an addition from Malory's version would involve recasting the language of contiguous lines in the poem (3, 6, 7, etc). Sometimes Malory's variation represents a rephrasing or an expansion of material in the poem. The two longer passages relating to Priamus (23, 28) are of this kind, but there are others too. Moreover, Malory also has many other details that are not in the Thornton text of the poem, although they are not put in alliterative style. The sheer number of these additional details, alliterating and nonalliterating, preclude their all being fitted into the Thornton text as emendations: and if they were taken from another text of the poem, that text could not have been simply a more correct copy; it would have had to be substantially a different version. Some scholars have in fact suggested that the poem from which Malory worked was very different from the one that appears in the Thornton MS. Since Malory's variations are the basis for this conjecture, however, it might be a safer procedure to seek an explanation from Malory himself.

Several of these alliterative additions (6, 7, 8, 10, 11, 12) occur in passages where Malory has a free précis of lengthier matter in the Thornton text; here his alliteration is sometimes his own, sometimes pieced out from scattered words in Thornton, and sometimes modelled on alliterating passages elsewhere. No. 16 completely rephrases a command in the poem, giving much the same meaning but using different alliteration.

No. 21, on the other hand, completely changes the meaning but retains the alliteration of the line in Thornton. Most significantly, at least ten of the alliterating passages appear in episodes and details that most critics agree must be Malory's own additions. The bulk of these (36-43) occur in the triumphant conclusion that Malory substituted for the tragic last part of the poem.

Conjectured poems, conjectured variants of poems, are as insubstantial as ghosts and as difficult to lay low. This conjectured variant of the *Morte Arthure* is the offspring of Malory's variations, particularly his alliterating variations. It may be significant therefore to examine his procedures when he was working with another English poem.

In the last section of his book, the story of Arthur's death, Malory worked from two sources simultaneously: a version of the French *Mort Artu* and an English poem entitled *Le Morte Arthure*. The poem was composed not far from the Humber in the late fourteenth century; it is written in rhymed stanzas, but its phraseology is strongly influenced by alliterative verse. This fact explains the abundance of alliteration in Malory's narrative at this point, viz:

1. Than had sir Gawayne suche a grace and gyffte that an holy man had given hym 1216.32	Than had syr Gawayne such a grace An holy man had boddyn that bone. *Le Morte Arthure* 2802-3
2. For wyte you welle, ye wynne no worshyp at thes wallis 1218.12	Ye wynne no worshyp at thys walle 2845
3. Com forth, thou false traytoure knyght 1219.1	Come forthe, launcelot, and prove thy mayne Thou traytour that hast treson wroght 2866-7
4. to ley the as low as thou laydest me 1219.13	Ne pees shall ther neuer be sayné Or thy sydes be throw sought 2873
5. and salved them with soffte salvys that full sore were wounded 1232.30	[Nothing corresponding to this in the poem]
6. brochys and bees 1238.2	
7. nothyng but wawis and wyndys 1239.14	They refte theym besaunt, broche, and bee 3419

8. nothynge but watirs wap and wawys wanne 1239.25	nothynge But watres depe And wawes wanne 3464-5
9. He wepte and wayled 1241.3	he went wepynge sore 3523
10. betwyxte two holtis hore 1241.5	by-twene ij holtes hore 3525
11. he seekened more and more and dryed and dwyned awaye 1257.2	That launcelot sekenyd sely sare 3835

Malory's alliterative passages here are far fewer than in Book V, and that is to be expected: the French *Mort Artu* is not alliterative, and the stanzaic *Le Morte Arthure* uses alliteration only decoratively. But they are enough to show that Malory's response here is the same as in Book V. In Nos. 2, 6, 10 he simply took over alliterative phrases from the English poem; in No. 9 he varied the alliterative pattern by substituting a synonym that also alliterates; in Nos. 1 and 8 he extended the alliteration; in No. 7 he repeated an alliterative phrase taken from the poem; in No. 3 he created an alliterative phrase on the basis of one word in the poem; in Nos. 4, 5, 11 he composed alliterative lines that do not appear in the poem at all.

No one has ever suggested that it is necessary to postulate a variant form of the stanzaic poem. These alliterative variations are clearly Malory's own doing.

In summary, these conclusions may be drawn from an overall survey of Malory's alliteration. He used some alliterations throughout his writing, even when translating from French, and these are largely phrases that were popular in northern alliterative verse. In Books XX and XXI, he transferred some alliterative phrases from the stanzaic *Le Morte Arthur* and added others; in Book V, he transferred many alliterative lines from the alliterative *Morte Arthure* and also used a great many that either vary from the phrasing of the poem or do not appear there at all.

In the full analysis of Malory's northern dialect words and forms, it was necessary to conclude that he added northernisms to his version of his northern sources and that this must have been because he was familiar with northern dialect and northern alliterative verse. The conclusion about his alliteration must be much the same: he was able and disposed to add alliterations because he was familiar with other alliterative poetry than the poem that he used for Book V. It seems, therefore, an unjustifiable procedure to emend the alliterative *Morte Arthure* extensively simply on the basis of Malory's prosing of it, and an unnecessary deduction that he used a text of that poem very different from that which appears in the Thornton MS.

BIBLIOGRAPHICAL NOTES

BIBLIOGRAPHICAL NOTES

Since it would be cumbrous to list every book, article, document, and picture that has been utilized during the eight years this book has been in the writing, these notes are restricted to items that a reader might want to look at. In particular, the notes do not reproduce the sources Hicks and Baugh cited in their contributions to the biography of the Warwickshire Malory.

GENERAL

The edition of *Le Morte Darthur* which is cited in this book is that of the Winchester Manuscript, published in Eugène Vinaver (ed.), *The Works of Sir Thomas Malory*, 3 vols., Oxford, 1947. Corrections of this, as noted in the discussion, are based on a photograph of the Winchester Manuscript. Comparisons with the Caxton text are drawn from Vinaver's footnotes and from H. Oskar Sommer (ed.), *Le Morte Darthur*, London, 1889.

BACKGROUND HISTORY

1. The historical settings in chapters i, ii, and iv, and some of the biographical details about public figures, are based mostly upon these authorities: E. F. Jacob, *The Fifteenth Century*, Oxford, 1961; H. S. Bennett, *The Pastons and Their England*, Cambridge, 1922; V. H. H. Green, *The Later Plantagenets*, London, 1955; C. Oman, *The History of Eng-*

land, 1377-1485, London, 1906; C. Oman, *Warwick the Kingmaker*, London, 1891; A. H. Burne, *The Agincourt War*, London, 1956; P. M. Kendall, *Warwick the Kingmaker*, London, 1947; J. J. Bagley, *Margaret of Anjou*, London, n.d.; J. H. Wylie, *The Reign of Henry V*, 3 vols., Cambridge, 1914-1929; Sir J. H. Ramsay, *Lancaster and York*, 2 vols., London, 1892; and, most importantly, Cora L. Schofield, *The Life and Reign of Edward the Fourth*, London, 1923.

2. Particular details, both historical and biographical, have been provided by these contemporary documents: *Registrum Johannis de Whethamstede*, Rolls Series, 1873; A. H. Thomas and I. D. Thornley, *The Great Chronicle of London*, 1938; R. Flenley, *Six Town Chronicles*, 1911; William Gregory's *Collections of a London Citizen*, ed. J. Gairdner, Camden Society, 1876; *The Brut or the Chronicle of England*, ed. F. W. D. Brie, EETS 131, 136, London, 1906-1908; *The English Chronicle from 1377 to 1461*, ed. J. S. Davies, Camden Society, 1856; *The Chronicle of John Harding*, ed. Sir H. Ellis, 1812; H. L. Kingsford, *English Historical Literature in the Fifteenth Century*, 1913 (Contains the "Latin Brut 1399-1437," "Chronicle of 1445-1455," "Collections of a Yorkist Partisan."); John Warkworth's *Chronicle*, ed. J. O. Halliwell, Camden Society, 1839; John Rous, *Historia Rerum Angliae*, 1716; J. Gairdner, *Three Fifteenth Century Chronicles*, Camden Society, 1880; Robert Fabyan's *Newe Chronycles of England*, ed. Sir H. Ellis, 1811; Edward Hall's *The Union of the two Noble and Illustrious Families of Lancaster and York*, ed. Sir H. Ellis, 1809; Sir H. Ellis, *Three Books of Polydore Vergil's English History*, Camden Society, 1844; G. Baskerville (ed.), "London Chronicle of 1460," *English Historical Review*, XXVIII; James Gairdner, *Paston Letters*, London, 1904; *Plumpton Correspondence*, ed. T. Stapleton, Camden Society, 1839; *The Official Correspondence of Thomas Bekynton*, ed. C. Williams, Rolls Series, 1872; *Letters of Queen Margaret of Anjou*, ed. C. Monro, Camden Society, 1863; *Rotuli Parliamentorum*, Vols. III-V, 1767; Samuel Bentley, *Excerpta Historica*, London, 1833.

Many details, biographical ones particularly, have been gleaned from: *Calendarium Inquisitionum post Mortem*, IV, 1828; *Early Chancery Proceedings*, I, 1907; *Calendar of Close Rolls*, 1468-1476; *Calendar of Patent Rolls*, 1452-1461, 1461-1467, *Calendar of Fine Rolls*, 1437-1445, 1445-1452, 1461-1467.

Chapter I

1. The account of the Welsh candidate is based mostly on Kittredge's essay and an Appendix in Vinaver's *Malory*.

2. The Papworth Malory's claims are reported from Martin's articles, Kittredge's essays, the genealogies cited in Appendix A, Early Chancery Proceedings, and Pro. C. I. bundles 27 and 28.

3. Our account of Warwickshire in the late Middle Ages is based mainly upon: *Victoria County History, Warwickshire*; W. H. Hutton, *Highways and Byways in Shakespeare's Country*, London, 1914; Sir James D. Mackenzie, *The Castles of England*, London, 1897; Alfred Harvey, *The Castles and Walled Towns of England*, London, 1911; H. A. Cronne, "The Borough of Warwick in the Middle Ages," *Dugdale Society Occasional Papers*, X, 1951; R. T. Hilton, "Social Structure of Rural Warwickshire in the Middle Ages," *ibid.*, IX, 1950; Charles Ross, "The Estates and Finances of Richard Beauchamp," *ibid.*, XII, 1956; *Memorials of Old Warwickshire*, ed. Alice Dryden, London, 1908; *The Rows Rol*, London, 1908; Viscount Dillon and W. H. St. John Hope, *Pageant of the Birth, Life and Death of Richard Beauchamp, Earl of Warwick*, London, 1914; article on Richard Beauchamp in the *Dictionary of National Biography*; and William Dugdale's *Antiquities of Warwickshire*, London, 1656.

4. Details of the Newbold Revel Malorys and the career of Sir Thomas Malory are drawn mainly from *Victoria County History, Warwickshire*, VI (Monks Kirby); Dugdale Manuscript No. 2 (Bodleian Library); Dugdale, *Antiquities*; G. L. Kittredge, *Who Was Sir Thomas Malory?* (first published in Harvard *Studies and Notes in Philology and Literature*, V, 1897); T. W. Williams, Letter to *The Athenaeum*, July 11, 1896; T. W. Williams, *Sir Thomas Malory and the "Morte Darthur*," Bristol, 1909; A. T. Martin, "Sir Thomas Malory," *Athenaeum*, 1897; A. T. Martin, "The Identity of the Author of the Morte Darthur," *Archaeologia*, LVI, 1898; Sir E. K. Chambers, *Sir Thomas Malory*, English Association, London, 1922; Edward Hicks, *Sir Thomas Malory, His Turbulent Career*, Cambridge, Massachusetts, 1928; Eugène Vinaver, *Malory*, Oxford, 1929, Appendix I; A. C. Baugh, "Documenting Sir Thomas Malory," *Speculum*, VIII, 1933; Josiah Wedgewood, *History of Parliament*, London, 1936.

Genealogies and some details of the Warwickshire Malorys and other branches of their family in the Midlands appear in: Dugdale, *Antiquities*; John Nichols, *History and Antiquities of the County of Leicester*, 1807-

1811; William Burton, *The Description of Leicestershire*, 1622; Peter Whalley, *The History and Antiquities of Northamptonshire*, 1791; George Baker, *History and Antiquities of Bedfordshire*, 1884; F. A. Blaydes (ed.), *Visitations of Bedfordshire*, 1884.

5. Notes on the persons associated with Malory are derived from the works by Baugh, Dugdale, Wedgewood, cited previously, and also from: the *Dictionary of National Biography*; *Complete Peerage*; *Paston Letters*; Wedgewood's *Parliamentary History*; Thomas (Fortescue), Lord Clermont, *The Works of Sir John Fortescue*, 1869. For Brigham, see *Calendar of Patent Rolls*, 1461-1467, 1467-1471.

6. The account of Greyfriars is based upon Charles L. Kingsford, *The Grey Friars of London*, London, 1915, and the documents that he there reprints.

Chapter II

1. The various ways of dealing with the moral paradox in Malory will be found, for example, in: Eugène Vinaver, *Malory*, Oxford, 1929; Vinaver, *Works*, Introduction; Richard Altick, *The Scholar Adventurers*, New York, 1950; M. C. Bradbrook, *Sir Thomas Malory*, London, 1958; Hicks, *Sir Thomas Malory*; Wedgewood, *History of Parliament*; Vinaver's and C. S. Lewis' essays in *Essays on Malory*, ed. J. A. W. Bennett, Oxford, 1963; Richard Barbour, *Arthur of Albion*, London, 1961; Sir E. K. Chambers, *English Literature at the Close of the Middle Ages*, Oxford, 1947. A different view is expressed in R. M. Lumiansky, *Malory's Originality*, Baltimore, 1964.

2. Statements about the fifteenth-century social climate are based upon the general and particular histories cited in the introductory note on sources, and especially: Bennett, *The Pastons*; Gairdner, *Paston Letters*; *Rotuli Parliamentorum*, Vol. V; *Calendar of Proceedings in Chancery*, I, 1827; *Early Chancery Proceedings*, I, 1901; PRO, C.I bundles 27 and 28.

3. The account of Newgate and its environs is derived from: Kingsford, *The Grey Friars*; Margery Bassett, "Newgate Prison in the Middle Ages," *Speculum*, XVIII, 1943; Marjorie B. Honeybourne, "The Precinct of the Grey Friars," *London Topographical Record*, XVI, 1932; *idem*, "The Fleet and Its Neighbourhood in Medieval Times," *ibid.*, XIX, 1947; Walter Besant and James Rice, *Sir Richard Whittington*, London, 1902.

For Malory's imprisonment, see Baugh's "Documenting Sir Thomas

Malory." The pardon roll is reported in the article on Malory in Wedgewood, *Parliamentary History*. The witnessing of the Fielding conveyance is reported in John Nichols, *History . . . of Leicester*, IV, p. 368.

4. The report on the Greyfriars library and other medieval English libraries relies upon: Kingsford, *The Grey Friars*; N. R. Ker, *Mediaeval Libraries of Great Britain*, London, 1941; M. R. James, *The Ancient Libraries of Canterbury and Dover*, Cambridge, 1903; Dom David Knowles, *The Religious Orders in England*, Vol. II, Cambridge, 1955; J. W. Thompson, *The Medieval Library*, Chicago, 1938.

5. The literary arguments in support of the Newbold Revel knight appear in Kittredge's essay; Hicks, *Sir Thomas Malory*; Vinaver, *Malory and Works*; W. H. Schofield, *Chivalry in English Literature*, Cambridge, 1912.

6. On place-names in Malory, see George R. Stewart, "English Geography in Malory's 'Morte D'Arthur,'" *Modern Language Review*, XXX, 1935; F. J. Snell, *King Arthur's Country*, 1926. Names of Arthurian knights are recorded in Robert W. Ackerman, *An Index of the Arthurian Names in Middle English*, Stanford, 1952. The location in Malory's text of the names discussed here and elsewhere is reported in the Index to Vinaver, *Works*.

7. Information on the dialect of Coventry is derived from analysis of the EETS editions of *Two Coventry Corpus Christi Plays* and the *Coventry Leet-Book*, and also C. F. Northall, *A Warwickshire Word-Book*, EDS, London, 1896.

The authorities for the general statements about Middle English dialect characteristics that are made here and in the next chapter are: R. Jordan, *Handbuch der mittelenglischen Grammatik*, Heidelberg, 1934; Karl Luick, *Historische Grammatik der englischen Sprache*, Leipzig, 1921-1940; Samuel Moore, *Historical Outlines of English Sounds and Inflections*, Ann Arbor, 1951; S. Moore, S. M. Meech, and H. Whitehall, "Middle English Dialect Characteristics and Dialect Boundaries," *University of Michigan Publications in Language and Literature*, XIII, 1935; L. Morsbach, *Mittelenglische Grammatik*, Halle, 1896; Fernand Mossé, *A Handbook of Middle English*, Baltimore, 1952; J. P. Oakden, *Alliterative Poetry in Middle English*, Vol. I; *The Dialectal and Metrical Survey*, Manchester, 1930; J. and E. M. Wright, *An Elementary Middle English Grammar*, Oxford, 1928; H. C. Wyld, *A Short History of English*, Oxford, 1927.

8. The "siege" of Calais in 1436 is described in the modern histories

and several of the medieval chronicles listed in the foregoing note on general sources and in the Beauchamp *Pageant*. Details of the military indenture system appear in Wylie, *Reign of Henry V*. Dugdale's copies of the documents that he used for the notes on the roles of Malory and other Warwickshire knights, which he printed in the *Antiquities*, are collected in Dugdale Manuscript No. 2 (Bodleian Library). The details about Malory's companions in this military service are drawn from: Dugdale Manuscript No. 2; Dugdale, *Antiquities*; Wedgewood, *History of Parliament*; *Dictionary of National Biography*; *Victoria County History, Warwickshire*.

Chapter III

1. The full linguistic analyses upon which these sections rely are set out in Appendixes B, C, D, and E. Mrs. Sally Shaw's discussion of Malory's language appears in her essay in Bennett, *Essays on Malory*. The chief sources of information on the spelling and grammatical characteristics of Northern Middle English are the handbooks of Jordan; Luick; Moore; Moore, Meech, and Whitehall; Mossé; Oakden; Wright; and Wyld—cited in Note 7 to the previous chapter—together with Asta Kilbohm, *A Contribution to the Study of Fifteenth-Century English*, 1926; Tauno Mustanoja, *Middle English Syntax*, Helsinki, 1961; Angus McIntosh, *A New Approach to Middle English Dialectology*, 1959 (mimeographed); Charles S. Baldwin, *The Inflections and Syntax of the Morte d'Arthur*, Boston, 1894; Mary Serjeantson's article on Middle English dialects in *Review of English Studies*, 1927; A. Dekker, *Some Features Concerning the Syntax of Malory's Morte Darthur*, Amsterdam, 1932; and Jan Simko, *Word-Order in the Winchester Manuscript and in William Caxton's Edition of Thomas Malory's Morte Darthur (1485)—A Comparison*, Halle, 1957; Sally Shaw's essay in *Essays on Malory*, ed. Bennett.

Authorities relied on for Middle English dialect lexicography are: *OED*; Hans Kurath and Sherman Kuhn, *Middle English Dictionary*, Ann Arbor, Michigan (in progress); Rolf Kaiser, *Zur Geographie des mittelenglischen Wortschatzes*, Palaestra 205, 1937. Details of recent Yorkshire (and generally northern) dialect usages are reported from: Joseph Wright, *English Dialect Dictionary*; C. Clough Robinson, *A Glossary of Words Pertaining to the Dialect of Mid-Yorkshire*, London, 1876; Sir Alfred E. Pease, *A Dictionary of the Dialect of the North Riding of Yorkshire*, Whitby, 1928. The Yorkshire, Warwickshire, and

London texts that were used for the dialect comparisons made in this chapter are set out in Appendix D with the fuller analyses.

2. For the relationship of the stanzaic *Le Morte Arthur* to Malory, see: J. D. Bruce (ed.), *Le Morte Arthur*, EETS, 1903; E. T. Donaldson, "Malory and the Stanzaic *Le Morte Arthur*," *Studies in Philology*, XLVII, 1950; Lumiansky, *Malory's Originality*; and Vinaver, *Works*, pp. 1573-99.

3. The Thornton Manuscript, which contains the only medieval text of the alliterative *Morte Arthure*, is now in the library of Lincoln Cathedral; the text cited here is Edmund Brock's EETS edition of 1865, reprinted in 1961. See also: Angus McIntosh, "The Textual Transmission of the Alliterative *Morte Arthure*" in *English and Medieval Essays presented to J. R. R. Tolkien*, Oxford, 1962.

4. The texts of Arthur's epitaph are cited from J. Armitage Robinson, *Two Glastonbury Legends*, Cambridge, 1926. See also, F. J. Furnivall (ed.), *Arthur*, EETS, 1864.

5. The romances compared with Malory are: *The Awntyrs off Arthure at the Terne Wathelyne*, in F. J. Amours, *Scottish Alliterative Poems*, STS, XXVII, XXXVIII, 1892, 1897; *The Avowing of King Arthur, Sir Gawain, Sir Kay, and Sir Baldwin of Britain*, in W. H. French and C. B. Hale, *Middle English Metrical Romances*, New York, 1930; *Syre Gawene and the Carle of Carelyle*, ed. R. W. Ackerman, in *University of Michigan Contributions in Modern Philology*, VIII, 1947 (The romance was reëdited by Auvo Kurvinen, Helsinki, 1951); *The Turke and Gowin*, in J. W. Hales and F. J. Furnivall (eds.), *Bishop Percy's Folio MS.*, London, 1867-1868; *Sir Gawain and the Green Knight*, ed. Sir Israel Gollancz, EETS, 1940.

6. For Guildford and vicinity, see *Victoria County History, Surrey*. On Watling Street and "suffragan," see *OED* entries. Patten's comment is reported in Edward Bateson, *A History of Northumberland*, 1893.

7. The Ribston *Suite* is now Cambridge University Additional Manuscript 7071. (With it are the letters referred to in this discussion.) The Ribston deeds are now shared by the Leeds Public Library and the library of the Yorkshire Archaeological and Historical Society at Leeds, and a report on them appears in R. V. Taylor, "Ribston and the Knights Templars," *Yorkshire Archaeological and Topographical Journal*, VII, 1881-1882. For Vinaver's comments on the Ribston *Suite*, see his edition of *The Works*, pp. 1277-80.

8. The Mauleverers are reported in *Genealogy of the Family of*

Mauleverer, London, 1869; wills are in York Registry and *Testamenta Eboracensia*.

Chapter IV

1. Our account of medieval Yorkshire and the border counties is based on a variety of sources, including: *Victoria County History, Yorkshire*; Arthur H. Norway, *Highways and Byways in Yorkshire*, London, 1899; P. Anderson Graham, *Highways and Byways in Northumbria*, London, 1920; A. M. Wilkinson, *Ripon Five Hundred Years Ago*, Ripon, 1959; idem, *The Fountains Story*, Ripon, 1957; *Ripon Chapter Acts*, 1452-1506, Surtees Society, 1873 (also the manuscript in Ripon Cathedral Library); *The Darnborough MS.* (Ripon Cathedral Library); Robert Surtees, *The History and Antiquities of Durham*, 1823; J. R. Walbran, *Memorials of the Abbey of St. Mary of Fountains*, Surtees Society, 1863; *Memorials of the Church of SS. Peter and Wilfrid*, Surtees Society, 1882-1908; Arthur E. Henderson, *Fountains Abbey Then and Now*, London, 1958; William Sitwell, *The Border*, 1927; Alexander Eddington, *Castles and Historic Homes of the Border*, 1949; Crawford, "Arthur and his Battles," *Antiquity*, IX, 1935. The historical data is drawn mainly from Schofield, *Edward the Fourth*; and the details of doings at Ripon come from the *Acts of the Ripon Chapter*.

The reports on Northallerton worthies derive largely from Leland's *Collectanea*; *Victoria County History, Yorkshire*; wills in the Register of Probates, York District (Borthwick Institute, York); Geoffrey H. White, *The Complete Peerage*, 1959.

2. The sources for our account of the Yorkshire Malorys are the documents—mainly court rolls, leases, wills, and similar deeds—which are now housed in the Estate Office at Studley Royal, Yorkshire. They have been calendared in a mimeographed volume, copies of which are at the Estate Office, Leeds Public Library, and the National Registry of Archives in Chancery Lane. The items that proved particularly informative for the present book are those numbered in this calendar: 936, 1674, 1676, 4410-14, 5157, 5518, 5278-81, 5288, 5374, 5283-5, 5397, 5398, 5402, 5457, 5497, 5498, 5821, 5822, 6071. The chief modern account and genealogy of the family is, J. R. Walbran, *Genealogical and Biographical Memoir of the Lords of Studley*, 1841. The early documents that give genealogies are: *A Visitation of the North circa 1480-1500*, Surtees Society, 1930 (see Anthony Wagner, *English Genealogy*, Oxford, 1960, pp. 308-10, for further copies of this visitation); Wil-

liam Flower, *Visitation of Yorkshire, 1563–1564*, London, 1881; Robert Glover, *Visitation of Yorkshire, 1584–1585*, London, 1875. Manuscript materials which confirm these earlier records are: Thomas Beckwith's "Pedigrees of Yorkshire Gentry" and Walbran's "Yorkshire Genealogies" (both manuscripts in the library of York Cathedral) and Dodsworth Manuscript No. 50 (Bodleian Library). Detailed sources are given in the notes to the genealogy of the Yorkshire Malorys in Appendix A.

Further details about the activities of various members of the family derive from *The Register of the Corpus Christi Guild of the City of York*, Surtees Society, 1872; "Acts of the Ripon Chapter"; *Testamenta Eboracensia*, Surtees Society, I-IV, 1836-1902; Warkworth's *Chronicle*; Hall's *Chronicle*.

The account of Hutton and Markenfield Hall is based partly on direct observation, but formally on T. Hudson Turner, *Domestic Architecture of the Middle Ages*, Vol. II, Oxford, 1853.

Details of the Vavasours come mainly from their wills in *Testamenta Eboracensia*.

3. The 1462 list of *milites* appears in Lambeth Palace Manuscript No. 448, which is printed in Gairdner, *Three Fifteenth-Century Chronicles*. Details about the men listed in this document derive from many sources, notably: Wedgewood, *History of Parliament*; A. R. Myers, *The Household of Edward IV*, 1959; *Victoria County History, Yorkshire* (and other counties); *Testamenta Eboracensia*; *North Country Wills*, Surtees Society, 1908; *Dictionary of National Biography*; *Calendar of Patent Rolls 1461–1467*; *Close Rolls*, 1468; and the chronicles listed in the first general note.

4. Our account of the siege of the northern castles derives mostly from Schofield's *Edward the Fourth* and Warkworth's *Chronicle*.

5. The location of the Earl of Warwick in October, 1462, and the recruitment of Yorkshiremen is reported in: Kendal, *Warwick*; *Victoria County History, Cumberland*; R. Davies, *Extracts from the Municipal Records of the City of York*, 1843.

6. Copies of the 1468 pardon are in *Liber Albus*, II, ff. 199-200, and III, ff. 227-8 (in the library of Wells Cathedral), the archives of the Borough of Nottingham, and British Museum Additional Charter 17,248. See T. W. Williams, *Athenaeum*, July 11, 1896, who first reported the Wells copy. Details of the court group in the list of exceptions come from *Letters of Margaret of Anjou*, and Lord Clermont's *For-*

tescue. The Welshmen are annotated from Sir John E. Lloyd, *A History of Carmarthenshire*, Cardiff, 1935, and Howell T. Evans, *Wales and the Wars of the Roses*, 1915; see also *Calendar of Patent Rolls*, December 16, 1469. The London plot and the participants are recorded in William of Worcester's *Annals*, and the fullest modern accounts appear in Ramsay's *Lancaster and York* and Schofield's *Edward the Fourth*.

7. The London Robert Marshall is mentioned in *Calendar of Close Rolls 1468–76*; the Nottingham one in *Calendar of Patent Rolls, 1461–7*. These and other rolls also mention a King's minstrel of the same name; and a Yorkshireman similarly named appears in *Ripon Chapter Acts*.

8. Our account of Sir Humphrey Neville is derived from Schofield, *Edward the Fourth*; J. R. Lander, "Attainder and Forfeiture"; with additional details from: Henry J. Swallow, *De Villa Nova*, London, 1885; Cadwallader Bates, *Border Holds*, 1891; Sitwell, *The Border*; Hodgson, *History of Northumberland*; Surtees, *Durham*; *Memorials of Hexham Priory*, Surtees Society Vol. XLIV; *Rotuli Parliamentorum* for 1464; *Calendar of Patent Rolls, 1454–1461*, and *ibid., 1461–1467*.

9. For the pace of medieval translators, see: Caxton's statements in *Prologues and Epilogues*, EETS, 1927; the Prologue to Gavin Douglas, *The XII Bukes of Eneados*; and the Prologue to Stewart's *Scottis Originall*, Rolls Series.

10. Concerning the owners of manuscripts in England, see Margaret Deanesley, "Vernacular Books in England in the Fourteenth and Fifteenth Centuries," *Modern Language Review*, XV, 1920. Libraries in various countries are discussed in Thompson, *The Medieval Library*, and the particular collections of Arthurian romances are in: W. Braghirolli, *et al.* "Inventaire des manuscrits en langue française possèdés par Francesco Gonzaga I," *Romania*, IX, 1880; F. Novati, "I Codici Francesi de' Gonzaga," *Romania*, XIX, 1890; Pio Rajna, "Ricordi di codici," *Romania*, II, 1873 (Ercole d'Este); M. Van Praet, *Recherches sur Louis de Bruges*, Paris, 1831; C. Pickford, *L'Evolution du Roman Arthurien en Prose*, Paris, 1960; B. de Maudrot, "Jacques d'Armagnac," *Revue Historique*, XLIII, 1890; C. Samaran, *La Maison d'Armagnac au xve siècle*, Paris, 1907.

11. The report of resemblances between Malory's text and manuscripts that were owned by Jacques d'Armagnac is based upon Vinaver's statements in his notes in his edition of *Works* and upon Pickford's *L'Evolution*. Closer investigation along this line might be revealing.

12. For prisoners in Armagnac, see Thomas Carte, *Catalogue des*

Rolles Gascons, London, 1743; *Calendars of the French Rolls*, 1888; J. Stevenson, *Narratives of the Expulsion of the English from Normandy*; Philip de Commynes, *Mémoires*; E. de Monstrelet, *Chronicles*; Jean du Wauvrin, *Receuil de Chroniques*, Rolls Series, V, 1890; *Calendar of State Papers, Milan*, ed. A. B. Hinds, 1913.

13. The relative status of "knight" and "esquire" is discussed in Wagner, *English Genealogy*.

INDEX

INDEX

Addelsey, John, 27
Aldfield, Yorks., 120, 123
Algore, William, 27
Allerton, Yorks., 119, 123
Alliteration, Malory's, 96–98, 233–238
Alliterative *Morte Arthure*, Malory's handling of, 93, 96, 213–221
Alnwick, Nhb., 38, 64, 107, 116, 128, 130, 134, 137
Amesbury, Wilts., 64, 90, 103
Appleby, John, 17, 18, 19, 20, 21, 22
Arthur, King, 3, 12, 35, 44, 52, 56, 57, 61, 89, 90–92, 98–102, 106–109, 118, 119, 130, 137, 140, 145, 147
Arthurian romances, owners of, 52, 141–146
Arthur's epitaph, 98–99
Arundel, Suss., 30, 38, 64, 104, 130, 136
Astley, Sir John, 128
Attainder, 133, 135
Authorship of *Le Morte Darthur*: primary information, 3–4; criteria for, 39, 150; candidates and their claims (summary), 130, 135–136, 150–151
Axholme, Lincs., priory of, 21

Baldwin of Britain, Sir, 41, 62, 63, 100, 101
Bale, John, 5, 35, 36, 40

Bamburgh, Nhb., 64, 107, 128, 130, 131, 134, 137
Barham Down, Kent, 64
Barnard of Astolat, Sir, 104
Baugh, Prof. Albert C., 9, 37, 45, 58
Beauchamp, Richard, earl of Warwick, 8, 12, 14, 24, 40, 41, 60, 61, 63, 64, 68–72
Beaumains (nickname for Gareth), 60
Bedford (county), 6, 7, 9, 19
Bekyngton, Thomas, bishop of Wells, 130
Bernangle, Warw., 18
Beverly, Yorks., 115, 118, 127
Birmingham, Warw., 10, 22
Bishopeston, William, 71, 72
Bodrugan, Henry, 46, 47
Boethius, 51, 139
Bolton Castle, Yorks., 116
Boroughbridge, Yorks., 106
Bors, 99n, 148
Boys, Walter, 29
Brabeuf, Sry., 104
Braintree, Essex, 27
Bramcote, Warw., 72
Brampton, Yorks., 120
Brancepeth, Dur., 116, 133
Briggeham, William, 30
Brigham, Yorks., 30
Brinklow, Warw., 18

255

Broun, Adam, 17, 18
Buckingham, duke of. *See* Stafford, Humphrey
Burgundy, 91, 142, 144
Burnaby, Eustace, 18, 19

Calais, and sieges of, 14, 24, 30, 31, 40, 41, 60, 62, 68–73
Caludon, Warw., 21, 22, 24, 26
Cambridge (county), 7, 32, 38, 129
Camelot, 104, 106, 119
Camlan, battle of, 107
Canterbury, Kent, 55, 64, 142
Carlisle, Cumb., 19, 64, 92, 101–103, 106, 107, 129, 130, 136, 137
Carpenter, John, 56
Catterick, Yorks., 92, 106
Caxton, William, 3, 35–38, 42, 45, 49, 52, 65, 67, 68n, 76, 78, 81, 82, 84, 86–88, 91, 97, 102, 103, 109, 112, 113, 138, 142, 144, 145
Caxton text, language of, 67, 86–89, 193–197
Chamberlain, Sir Roger, 26
Charles V, 52, 53, 142
Chaucer, Geoffrey: language of, 24, 81; northernisms of, 205–206
Christ's Hospital, London, 33
Claro Wapentake, Yorks., 112, 123
Clerkson, John, 30
Clodsale, Sir Richard, 72
Clotherholme, Yorks., 119
Cobb, Edward, scholar, 8, 9, 14, 37
Cobham, Sir Thomas, 27
Colchester, Essex, 27, 28, 53
Coleshill, Warw., 15, 21, 27, 41, 46, 63
Colville, John, 130
Combe Abbey, Warw., 11, 13, 16, 22, 23, 24, 25, 30, 44, 46, 64
Constables, 112, 116; Joan, 112; John, 130; Sir John, 112; Sir Robert, 130; Robertus, 111, 112
Conyers, 110, 112, 116, 125; Sir John, 117, 123, 124, 130, 172 (*see also* Robin of Redesdale); Sir Roger, 130
Copt Hewick, Yorks., 120, 123, 125

Cornwall (county), 46, 105, 130
Coventry, Warw., 10–13, 17, 18, 21, 23, 64, 66, 82, 83
Coventry Leet-Book, language of, 66–67, 203–204
Cowper, Thomas, 13, 21
Culham, Oxon., 132
Cumberland (county), 101, 129

D'Armagnac, Jacques, duc de Nemours, 52, 142, 145, 146, 147, 149
De Ardern, Ralph, 71, 72
De Berry, Jean, duc, 52, 142, 145
De Gruthuyse, Louis, 52, 143–144
De la Rouse, duke, 42, 61
De Lile, Melias, 41, 62; Neroveus, 41, 62; William, 41, 62
De Montfort, Simon, 11
Denbigh (county), 37, 131, 132
Dent, Major J. G., 109–111
Dercet, John, 20
De Revel, Sir Hervise, 41, 61
D'Este, Ercole, 52, 143
De Troyes, Chrétien, 118, 144
Dialects, 38, 65, 75–88; Warwickshire, 66, 67, 203–205; Yorkshire, 78–89, 199–203; London, 81, 205–206
Dolorous Garde, 106, 107
D'Orléans, Charles, duc, 51, 53, 54, 140, 142
Douglas, Gavin, 139
Dover, Kent, 64
Dowde, William, 20
Dugdale, Sir William, antiquary, 8, 12, 32, 39, 40, 68, 69, 70, 72, 73, 73n
Dunstanburgh, Nhb., 107, 116, 128
Durham (county), 55, 116, 120, 132, 133, 135, 152
Durham Malorys, 153

Edgecote, Nhp., 105, 124, 135
Edward III, 33, 103, 141
Edward IV, 12, 24, 27, 31, 37–39, 76, 104, 105, 116–118, 121, 128, 130, 131, 133, 135, 143
Elaine, 104

Index

Essex (county), 26, 27, 46, 104, 129

Fauconbridge, Lord. *See* Neville, William
Fielding, William, 32
FitzAlans, 104; William, duke of Arundel, 104
Fitzwilliam, Edmund, 26
Forest of Arden, Warw., 13, 16, 19, 23
Fortescue, Sir John, 26, 28–30, 59, 133
Fountains Abbey, Yorks., 103, 110, 112, 115, 118, 120–122, 124, 152
Four sons of Aymon, language of, 205
Framlingham, Suff., 26, 27
Frysseby, John, 18, 20
Furneys, John, 18

Gahereit, 108
Galerans dis li Gallois, 101
Galeron of Galloway, Sir, 101, 102, 106
Gareth, Sir, 4, 40, 42, 49, 60, 61, 90, 137
Gascony, 33
Gawain, Sir, 40, 90, 93, 100–102, 108
Gillyng, Yorks., 134, 136
Glastonbury, Som., 57, 91, 98
Gonnot, Michel, scribe, 146–147
Gonzagas, 52, 142, 143
Gothgallus, 12
Great Easton, Essex, 27
Grene: John, 27; William, 27
Greswold, Thomas, 23, 29
Grey, Sir Ralph, 128, 134
Greyfriars, London, 52, 54, chapel, 33, 47, 59, 60; library, 52–56
Griffin, Geoffrey, 18, 20
Gromore Somyr Ioure, 102
Guenevere, 90, 98, 101–103, 106, 108
Guildford, Sry., 64, 104
Guy of Warwick, 12, 42, 53, 55
Guy's Cliff, Warw., 42, 61, 63

Hales, William, 17
Hall, William, 20, 22
Hampton, John, 26, 27, 28
Harlech Castle, 131

Harper, John, 20
Henry V, 10, 12, 14, 68, 69, 71, 72
Henry VI, 12, 15, 24, 26, 28–30, 32, 59, 68, 105, 117, 128, 131, 133, 137
Henry VII, 112, 118, 121
Hicks, Edward, scholar, 9, 38, 41–42, 52–53, 73n
Hornby, Yorks., 116, 124
Humber, river, 78, 80, 82, 106
Hungerford, Lord, 128, 134
Huntingdon (county), 5, 6, 7, 9, 32, 38, 60, 150
Hutton, Yorks., manor of, 119, 120, 122, 123, 125, 126, 136
Hutton Conyers, Yorks., 112, 121, 162
Hylton Floghen, Westm., 120, 124, 164

Inglewood Forest, Cumb., 101, 102, 120
Irishman, Richard, 20, 22
Iseult of the White Hands, 36
Isolde, 106

Jackson, Thomas, 111, 112
James I of Scotland, 51, 140
Jenyn, Bernard, 104
John, abbot of Tilty, 27
John, duke of Bedford, 52
Joyous Garde, 106, 107, 130, 137
Juries, 22, 25, 27, 28, 45, 47

Kay, Sir, 60
Kendals, 119
Kenilworth, 64
Kent (county), 103, 104, 129
Kirkby Malory Malorys, 159
Kittredge, Prof. George Lyman, 8, 14, 35, 37, 38–41, 44, 45, 60, 64, 67–69, 73–76, 113, 114, 126, 151
Knaresborough, Saint Robert of, 110, 115, 120, 123; *Metrical Life of*, language of, 200
Knaresborough, Yorks., 83, 84, 112, 116, 139
Knight, use of title of, 152–153
Knight-prisoner, meaning of, 139, 152

Lambeth, Sry., 38, 64, 104
Lamorak of Wales, 36, 108
Lancelot, Sir, 4, 36, 43, 45, 48, 51, 53, 55, 62, 90, 100–104, 106, 139, 140, 142, 148
Language of *Le Morte Darthur*, 65–67, 177–221
Lawlessness in fifteenth-century England, 7, 8, 12–14, 16, 18, 20–23, 27, 44, 46–48
Leghton, Thomas, 18, 19
Leicester (county), 7, 9, 10, 13, 17–20, 23, 25, 60, 64, 129
Deland, John, antiquary, 35, 56, 57, 98, 113, 119, 121, 122
Le Morte Arthur, stanzaic, alliteration of, 97, 236–237
Leventhorpe, John, 26
Libraries, 33, 52–57, 142-145
Lichborough Malorys, 160
Lile, John, 71
Lincolnshire, 21, 82, 90, 92, 120, 133, 134
Linton-in-Craven, Yorks., 120
Lionel, 139, 149
Literary parallels in *Le Morte Darthur*, 40–42, 60–63
Literary sources of *Le Morte Darthur*, 51–52, 89–99, 99–103, 140, 146–147
London, 19, 24, 26, 27, 29, 30, 33, 47, 56, 60, 64, 65, 67, 77, 81, 82, 86, 93, 104–106, 129, 131-133
Lot, Arthur's war with, 108
Ludgate, 30, 57, 59
Lynton, Yorks., 123

McIntosh, Prof. Angus, 91, 92
Mackershaw, Yorks., 120
Magowns, castle of, 130
Mailoria, 35, 37
Malory: Anthony, 60; Edward, 9, 60; Lady Elizabeth, 15, 157; John, 126; John, son of William Malory of Hutton, 124, 161; Sir John, 10, 71; Sir John, 126; Katherine, 121, 161; Margaret (of Clint), 112; Philippa, 10, 157; Richard, 18, 19; Robert, 9, 60; Roger, 29; Sir Stephen, 9, 10; Sir William, 6, 158; Sir William, 103, 105, 121–126, 136, 161. *See also* Tempest, Dionisia
Malory, Thomas, M.P. for Wareham and Bedwin, 151
Malory, Sir Thomas, of Bramcote, Warw., 72, 159
Malory, Thomas, of Hutton and Studley, Yorks., 78–86, 88–92, 94–107, 112–113, 117, 119, 125–128, 130–132, 135–142, 150–152, 161
Malory, Thomas, of Kent, 150n
Malory, Sir Thomas, of Newbold Revel, Warw., 75, 76, 82, 92, 93, 106, 114, 120, 127, 129, 130, 135, 138, 139, 151–152, 157; life and turbulent career of, 5–34; support for claim of, to authorship, 38–43, 60–63; moral paradox, 45–50; bibliographical paradox, 51–57; imprisonment paradox, 57–60; use of place-names by, 64–65; dialect of, 66–67; age of, 67–73, 129, 135; objections to claim of, 73–74
Malory, Thomas, of Papworth St. Agnes, Hunts., 5–7, 37–40, 64, 67, 114, 130, 135, 150, 158
Malory, Thomas, of Tachebrook Malory, Warw., 72, 150
Malory families: genealogies, 157–169. *See also* Durham Malorys; Kirkby Malory Malorys; Lichborough Malorys; Papworth Malorys; Walton-on-the-Wold Malorys; Warwickshire Malorys; Yorkshire Malorys
Manuscripts, 56–57, 65, 91–92, 108, 141–142, 147
Margaret (of Anjou), Queen, 15, 26, 29, 59, 117, 128, 129, 131, 132, 133
Markenfields, 110, 116, 119, 122
Marmions, 116, 119
Marshall, Robert, 131, 132
Marshalsea, Southwark, 16, 19, 24, 25,

27, 28, 29, 30, 53, 57
Martin, A. T., antiquary, 5, 6, 8, 37, 38, 67
Maryot, Thomas, 18, 19, 22
Masshot, John, 18, 20, 22
Mauleverers, 110, 111, 112, 113, 119, 142; Sir Richard, 112; Sir Thomas, 109, 112
Maxstoke Castle, Warw., 21, 64
Merlin, 51, 55, 57, 105, 108, 140, 141, 143-145
Minot, Laurence, language of, 81, 200
Moleyns, Adam, bishop of Chichester, 17
Monks Kirby, Warw., 13, 14, 17, 18, 21, 31, 43
Monkton, William, 125, 127
Mordred, 90, 91, 101-104, 106, 108, 137
Morgan le Fay, 108
Morholt, 108
Morton Corbet, Shrop., 6
Mountford: Baldwin, 41, 63; Thomas, 130; Sir William, 15, 16, 21, 63, 71, 72
Mowbray: John, duke of Norfolk, 15, 26, 31, 60; Thomas, 13
Mylner, John, 17

Nevilles, 116, 119, 121, 133, 136; Charles, 118; Sir Humphrey, 117, 118, 121, 132, 133-135, 136; John, 117, 134; Ralph, 133; Richard, earl of Salisbury, 133; Richard, earl of Warwick (the Kingmaker), 7, 12, 16, 17, 23, 24, 30, 31, 44, 45, 46, 59, 60, 72, 117, 118, 128, 129, 130, 133, 135, 137; Sir Thomas, 133; William, 30, 31
Newbold Revel, alias Fenny Newbold, Warw., 5, 9, 13, 15, 17, 21, 22, 26, 28, 30, 31, 32, 34, 46, 53, 58, 59, 63, 64, 66, 72, 73, 77, 92, 93, 106, 127, 129, 150
Newgate, 30, 31, 51, 52, 53, 54, 56, 57, 58, 60, 63, 73, 138, 139

Newgate Street, 33
Newton, Yorks., 91, 120, 127
Nidd, river, 115
Norfolk, duke of. *See* Mowbray, John
Northallerton, Yorks., 120, 123
Northallertonshire, 119
Northampton (county), 7, 9, 10, 19, 20, 31, 60, 64, 129
Northernisms in Roman war section, 84-86, 207-221
Northern rebellions, 105, 117-118, 124, 133-136, 175
North Riding, Yorks., 91, 115, 116, 117, 118, 120, 129, 133
Northumberland (county), 107, 116, 128, 133, 135
Nottingham (county), 129, 130, 132
Nuneaton, Warw., 10, 22, 23, 24, 26, 46, 64

Overton, Robert, 25, 29

Papworth Malorys, 5-7, 64, 67, 158-159
Papworth St. Agnes, Hunts., 6, 67, 77, 150, 158
Pardons, 27, 29, 31, 58n, 59, 118, 130-133
Parliament, 15-16, 18, 19, 46
Partrych, Thomas, 18, 19
Pastons, 26, 46, 142; William, 130, 131, 135
Pellinor, 61, 108
Perceval, 108
Percies, 107, 116, 117, 119, 121, 122, 136; Henry, 3d earl of Northumberland, 117; Sir Ralph, 128, 134, 136; Sir Thomas, 136
Petipace of Winchylse, Sir, 102, 103
Peyto, Lady Katherine, 20; Willelmus, 71
Philip the Good, duke of Burgundy, 68, 69
Piercebridge, Dur., 120, 123
Piggotts, 116, 119, 125; Sir Ralph, 130
Pinel, Sir, 90

Place-names in relation to *Le Morte Darthur*, 36, 38, 64–65, 103–107, 147–149
Plumpton Correspondence, language of, 89, 201–202
Plumpton Hall, Yorks., 119
Plumptons, 83, 116, 119; Sir William, 117, 121
Podmore, William, 18
Politics and the Malorys, 23–24, 26, 29, 30, 31, 45–47, 59, 60, 104–106, 121, 133, 135, 136, 137, 152
Price of Maleor, Edward, Welsh bard, 5, 37, 40
Prison books, 51, 139–141
Prisons, 24–31, 37, 42, 52, 58–59, 137–140, 149. *See also* Colchester; D'Armagnac; Ludgate; Marshalsea; Newgate; Tower of London
Pulton, Thomas, 29
Puritans, 33, 49
Pygot, Richard, 123

Revels, 41, 61; Margaret, 9
Rhys, Prof. John, 5, 37, 40
Ribston, Yorks., 110, 111, 141, 142
Ribston Hall, 109
Ribston *Merlin*, 107–113
Ribston records, 109–111
Richard, abbot of Combe, 12–13
Richard II, 117, 121
Richard III, 121
Richmond, Yorks., 119, 120, 133
Ripon, Yorks., 77, 83, 112, 115, 116, 118, 119, 120, 121, 123, 133, 136, 152, 153
Ripon Cathedral, 115, 119, 120, 122, 123, 125, 132n
Ripon Park, 119
Robin of Redesdale, 105, 117, 121, 124, 136, 152, 167, 172, 175. *See also* Conyers, Sir John
Rochester, bishop of, 106
Rolle, Richard, language of, 81, 118, 199–200
Roos, Robert, Lord, 110, 128, 134

Rous, John, 42, 61, 63
Rowe, William, 20
Ryton, Yorks., 29, 133

St. Albans, Herts., 24, 28, 29, 38, 105
St. Anthony, leper hospital of, Yorks., 122
St. Augustine's abbey, Canterbury, 55
St. Martin at Dover, priory of, 55
St. Mary's at Huntingdon, church, 6
St. Wilfrid's mile, Ripon, 122
Sand Hutton, Yorks., 120, 123
Sandwich, Kent, 64
Sawley, Yorks., 120
Schofield, Prof. W. H., 42, 61
Scotland, 65, 81, 107, 128, 139
Scropes, 116; Archbishop Richard, 117; Sir John, 121; Stephen, language of, 81, 205
Servage, Isle of, 36
Sewingshields, Nhb., 107
Shalott, Lady of, 90
Sharow, Yorks., 120, 125, 127
Shaw, John, 12; Mrs. Sally, 82, 83, 84, 86
Shawell, Leic., 20
Shelton, Beds., 6
Sherd: John, 18, 20, 22; Roger, 18, 20, 22; Thomas, 18, 20, 22
Sheriff Hutton Castle, Yorks., 116
Sherwood Forest, 64, 105
Siege of the northern castles, 31, 127–129, 171–174
Sigismund, emperor, 12
Skott, Richard, 27
Slingsby, Yorks., 133
Smith, William, 18, 20
Smyth: Hugh, 17, 44, 45; Joan, 17, 44, 45
Smythe, Thomas, 8, 14, 15, 22
Solihull, Warw., 22, 23
Somerset, Henry Beaufort, earl of, 128, 134
Sommer, Prof. Oskar, 40, 64, 113, 126
Sondes, Walter, 71
Southwark, Sry., 24, 30

Stafford, Humphrey, duke of Buckingham, 12, 16, 18, 21, 23, 24, 25, 31, 44, 46, 59, 69, 71, 131
Staffordshire, 129
Staveleys, 119
Stewart, William, poet, 139
Stodeley, John, 26
Stoneleigh, Warw., 11, 18, 64
Strangways, 110, 119; James, 130, 134
Straunge, Baudwyn, 71
Strete, Thomas, 27
Studley, Yorks., 120, 121, 122, 123, 125, 127, 136, 161–166
Sudburgh, Nhp., 6
Suffolk (county), 26, 104
Surrey (county), 64, 104, 150
Sussex (county), 104, 130, 150
Swinford, Leic., 10, 15, 20

Tachebroke Malory, Warw., 72, 150
Tarn Wadling, Cumb., 102
Tempests, 110, 112, 160; Dionisia, 121, 123, 125, 160, 161; Sir William, 123
Thomas, earl of Lancaster, 107
Thornton, Robert, scribe, 91, 92, 98, 99, 120, 141, 142
Thornton-le-Street, Yorks., 120
Thorpe, William, friar, 54
Thwaites: Henry, 123; John, 123
Topcliff, Yorks., 117, 119, 120
Tower of London, 28, 30, 57
Towton, Yorks., battle of, 117, 136
Trafford, Yorks., 120, 123
Translations, pace of medieval, 138-139
Trent, river, 105
Trevisa, John, 92, 106
Tristan, 4, 36, 42, 51, 62, 63, 89, 101, 106, 130, 139, 140, 141, 142, 143, 144, 145, 146, 147
Troy, Geste Historiale of the Destruction of, language of, 201
Tudor, Jasper, earl of Pembroke, 131, 132
Tyncock, John, 18, 19, 20, 22
Tyrlyngton, 18

Ughtreds, 116, 141
Upper Helmsley, Yorks., 120, 123
Urry, Sir, 49
Uther Pendragon, 109

Valens, John, 26
Vavasours, 116; William, of Gunby, 127; William, of Newton, 127
Vinaver, Prof. Eugène, 4, 36, 40, 42, 43, 60, 65, 68, 69n, 99, 102, 104, 105, 107–108, 109, 111, 147, 149, 158
Vincent, Robert, 10, 15
Viviene, 108
Vyners, 121

Wakefield, Yorks., 81, 115, 117, 118
Wakefield Plays, language of, 199
Wakes, 125
Waldtheve, John, 71
Wales, 36, 131, 132
Walshale, Gregory, 18, 19, 22
Waltham Cross, Herts., 27
Walton-on-the-Wold Malorys, 160
Warkworth, John, chronicler, 124
Warkworth, Nhb., 116, 128
Wars of the Roses, 28, 31, 32; Le Morte Darthur and, 104–106, 117–118, 124, 131–132
Warwick, earl of. See Beauchamp, Richard; Neville, Richard
Warwick, John, 18
Warwickshire, 5, 8, 9, 10–13, 14, 15, 19, 20, 22, 23, 24, 25, 28, 30, 39, 40, 41, 42, 43, 47, 57, 58n, 59, 60, 61, 62, 63, 64, 66, 67, 68, 70, 71, 72, 73, 75, 76, 82, 83, 93, 94, 114, 120, 127, 129, 150, 151
Warwickshire Malorys: estates, careers, genealogy of, 9–30, 157–158
Watford, Herts., 14, 18
Watling Street, 106, 136
Wells Cathedral, Som., 130–131
Welsh candidate, 35–37, 40, 64, 67
Westgate, Ripon, 120
Westminster, 15, 24, 25, 28, 31, 104

Westmoreland (county), 124, 129, 133
Weston, William, 17, 18
West Riding, Yorks., 115, 117
Wetherby, Yorks., 109
Whittington, Sir Richard (Dick), 52, 54, 56, 59
Whixley, Yorks., 110, 111
Winchelsea, Kent, 103
Winchester, Hants., 38, 51, 64, 65, 67, 76, 78, 79, 80, 82, 83, 84, 85, 86, 87, 88, 91, 97, 104, 143
Winchester College, 3, 42
Winchester Manuscript, language of, 67, 78–88, 177–197, 207–221
Windsor, Berks., 139, 140
Windsor Forest, 104
Winkelsey. See Winchelsea; Winksley
Winksley, Yorks., 103, 120, 123
Winwick, Nhp., 9, 15, 20
Wolverhampton, Warw., 10
Wolvey, Warw., 18
Worcester, 55
Worthington, Ralph, 26
Wressell, Yorks., 117
Writhe, John, herald, 125
Wyvilles, 119

Yonge, Thomas, 33
York, 55, 64, 83, 92, 106, 115, 117, 118, 120, 127, 128, 134, 139
York, Edward, duke of, 29, 116
Yorkshire, 30, 78, 81, 82, 83, 84, 85, 89, 90, 91, 99, 102, 109, 110, 112, 113, 115, 116, 117, 118, 119, 120, 127, 129, 130, 133, 135, 141, 151, 153, 199
Yorkshire families, 103, 110, 112, 116, 119, 123–125, 130, 171–174
Yorkshire literature, 118–119, 141
Yorkshire Malorys, 101, 103, 113, 114, 115, 116, 117, 119, 120, 121, 130, 136, 152; genealogy and careers of, 122–127, 161–167
Yorkshire scene in fifteenth century, 115–119
Ywain, 108, 144
Ywain and Gawain, language of, 200–201